SPIES, DUPES, *and* DIPLOMATS

Books by Ralph de Toledano

FRONTIERS OF JAZZ
  (AN ANTHOLOGY)

SEEDS OF TREASON

DAY OF RECKONING

NIXON: A BIOGRAPHY

LAMENT FOR A GENERATION

THE GREATEST PLOT IN HISTORY

THE WINNING SIDE

SPIES, DUPES,
and DIPLOMATS

by Ralph de Toledano

ARLINGTON HOUSE
New Rochelle, New York

Library of Congress Card Catalog Number 66-25070

MANUFACTURED IN THE UNITED STATES OF AMERICA

for my uncle
MARC J. NAHON

*who took my hand when
I was young*

Foreword

History, whatever the historians of the Establishment may argue, does not just happen. If it is seen as the confluence of great impersonal forces, then those forces are set loose by men. Whether in the cloisters of government, the stage of events, or the cellars of the Lubianka, history is the function of the men who make it. The captive historians have waved their concept of history as something beyond the control of men to excuse the staggering failure of postwar policy in the Far East. For them to do otherwise would compel the admission that in the years between 1945 and 1950, the United States, by omission and commission, delivered to the Communists the vast areas of mainland China.

To some degree this surrender was conditioned by an officialdom of stunning blindness, to some degree by the careful work of men whose motivations may have differed but whose acts were all designed to destroy the legitimate and war-weakened government of China under Chiang Kai-shek and his Kuomintang party. If these men and their acts are included in that comforting alibi, if they are designated the "forces" of history which no man could challenge or assail, then the Establishment is correct. But at every turn, as this book — and the mountains of evidence from which it is derived — will show, China could have been spared the brutal consequences of Communist capture. The United States would not have been plunged into the bloody interlude of the Korean war or its Vietnamese aftermath.

Had adequate security and political sensibility safeguarded the high echelons of American policy makers from the double-gaited counsel of their subordinates, the course of events in China, Korea, Burma, Indonesia, Malaya, the Indochinese states, and India would have led to peaceful development, to an improvement of the human condition in these areas of densely-packed misery, and to the creation of viable institutions of governance suitable to the time and the place of Far Eastern progress. Instead, innumerable lives and vast treasure have been sacrificed to contain the rampaging ideological hatreds of the Chinese Communists and the allies they have recruited in the Asian continent. Africa, now torn and disabled by reverse racialism and a national communism, might now be breaking through the curtain of time and technology which separates it from the Twentieth Century.

The background of this great and semi-conscious betrayal of a China which had suffered rapine and war ever since 1931, when the China Incident—the invasion of the mainland by Japanese imperialists—brought to a halt the move toward representative government and the development of an industrialized society, has been systematically ignored by the Establishment and its official chroniclers. It is not that the facts were not available to the patient researcher. But decades of falsification—of doublethink and doubletalk—distorted the Western world's thinking on the root evil of our times. Decades of one-party hegemony had preempted the market place of ideas and set up insurmountable barriers against the free trade of thought. To this day, even the most scholarly and annotated work is tossed aside if it runs counter to the "historical inevitability" propositions of those dominating the academy and the media of mass communications.

I am speaking of the past, of the years when the deeds were done. But the story of America's suicidal Far Eastern policy assumes more pressing significance than a re-play of a sad and shameful era. For in this state of international crisis, an old *dramatis personae* may be seen repeating the same old myths and uttering the same old shibboleths to a new cast of characters still bemused by worthless formulations. Ignoring all the facts and resorting to a discarded rhetoric, J. William Fulbright, the chairman of the Senate Foreign Relations Committee, tells the nation what even the *Washington Post* describes as "simply rubbish" — that the Chinese Communists "won patriotic support by actively fighting the Japanese while the Kuomintang remained passive, waiting for the United States to overcome Japan."

Senator Fulbright's pronouncements have never been known for logic, historical accuracy, or particular sense. But he would have been aware, had not the whisperings of some not-so-mysterious birdie confused him, that the Kuomintang was fighting the Japanese for ten years before the United States entered the Pacific war. He might have known that during the period from the beginning of the China Incident to the eventual collapse of President Chiang, the government of China fought a two-front war. In the terrible days after Pearl Harbor, it was the Chinese Reds who avoided contact with the Japanese army while they sabotaged Chiang Kai-shek's war effort — confident that Japan would eventually fall and conserving their arms and men for the final conflict for control of China. The Free Chinese had suffered more than three million casualties in the war against Japan when freshly equipped and unbloodied Communist troops launched their great offensive.

That America stood by, praising the Chinese Reds and withholding aid from the Free Chinese in those days of confusion and despair, is demonstrable historic fact. Yet the voices which hailed Mao Tse-tung and Chou En-lai as "agrarian reformers," latter-day "democrats," and the "George Washingtons" of the Chinese revolution are once more abroad in the land, sounding from positions of importance on the nation's campuses and given seats of honor before the TV-ridden sessions of the Fulbright Committee. John Stewart Service, whose activities are detailed in this narrative; Owen Lattimore, one of the major architects of the Far Eastern policy that lives to haunt us today; Professor John K. Fairbank, Harvard's chronic contribution to the general confusion — these have again been called back to stir up the entrails of small animals and read the auguries of a future which would be shiny, so they tell the world, if only the strategists of past defeats were called back to place and influence where they could open the gates of the citadel to Asia's Communist cabal.

It is too late in the day for them to repeat their former adulatory exercises. They tell us now that, yes, the Chinese Communists have visited their form of destruction on such countries as have stood in the way of total Asian conquest. The persuasion for admission of Red China into the community of civilized nations is more sophisticated. It must be "contained but not isolated" — a slogan that America's soldiers in the Vietnamese jungles must find hard to stomach. Red China's leaders are aggressive in speech but do not translate words into action, we are told — an argument which a Tibet decimated by Chinese Communist genocide must find somewhat tactless.

The United States, at every turn, is urged to reach out the hand of friendship to those leaders and countries which applauded most enthusiastically when Nikita Khrushchev promised, "We will bury you." The arguments and the blandishments may change, but the desired result is the same. The "natural aspirations" of inferior nations, the push of a "new nationalism," the desire for "a share of the world's goods" — these are held up before the nation like cue cards at a television production. But the focus of *Spies, Dupes, and Diplomats* is on the Far East. Much of the material in this book is as pertinent now as it was when it appeared in its 1952 edition, if only because the Establishment has refused to give it the exposure it would have, under other circumstances, received. In the original edition, I wrote:

"The writer of contemporary history does not look for skeletons in the closet. They are all walking about with flesh on their bones. Yet he must treat his cast of characters as if they were both living people and heads impaled on the point of a chronicle. Carelessness in characterization often leads to unpleasant correspondence—or worse. I have, therefore, made it a point to . . . carefully separate the sheep from the Reds, and labeled each meticulously. Because the language has so far not devised a word to describe certain of the *dramatis personae* of our sorry era, they move through these pages unticketed. I have tried to lay aside motives and to deal with the acts which have affected the course of our contemporaneity.

"In politics, as in war, it is the act which counts—not the motive. For motive is important in meting out punishment, not in assessing error. Perhaps some of those who sheltered the Communists, both in and out of government, as this account notes, did it for reasons we might respect. So be it. But I have only anger and scorn for a new strategy of "liberalism" which defends the motive by denying that the overt act was committed. The function of this book is to describe those acts. When they are admitted, that will be time enough to discuss motivation."

The strategy of defending the motivation by denying the act persists. Of the men who made China policy in the late Forties and early Fifties, the best that can be said of them is that they were disastrously in error. Of the men in error during the Sixties, the best that can be offered is that they have with determination shut their eyes to the past, ascribing the most scabrous of motives to those who have benefited from the lesson of history. They stand self-condemned of combining dogmatic innocence with unmitigated duplicity. And in so doing, they lend credence to the troubled men who cannot explain the record of past years except in conspiratorial terms. There is enough conspiracy in the Sorge story and the *Amerasia* episode to satisfy the most avid. It is not necessary to carry it over to the grim pageant that makes up the rest of these pages.

All of this is perhaps unnecessary explanation. A book speaks for itself. A note on sources may, however, be pertinent. Some of these are primary — the 30,000-word confession of Richard Sorge; excerpts from the confession and statements of Ozaki Hozumi and other participants in the Sorge *apparat*; interviews with former Soviet *apparatchiks* and with their American opposite numbers; such court records of the trial of the Sorge *apparat* as were translated from the Japanese by Intelligence personnel of the United States Far East Command in Tokyo; correspondence from the hidden files of the Institute of Pacific Relations; transcripts of hearings before the Senate Internal Security subcommittee; transcripts and exhibits of the Pearl Harbor inquiries; transcripts of Senate hearings into the dismissal of General Douglas MacArthur by President Truman; Communist documents in my possession; the secret transcript of a meeting of the State Department's Loyalty Review Board; and the memoirs of participants in the events detailed here.

There are also secondary sources: the SCAP Intelligence report, *The Sorge Spy Ring,* issued by the Defense Department in 1949 and then withdrawn after leftwing protest; my own voluminous files on Communist activities and espionage, and on politics in general; the reports of various Congressional committees; and a library of New/Fair Deal Americana.

I have described *Spies, Dupes, and Diplomats* as a narrative — which is how Professor Allan Nevins defines history. "Without life, there is not truth to history," he has written. In this sense, the narrative I have written is history. It is also a declaration of conscience, uttering and documenting a point of view stifled in our times. It invigorates a forgotten theorem — that men's ideas calcify, but history is organic and changing as new materials present themselves to the professor or newspaperman who continues the long narration which is the story of mankind.

RALPH DE TOLEDANO

Washington, D. C.
July 1966

Contents

Foreword   vii

I   Love — and Death — Is a Falling Star   3

II   All Quiet on the Western Front   11

III   No Dogs or Chinese Allowed   24

IV   Comintern to Fourth Bureau   35

V   Shanghai Gesture: Red Version   42

VI   Sorge at Work   49

VII   Ring around Shanghai   58

VIII   Japan Is the Focus   64

IX   Mission to Tokyo   72

X   Tokyo Marching Orders   80

XI   Price $40,000   90

XII   Prelude to Pearl Harbor   102

XIII   Links of American Policy   122

XIV   Amerasia, I: 1700 Stolen Documents   134

CONTENTS

x v   Amerasia, II: Justice in Reverse   155

x v i   IPR: Carter's Pink Pill   172

x v i i   Strategy of Defeat   194

Appendices   211

    i. Service's Report to Stilwell   213

    i i. Lattimore and OWI   220

    i i i. Dubinsky on Carter   232

    i v. Memo to Marshall   235

    v. Investigation of State Department   237

    Index   251

SPIES, DUPES, *and* DIPLOMATS

I

Love — and Death — Is a Falling Star

SITTING in death row, a man may think of the gallows. But he does not really believe they exist. He may accept the hour of his death, but he does not really believe in death itself. Extinction and dissolution center in the pit of the stomach. The condemned man lives in suspension; he merely thinks. From each according to his nature, and to each according to his soul, the thoughts come and are separated out. Pacing his cell or staring at the cold sky, he asks: "What was the wrong turning, where was the false step?" These are questions less academic to him than: "Will I die?"

In the grim row of cells in Sugamo Prison, where the Japanese Empire sequestered men about to die, Richard Sorge and Ozaki Hozumi sought to make a pattern of their lives as they waited for the knock on the door which would admit their last minutes. The year was 1944, the month November. The country which one had spied on and the other betrayed still fought against Britain and the United States. But it had already begun to move inexorably toward the defeat which exploded over Hiroshima and was formalized by General MacArthur on the deck of an American battleship.

Neither Sorge nor Ozaki knew this. Within Sugamo's walls, their punctilious guards bandied only words of victory, the triumph of a brutal and calculated imperialism. To Sorge, Japanese successes meant little that could touch his emotions. The wars of capitalist powers meant only a struggle for temporary hegemony before the great and concluding triumph of the Soviet power over the human race. A hard mind that categorized all facts and ordered all existence within the Leninist dialectics of his creed, Sorge had set for himself the task of re-examining the details of his life, his work, and his achievement. These *obiter scripta* to a life he had put down on paper, at the urging of his Japanese captors.

They were in no sense a confession. For though the document, in its thirty-two thousand words, meticulously recorded his espionage activities in China and Japan, it was more in the nature of an epistle to the Nipponese heathen, an explanation of the magnitude and patience of Soviet method. It betrayed no secrets the Japanese secret police did not know already. Where it dealt with Sorge, the man and the Communist, it was almost openly addressed to his masters in the Kremlin. See, the Sorge story seemed to say, though I have committed the grievous sin of letting myself be caught, I am still a sound Leninist. Almost the last words of the document were a confession of a youthful ideological fault in evaluating Rosa Luxemburg, the German revolutionary.

Sorge was proud of his Communist record. He had moved into the Marxist orbit as a young soldier, consciously, carefully, in all premeditation. He had served Stalin well. He had fulfilled one of the most fabulously difficult missions in the history of espionage. Working as a confidant of Gestapo agents, this Soviet spy had wormed his way into the highest councils of the German Embassy in Tokyo. He had whipped the cream of this jest to solid consistency by helping his Nazi "friends" and Japanese "allies" draft the Anti-Comintern pact. Through his accomplice Ozaki, he had discovered Japan's most guarded military secret, the time and the place of the next onslaught — Pearl Harbor. And he had transmitted this information to Moscow months before Japanese planes virtually obliterated the United States Pacific Fleet. This one piece of intelligence had shifted the course of history; Siberian troops had been moved to the German front.

And out of the intuition which often cohabits with rigorous logic,

Sorge knew that his work in the Far East would continue to an overwhelming conclusion for Communist arms. His agents — the Agnes Smedleys and Guenther Steins — were busy creating the intellectual climate which would permit a frustration of American self-interest and lead to a disastrous Chinese Communist victory in the postwar years. The road from Sorge's cell to the State Department White Paper was long and tortuous, but his logical brain could trace it out.

Perhaps some regrets flickered through Sorge's mind — no man wants to die — but these were probably sensual. Throughout his adult life, he had drunk boisterously and fornicated with determination. A random check by the Japanese secret police, after Sorge's arrest, had netted them the names of thirty women who had moved in and out of his bed during the Tokyo years. Among them were the hetaerae of the Communist netherworld, the wives and mistresses of his espionage colleagues, and even the wives of German Embassy colleagues — the very men whose suspicion could have destroyed him at any moment. For liquor — since it might lead to political indiscretion — and sex were the calculated risks of his existence, the measure of his blood and arrogance. In bed or at the bottle, the steeled Bolshevik could disappear and the undisciplined Teuton take over.

Ozaki Hozumi was another man altogether. He had come to Communism out of an overblown guilt sense, an easy sentimentality, and a large measure of thoughtless idealism. Espionage had followed painlessly when Agnes Smedley had convinced him that he "would be doing something of real importance." He believed that his meeting with her, and his "decision to follow the narrow road," had been "predestined." He had been captured by slogans and snared by a hope of unearned green pastures for all men. When the means enslaved the ends, he was raddled by conscience. He knew his moral crime was greater than Sorge's, for Ozaki had betrayed his own country. He had a wife whom he loved, a child.

Ozaki, too, wrote a memoir, but it was no dialectical account of his deeds. Instead, he turned out long, emotional letters to his wife and an apologia for the Japanese court in which he traced the course of his spiritual downfall and sadly seconded his coming extermination. The letters, written with all the petaled detail of a Japanese print, were later published, and their title reflected the ambivalence of the Japanese character: *Love Is Like a Falling Star*. But the apologia, the thoughts of a man who took a wrong turn and knew that he would live just long enough to regret it, lies buried in Tokyo court records.

"I am now awaiting my final judgment," he wrote in the concluding pages. "I am well aware of the importance of the laws I violated. . . . To show my face, to live among my friends, even after many years shall have passed, is impossible from both the standpoint of my conscience and that of my powers. . . . I am happy in the thought that I was born and will die in this, my country. . . . I finish writing in my cell at the Tokyo Detention House at a time when the clouds hang low over the earth, warning of a storm to come."

But before arriving at this serenity, he lived through torture, doubt, and the dark night of a creed destroyed. "Besieged by justice and charity, kindness and affection . . . I have begun to feel that perhaps I have overlooked some grave error in the reasoning behind my actions. At first the mere thought of such a possibility was torture. . . . I guiltily felt that I had lost faith." He shucked off that guilt because he was no more a real Bolshevik than, let us say, Frederick Vanderbilt Field. In time, he accepted the "Greater East Asia War" as a patriotic struggle. Typically, he never really understood the political and moral significance of his crimes.

His revulsion to Communism was emotional and personal. "My love for my family surged up anew as an unexpectedly powerful force. . . . At first it was so painful for me to read my wife's letters that I could not even bear to look at the enclosed pictures of my child. Sometimes I wept and sometimes I was filled with resentment and thought how glad I would be if I had no family. . . . Professional revolutionaries should not have families. . . . The future of my father, to whom I usually gave little thought, also weighed heavily. . . . I picture him standing with his back towards me, bowed down with anxiety and sorrow."

He was filled with tremendous gratitude because, after his arrest, his wife and daughter had not been stoned. "The teacher in charge of my daughter's class made a special visit to my home," he recorded, "to tell her that she should continue to attend school as before."

Almost placidly, he could write: "I am not a coward and I am not afraid to die."

Both Sorge and Ozaki had been sentenced to death by the Tokyo District Court in September 1943. In the midst of war, they were given the full protection of civil law and permitted to appeal the espionage conviction before the Japanese Supreme Court. Their defense was typical — and one used half a dozen years later by some of Alger Hiss's more subtle supporters. They had done nothing illegal, Sorge and Ozaki pleaded. They had used no force to gather the information; and what had been transmitted to Moscow had not been secret intelligence but facts which could have been available to any intelligent man.

Sorge's appeal to the Supreme Court was, in a small way, a classic of Communist reasoning:

Japanese laws are subject to interpretation, either broadly or according to the strict letter of the text. Although leakage of information may, strictly speaking, be punishable by law, in practice the Japanese system is not amenable to the keeping of secrets. . . . I consider that in the indictment insufficient consideration was given to our activity and to the nature of the information which we obtained. Data which [one of my agents] obtained was neither secret nor important; he brought in only news that was well known to every press correspondent. . . . What may be termed political information was obtained by Ozaki and by me.

I obtained my information from the German Embassy, but here again I consider that little if any of it could be termed "state secret." It was given to me voluntarily. To obtain it, I resorted to no strategy for which I should be punished. I used no deceit or force. . . . I placed much trust in this information because it was compiled . . . for the use of the German General Staff. I believe that the Japanese Government, in giving data to the German Embassy, expected some of it to leak out. . . . Even such data as Ozaki considered important and secret was actually no longer so, because he procured it indirectly after it had left its secret source.

The Japanese courts acted with moderation. For the secondary conspirators there were varying jail terms; for Sorge and Ozaki, death. The Supreme Court upheld Sorge's sentence in January 1944, Ozaki's the following April. Neither man was told on what day the court's mandate would be carried out. In the succeeding months, both men were intermittently questioned by military and police authorities on the wider implications of their conspiracy. Ozaki talked freely and without compunction. Sorge remained guarded. But he boasted that Stalin would somehow come to his rescue. He was too valuable a man to the Red Army's Fourth Bureau (Intelligence) to be sacrificed. The U.S.S.R. and Japan would come to some agreement over him.

On the morning of 7 November 1944, just as Ozaki had finished writing a letter to his wife, the governor of Sugamo Prison entered his cell. This, Ozaki knew, was his summons to the gallows. He had put aside clean clothing for this moment, and he changed into it. Ceremoniously, the prison governor asked him his name, age, and domicile to ascertain officially that Ozaki was the condemned man. Then the prisoner was led from the death row, across the prison yard, to the small concrete execution chamber. In the anteroom of this building, lit by tapers, a great golden altar celebrated the Amidha Buddha.

The Chief Chaplain, a Buddhist priest, offered Ozaki tea and cakes. He listened to Ozaki's explanation of the instructions in his written will, asked who was to be notified of Ozaki's death, and said:

"Life and death are the same to one who has attained impersonal beatitude. Impersonal beatitude can be attained by entrusting everything to the mercy of Buddha."

Ozaki kneeled and the priest recited the Three Promises of the Great Sutra of Constant Life. Ozaki burned incense, closed his eyes, and bowed. Rising to thank the officials for their courtesy, he said:

"I am ready."

Behind the altar, in a windowless room, stood the gallows. Ozaki was ordered to stand beneath it and the noose was placed around his neck. Twice Ozaki repeated a simple Buddhist ritual of comfort. At 9:33, the trap beneath his feet was sprung. At 9:51, he was declared dead.

Minutes later, the prison governor paid another visit — to Sorge's cell. The ritual of identification was repeated and he was informed that the Minister of Justice had ordered his execution for that morning. Did he have any further words to add to his will? Sorge was asked.

"My will is as I have written it," Sorge said.

"Have you anything else to say?" the governor asked.

"No, nothing else," Sorge said. Turning to the officials in the cell, he added, "I thank you for all your courtesies."

From the death row, he too crossed the wide prison courtyard, skirted the gray walls of the death house, and entered the single door. He walked past the golden altar and into the gallows room.

The prison records say that the trap was sprung at 10:20, that he was declared dead at 10:36.

But a German career diplomat, attached to the Tokyo Embassy, who knew Sorge and had talked to him in his last days, does not believe the prison records. In 1949, on a mission to Washington, he stopped off in New York.

"If Sorge walked into the execution chamber," he told friends, "he walked out on his own feet. Sorge is not dead. Stalin made a deal with the Japanese. After the war, I heard reports that Sorge was still alive. I believe those reports. The prison records? Every Bolshevik knows that records are kept only to be falsified. . . ."

But dead or alive, Richard Sorge had left his mark on history. And it was quite a mark.

I I

All Quiet on the Western Front

THE Sorge story begins in Germany. In a personal sense, it is a story of adventure and misguided idealism, souring into adventurism and political cynicism. But in an ironic sense, Sorge's story is one of Germany itself. Present-day Communism is a Russian excrescence, but the German genius for organization created the worldwide Communist *apparat* (a German word) in which Richard Sorge played such an outstanding part. The complex system of Communist-front groups which grew like cancers on every country on the face of the globe was conceived and developed in Germany by a German, Willi Muenzenberg. The language of the Comintern's secret operatives and of the Red Army's Fourth Bureau agents was, for many years, German.

And, if we have forgotten, "scientific socialism," cramped and bludgeoned into doctrinaire shape from the dreams and aspirations of civilized Europeans, was a product of Karl Marx, a German whose passion for order dictated a belief in a rigid society, the elimination of human differences, and a scholarly anti-Semitism. American and British Fabians gloss over the fact that, in pre-World War I years, the most disciplined socialist party in the world — and the most influential — was Germany's Social Democracy. When the Great War broke out, the German Social Democratic Party moved easily behind Kaiser Wilhelm's clicking footsteps.

The militarists said, *Gott mit uns;* the socialists said, *Marx mit uns;* the effect was the same. And the rationalization for "pacifist"

Social Democrats bore a startling resemblance to Stalin's current peace line. Only by the establishment of German "progress" over Europe could the endless wars between shifting alliances come to an end. The argument made sense if you were a German; but the French, British, and Italian socialist parties in the Second International were not quite progressive enough to grasp it. The Second International broke up, preparing the ground for Lenin's Third International — and only the impractical Italians clung to an antiwar position.

This marriage of social democracy and imperialism was successful just so long as the honeymoon lasted and the German armies swept forward. It began to founder during the stalemated war of position on the Western Front. In the fragmentation of the German state on the rocks of defeat, Armistice, and Versailles, the marriage was dissolved. The bill of divorcement and the patchwork design for living which followed left a great political void which was never filled until the victory of *National* Socialism. (Even in the 1920s, the German Left had flirted with Karl Radek's theories of National Bolshevism, only to be dissuaded by Zinoviev, the head of the Comintern.)

All of this is important to Germany. It explains the high hopes of 1914, the crashing moral bust of 1918, the spread of nihilism and negation among German intellectuals, the startling disintegration of sexual mores, and, eventually, the organized political prostitution of Stalinoid leftism. It explains the unbearable fatalism of *All Quiet on the Western Front* and the overripe cynicism of *Die Dreigroschenoper* — a glorification of pimps, whores, and thieves by two men who were significantly to shine in the Communist artistic heavens, Bertold Brecht and Kurt Weill. And it explains Richard Sorge.

Man or boy, Sorge was a German. The ease with which he duped the Nazis during his final, and fabulous, Tokyo adventures, shows that but for choice of masters the Communist activist was little different from the Gestapo careerist. (Even anti-Semitism, as the world is belatedly learning, was endemic to both ideologies; in any closed system the Jew is an abomination.)

The First World War caught Richard Sorge, at the age of eighteen, on a visit to Sweden. He returned to Germany by the last boat and enlisted so precipitously that he never bothered to take his final examinations at the Richterfelder District high school of Berlin, or even to inform his mother. Two things set him slightly apart from other German boys — he had been born in Baku, in the southern Caucasus, and he was the grandson of Adolph Sorge, secretary of the First International during Karl Marx's lifetime. His early years, summed up in the "confession," show strains of intellectual pride and a nagging sense of "difference":

Until the war, my boyhood was passed amid the comparative calm common to the wealthy bourgeois class of Germany. Economic worries had no place in our home. . . . The peculiarities of the Sorge family endowed my early childhood with certain distinguishing features. . . . I was a bad pupil, defied the school's regulations, was obstinate and willful and rarely opened my mouth. In history, literature, philosophy, political science, and, of course, athletics, I was far above the rest of the class, but I was below average in my other studies.

At the early age of 15, I developed an avid interest in Goethe, Schiller, Lessing, Klopstock, Dante, and other difficult authors and, in addition, struggled in vain with the history of philosophy and Kant. My favorite parts of history were the French Revolution, the Napoleonic Wars, and the time of Bismarck. I knew Germany's current problems better than the average grownup.

At school, I was known as "the Prime Minister." I knew what my grandfather had done for the labor movement and I also knew that my father's ideas were diametrically opposed to his. Father was unmistakably a nationalist and imperialist, and throughout his life he was unable to shake off the impression made upon his youth by the building of the German Empire during the war of 1870–71. He was strongly conscious of the property he had amassed and the social position he had achieved. . . . I was a member of a workers' athletic association for many years, which meant that I had constant contacts with the workers, but I had no clear political stand as a student. I was interested only in collecting political knowledge; I neither desired nor was able to adopt a definite attitude of my own.

Much of this is hindsight rationalization. Sorge's enlistment and his reaction to war were clearly those of a young man who was part of his social environment, "nationalist and imperialist" like other German youths who flocked to the colors. He joined the army, he recalled, because of a "strong urge to seek new experiences, a desire to liberate myself from school studies and what I considered the whole meaningless and purposeless pattern of living of an eighteen-year-old, and the general outburst of excitement created by the war." This is the reaction of a bright, moody adolescent, given to the *Weltschmerz* of his age, and hungry for physical adventure — not the reasoning of a politically sophisticated but uncommitted mind.

A "completely inadequate six-week training course at a drill ground in the outskirts of Berlin" was his preparation for combat. Then — "I was shipped out to Belgium to take part in a great battle on the banks of the Yser. This period may be described as 'From the Classroom to the Battlefield' or 'From the School Chair to the Slaughter Block.'" Sorge's reaction to the "fierce and sanguinary conflict" was a stirring up of what he realized to be his first serious psychological unrest. The battle was followed by one of those long and terrible stage waits of a war of position. "After our thirst for battle and adventure had been glutted," Sorge wrote, "several months of silent and pensive emptiness began."

All wars are fierce, sanguinary, and horrible. The first great European conflict was no more so than most; statistically, and in terms of human suffering, it was less terrible than the American War Between the States. But this war, entered into so lightheartedly by the young men of the time, caked the soldier's soul with mud. Carnage is bearable; living in trenches is not. Combat was a function of masses, not individuals — huge, insensate masses of men beating against each other — and a contest for yards of pulverized and useless earth. The individuals within that mass, moreover, were not prepared by their rosy nineteenth-century ideas of progress and increasing material good. Soldiers fight for one thing: to return home; but it must have seemed to many men in the trenches that home no longer existed.

"How many times before me German soldiers had fought in Belgium to invade France and the armies of France . . . had poised here ready to overrun Germany," Sorge thought. "Nobody knew the real purpose of the war, not to speak of its deep-seated significance. Most of the soldiers were middle-aged men, workers and handicraftsmen by trade. Almost all of them belonged to industrial unions, and many were Social Democrats. . . . I mused over my knowledge of history." Reaching for answers, perhaps much as the hero of *All Quiet* had reached for a butterfly, Sorge was wounded.

Returning to Germany to nurse his wound, he was thrust into another psychological morass. Instead of the jumping patriotism he had left, he found the "true standards" which governed home-front life. "Money could buy anything on the black market. . . . Wartime profiteering and surreptitious buying and selling were beginning to appear, and the lofty ideals underlying the war were receding farther and farther into the background. . . . The material objectives of the struggle were gaining increasing prominence."

The signs of deterioration were there, and they disturbed him — but not enough to prevent him from picking up his studies during the period of convalescence. He was not happy back in civilian life, however, and the political works which he studied seemed somehow meaningless in the face of the war and his front-line experiences. They were, in his words, "deprived of real significance." Before his convalescent leave was up, he volunteered for service again. Back in his old outfit, he found few of his comrades alive.

This time he was sent to the Eastern Front. Morale was high there. The German armies were scoring massive victories against the ill-armed and ill-led Imperial Russian forces. But the war had been going on for some time, and along with the other troops, Sorge succumbed to the occupational hazard of all soldiers. "The fact that, although we had already pierced deep into the heart of Russia, there was still no end in sight made some of them begin to fear that the war would go on forever." It ended abruptly for him a second time when he was wounded again. After a long trip across occupied Russia, he returned home to find the situation, early in 1916, critical.

As after his first convalescence, Sorge volunteered for combat duty, feeling "that I would be better off fighting in a foreign land than sinking deeper into the mud at home." In the army he found the beginning of the disintegration which comes with imminent defeat. "The general atmosphere in my unit was even gloomier than before, but more of the men were showing an interest in political problems and the issues involved in terminating the war. The notion was growing among them that a violent political change was the only way of extricating ourselves from this quagmire."

At first, these discussions were limited to possibilities of ending the war without capitulating to the enemy. There was much talk of a permanent solution to the problem of war's elimination. Morale was still not at the surrender point. But among the troops, the radicals were already circulating the idea of revolution. The names of Karl Liebknecht and Rosa Luxemburg, left-wing socialists who had taken an antiwar position, began to have meaning. The German government was bombarding the troops with propaganda, explaining its long-term objectives and detailing the reasons for Germany's demands on other countries. But the increasing number of leftist agitators within the army seized upon every official piece of paper and used it as a counterweapon.

When Sorge suffered his third wound — he was struck by shell fragments, two of which smashed bones and left him with a permanent limp — he was about ready to assume an active role in the coming struggle for Germany. Fate is not blind, and it placed the wounded soldier in care of a doctor and a nurse — father and daughter — who were left-wing socialists. For several months, as his body mended, they plied him with books and talk. They gave him a detailed account of revolutionary developments on the home front. Books by Kant and Schopenhauer were combined with political treatises. "Despite the seriousness of my injuries and the excruciating pain, I was happy for the first time in many years," Sorge was to recall.

Still a soldier, and still under treatment, he resumed his studies at the University of Berlin. "During the summer and winter of 1917, I realized most thoroughly the meaninglessness and the devastating effects of the Great War. Already several millions had perished. . . . The highly vaunted German economic machine had crumbled into ruins. . . . Capitalism had disintegrated into its component parts, anarchism and unscrupulous merchants." The answer, he found, "the only fresh and effective ideology," was in the labor movement. At the university, he spent all his time reading the Greek philosophers, and Hegel, Marx, and Engels; he delved into the whole history of the labor movement. The collapse of the Tsar and the early Russian Revolution "indicated to me the course which the international labor movement should adopt."[1] He decided to become a part of it.

In January 1918, a demobilized Richard Sorge continued his studies at Kiel University. At the same time, he joined the Independent Social Democratic Party. The second move was more in keeping with the times. Germany was in ferment. The Brest-Litovsk treaty, terminating the war with Russia, was signed, but the defeats on the Western Front continued. From over the Eastern border came electrifying news of Workers' and Soldiers' Soviets, of red flags flying. Karl Liebknecht, Germany's fiery socialist, was elected an honorary member of the Petrograd Soviet. Revolutionary pamphlets

---

[1] This is definitely *arrière-pensée*. The Kerensky revolutionary government, overthrown a year later by Lenin, was democratic and middle-class. It was a labor government only in a broad sense. But the Soviets have conveniently forgotten this.

by Trotsky, Lenin, and Bukharin reached the country. Bolshevik slogans were broadcast widely by soldiers returning from the Eastern Front.

On the Western Front, a new offensive punched holes in Allied lines, but it did not turn the tide in favor of Germany. Everywhere there was weariness and discontent. American troops, fresh to the conflict, surged into the trenches and across No Man's Land to be met by tired Germans carrying years of war on their shoulders. The German General Staff hoped for miracles, for compromises, and finally for death with honor. The German people hoped for peace — and eventually for peace at any price. The troops seethed with revolutionary propaganda; mutiny flickered here and there.

In this atmosphere, Sorge took up left-wing activities. He started a socialist youth movement at Kiel, became the head of a training group "teaching the history of the labor movement and the difference between revolutionary and counterrevolutionary movements," and recruited new party members from among students and friends.

Again fate moved with design for Sorge. Late in October, sailors of the German Navy refused to steam out to do forlorn-hope battle with the British Navy. Admiral von Hipper hastily canceled plans for the "death cruise" and ordered the Third Squadron to return to its home base at Kiel, hoping that shore leave would quiet the sailors. This miscalculation launched the German revolution. Sailors and workers met and fraternized; the local mutiny spread to Hamburg and Bremen, where tens of thousands marched in the streets singing socialist songs and proclaiming a republic. Soldiers deserted their barracks and joined in the parades. The red flag flew from battleship masts. The rebellion continued to spread. By 10 November, Berlin was in the hands of a Workers' and Soldiers' Council, and the German Empire had collapsed.

Sorge's career as a revolutionary activist began with the Kiel rebellion. He was busy agitating, speaking to insurgent sailors, organizing meetings, lecturing on socialism, and organizing for his party. His activities were noticed, and he was summoned to Berlin to work at the headquarters of the Independent Socialist Party. The city was in chaos. The Social Democratic government of Friedrich Ebert, supported by the German officers' corps and the troops that remained loyal to their commanders, was under constant attack by the revolutionary Spartacus Bund, led by Rosa Luxemburg and Karl Liebknecht, and half-heartedly by the Independent Socialist Party. In January 1919, a march on Berlin of armed workers was being suppressed by Ebert and his Minister of Defense Gustav Noske — just at the moment that Sorge was arriving at the capital city. He was seized at the station and searched for arms, then held for several days and returned to Kiel.

Going on to Hamburg, to prepare for his doctoral examinations at the university there, Sorge moved even deeper into revolutionary activities. When the Spartacists and the Independent Socialists merged with the Communist Party, he had already become one of the active men in the Hamburg area. He had by now chosen his sphere of Communist work, organization and agitation. The speechmaking and parliamentary intrigue was the prerogative of the big men of the party like Wilhelm Pieck, destined to become a Soviet *gauleiter* in Eastern Germany after World War II. The central committee assigned Sorge to agitational and training work in Aachen, in the zone of Allied occupation. To cover this activity, he secured a teaching job.

An instructor by day, he was busy at night doing propaganda among the miners, training Communist cadres, and running the local party. The scope of his influence spread to Cologne, where he attended secret meetings and helped edit the Communist newspaper. As a representative of the Rhineland region, he was consulted by the Communist central committee. In time, however, Sorge's double life caught up with him; he was expelled from his academic position at Aachen. In his Tokyo cell, Sorge wrote:

After consulting with the party, I decided to intensify my activities among the mineworkers and to work with them in the Aachen coal-mining region to cover my living expenses. I was able to find employment in a mine near Aachen as an inexperienced worker without being detected. It was a hard life, and I suffered immensely because of the serious injuries I had received at the front, but I never regretted the decision. The experiences I went through were just as valuable as those I gained on the battlefield, and my new vocation was equally significant to the party.

Within a short time, my work among the miners had produced a number of beneficial results. I organized a Communist group in the first mine at which I was employed, saw it develop soundly, and moved on to another mine. During the same year, I changed mines again. An effort to do similar work for the party in the coal-mining district of Holland failed. I was discovered immediately, expelled from the mine, and deported from the country. In the meantime, I had become known in the Aachen mines, with the result that I was no longer able to find work. The authorities threatened to turn me over to the Allied military authorities, so I was forced to leave the occupied area.

Sorge returned to Berlin for further instructions from the central committee. He was offered a paid job in the party's growing bureaucracy — slowly being bought by these salaries, and sold into subservience to Moscow control. Sorge refused, pleading that he needed more practical experience and wanted also to complete his academic training. Through the party, he was able to get a position as assistant to the director of the Social Science department of the University of Frankfurt. He was instructed to keep his party work and party affiliations under cover. It was at this point that his secret work for the Communist International began.

I handled all the secret documents and the membership register and maintained secret liaison between the central committee in Berlin and the organization in Frankfurt. The party funds and propaganda material were sent to me. I hid most of the party's property in my study room at the university or in the Social Science library, concealing large bundles in the coalbin in the classroom. There were two or three party members working there, so there was no need to fear discovery. Concealment of these materials permitted the party to use them constantly, with the result that, despite the ban on the Communist Party, there was no slackening of its activities in Frankfurt. Meanwhile, over in Saxony, an armed rebellion had set up a workers' republic with which, by party orders, we were in constant communication. I visited Saxony frequently on special missions to deliver essential political and organizational reports and directives which it was possible for the party to route through Frankfurt.

Sorge the idealist and Sorge the activist were well on their way to becoming Sorge the spy. The Comintern domination of the German Communist Party made this not only possible but essential. The "Twenty-One Conditions" for admission into the Comintern, following Lenin's doctrine, demanded that Communist Parties "create everywhere a parallel illegal apparatus." And the Comintern further exacted: "All legal work must be carried on under the practical control of the illegal party." To this underground *apparat,* the most effective, brilliant, and promising comrades were assigned. With the formation of the German Communist Party, Russian agents moved in to set up what was to become the classical pattern of Communist organization throughout the world.

The haphazard revolutionary undergrounds of the romantic past were not good enough. Almost from the inception of the Comintern, its leaders conceived of member parties as adjuncts of the Soviet State, supplying political and espionage effectives. The illegal party was broken down into groups, each with distinct training and specific function:[2]

The M-Group. The cadres and framework for a German Red Army. Its members were given basic training, went on night marches, and held secret maneuvers. It had its own arsenals.

[2] The author is indebted for this breakdown to *Stalin and German Communism* (Cambridge, 1948) by Ruth Fischer, sister of Gerhart Eisler and charter member No. 1 of the Austrian Communist Party.

The N-Group. The N stood for *Nachrichten* (Intelligence). By far the best equipped and financed, the N-Group was responsible for protecting party leaders, serving as bodyguards for Russian agents passing through the country. As it developed it took on infiltration and espionage functions. In time, it became the most important of the underground groups. Sorge belonged to it.

The T-Group. These terroristic units were assigned to sabotage missions, to kidnapping and liquidating traitors to the party and "class enemies."

The Z-Group. The Z stood for *Zersetzung* (disruption). This was a subdivision of the N-Group. The mission was to "bore from within" in hostile organizations, and either disrupt them or take them over. The rebellion in Saxony had been organized by M- and Z-Groups.

Every one of these groups, however, had a super-function: to keep a tight grip on the party machinery for the Soviet State. Leaders of the groups were appointed and received their pay from the Kremlin. Their livelihood depended on outright obedience to the Kremlin. Simultaneously, the Comintern was prostituting the entire leadership of the German Communist Party. Of 135,000 members in the early 1920s over 4300 were on the Russian payroll. If they put the interest of the German party above that of the Comintern, they were summoned to Moscow where they quietly disappeared into darkness or saw the light. If they ignored the summons, they were either kidnapped or "exposed" as Communists and turned over to the German police authorities. The Left Opposition in the German party was thus systematically destroyed and the "loyal" Communists completely Stalinized. Party members were expelled for having said "hello" on the street to a Left Oppositionist.

As the Soviet secret police assumed greater and greater power in Germany, Berlin was set up as a secondary center for world espionage operations. This "invisible hierarchy, a secret elite" (according to Ruth Fischer and to General Walter Krivitsky, the Red Army's Chief of Western Intelligence) was stringently organized. It was frankly a GPU (later NKVD) operation. Its members had rank and title, and a regular pay scale on a paramilitary basis.

Sorge, the intellectual and the man of action, fitted in perfectly with the discipline of this invisible hierarchy. Brave and tested, he rose gradually to a position of trust. He very delicately hinted at this in his Tokyo confession: "As I was engaged in secret liaison for the party, it was not surprising that at the Communist convention held at Frankfurt-am-Main in 1924 I was selected to protect delegates from the Soviet Communist Party who had entered the country illegally to represent the Comintern."

Because the German party was then torn by the Stalin-Trotsky battle, the Comintern had sent top-level men — Piatnitsky, Manuilsky, Kuusinen, and Lozovsky. As "security officer," Sorge's responsibility — and the trust placed in him — was tremendous. "Of course, my relations with the Comintern delegates were very intimate, and we grew more friendly every day. At the close of the session, they asked me to come to Comintern headquarters in Moscow to work for them." Sponsored by these top Soviet leaders, Sorge was transferred from the German to the Soviet Communist Party — the first step toward becoming a high-ranking *apparatchik*.

Late in 1924, Sorge reported in Moscow. His work in the conspiracy was about to begin.

III

No Dogs or Chinese Allowed

In the creation of a Communist espionage apparatus, many people and many types are needed. At the center is the trained leader, hardened by experience and inextricably committed to the victory of Soviet imperialism. Richard Sorge was one such. There are the equally committed adventurists, ideological camp-followers, the neurotically bound, the sexual or social misfits who, in the Army phrase, have "found a home." Some, like Agnes Smedley, are drawn in by their hatred of men and their fear of mankind. Others, like Alger Hiss, succumb to the most mortal of sins — pride. They become functionaries of betrayal because of their deep contempt for humanity and the fumbling processes of human salvation.

As a kind of protective cover for the apparatus, there are the politicians, and the do-gooders, and the patsies of deception who never know what they are doing, and the clever operators who believe that evil can be harnessed for purposes of selfish interest. Many of these types are convinced that they are anti-Communist, but when the consequences of their blind or self-seeking acts are made public, they are astounded and cry out rancorously. At the moment of crisis, these present-day Catilines put career or ego above the national interest. While the apparatus scampers behind their wide skirts, they steadfastly insist that it does not exist. The Hiss case and the so-called Tydings investigation turned them up by the score.

These, perhaps, are the most dangerous — for they protect Communist cells at the moment when their extermination is possible.

But the most effective, before the apparatus is discovered, are those who love Communism because they love humanity, who betray their countries because they love Communism, and who wrap both the betrayal and the Communism in a mesh of morality. Among these smug spinners serving the party more faithfully than a thousand dues-payers was Ozaki Hozumi, the befuddled idealist who became Richard Sorge's chief accomplice.

The birth records say that Ozaki was born in Tokyo, on 1 May 1901. He was still a young child, however, when his father transplanted the family to the island of Formosa. The move was dictated by the father's appointment as editor of the *Taiwan Nichi Nichi Shimbun,* and Ozaki spent all his childhood and most of his adolescence on the island. His life there was quiet and well ordered, as it would be in an upper-class Japanese family. But Formosa was occupied territory, wrested from China a scant six years before Ozaki's birth. "The many instances of discrimination between the subjugated natives and their Japanese conquerors caused humanitarian doubts to assail my mind," he wrote shortly before his death.

Japanese society was in turmoil. Roused out of her feudal sleep by American enterprise, the small, tightly knit country had transformed herself into a modern industrial state almost in a day. An economy based on handicrafts and home piecework was developing into a prodigious mass-producer, competing in the Asiatic market with Great Britain. From a military and political standpoint, the defeat of Russia in 1905 had made Japan the England of the Far East — the England of 1588 and the industrial revolution rolled into one. A single exception made the situation more explosive, more tempting. Japan was not faced across the China Sea by strong national states. A weak and divided empire tottered before her. Only the Western imperialists stood between Japan and Asiatic hegemony.

From the turn of the century forward, Japan's foreign policy was directed toward driving out Western influence and destroying the Open Door Policy which guaranteed China's political and economic integrity. Everywhere, this Japanese determination was visible. After Formosa, the next step was seizure of Korea. When, during World War I, the Western powers were otherwise occupied in Europe, Japan was taking advantage of the opportunity by pressing on China her infamous Twenty-one Demands, which would have given her virtual control of the mainland.

The Nipponese imperial muscles were not yet sufficiently developed for her to withstand British, French, and American pressure to withdraw the demands. But the "temporary" grab of German interests in Shantung province became permanent — the first move in the steady penetration of the Chinese state and the creation of a Greater East Asia Co-Prosperity Sphere. The handwriting could not have been clearer on the tattered map of Asia.

In the Japanese homeland, the concomitants of industrialization were everywhere apparent. Deprived of his tools by the machine, the worker was defenseless. The rigid, paternalistic society barred him from the protection of trade-union organization. A tradition of subservience to authority made this organization slow and timid. Hours were long, wages pitifully low, child labor was widespread. The military was already on the ascendant and war budgets piled taxation on the people. The upper classes still honored the cultivation of the arts and literature, but this was the façade behind which lurked the busy realities of modern exploitation.

It was in this environment that Ozaki grew up. During the final years of World War I, there was an upsurge of hope in the American dream. Ozaki was influenced, he would recall, by "the frivolous American propaganda concerning freedom and peace which was sweeping the world." It was neither frivolous nor propaganda, but unfortunately this pro-American sentiment was quickly dissipated in the cynical emanations from Versailles. President Wilson went to the Peace Conference clothed in ideals; he returned in a barrel. The deals and counter deals, the land and power grabs, of the victorious Allies destroyed America's moral ascendancy. In the dismemberment of the Austro-Hungarian federation, the snatching of colonial loot, the hodge-podge remaking of maps, the seeds of wars to come and a hardshell international immorality to justify them were planted. And no one knew this better than the Japanese.

To fill the propaganda void, however, a new-born system of illusions galvanized the world — the Russian Revolution. Out of the ashes of war, "freedom" was being reborn — and everywhere Lenin's finger poked at men's minds.

Ozaki's reaction to these events came later. The external events of his life were still ordinary. By 1919, he had been graduated from Taihoku Middle School. Before he left for Tokyo for the First Higher School (the American equivalent of undergraduate study), his father took him "to worship at the Taiwan Shrine and told me to be a man of service to my country." In Sugamo Prison, he wrote, "I have a fond recollection of this." The irony of his recollection was only partly apparent to him.

It was in Tokyo that the pattern of his life began unfolding. As a student in Course B, Literature Department, he plunged into the study of European classics. He learned German, began reading the German philosophers, and absorbed the historical materialism without which Marxism is both meaningless and impossible. In 1922, he had advanced to the Tokyo Imperial University, where he studied law. His ambition still was to become a government official. But his early seethings against Japanese society came to a boil the following year, when he witnessed the first roundup of Communists and Communist students. This event produced "a righteous social indignation." It did not affect him quite as much as an unhappy love affair which sent him back to Formosa in a state of deep depression.

Ozaki touches lightly on this break of heart. If it had any significance in the formation of the man, it was only tangential. At home, recovering from his *mal d'amour,* he came across a biography of Ferdinand Lassalle, a founder of the German Social Democratic

Party and a non-Marxist socialist. From Lassalle, Ozaki moved on to Hegelian dialectics, to historical determinism — the opening door to dialectical materialism and Communism. Ozaki notes in his confession only that he was "impressed" by Lassalle's ideas.

Social consciousness having soothed the pains of unrequited love, Ozaki returned to Tokyo in 1924 to pass his examinations for the political science degree. Then he again took up law studies at the Tokyo Imperial University. But his main interest was no longer in the government officialdom to which he had once aspired. Out of college, he immediately joined the Nipponese equivalent of a social problems club. Throughout the world such clubs were being set up by the Communists in colleges and universities — a handy way to indoctrinate and recruit party members. A young assistant professor headed the club, and it was he who introduced Ozaki to Bukharin's *Historical Materialism*. "I devoted most of my time to it," Ozaki wrote of his meetings with the Communist seminar.

Earnestly, he began the systematic study of Marxist literature. The *Manifesto, Das Kapital*, and the older classics were the first steps into the movement. But in pretty short order, he was reading Lenin's *State and Revolution*, Stalin's *Problems of Leninism*, the polemical writings of Karl Radek, and the steady flow of Communist propaganda in the Comintern's *Inprecorr* (International Press Correspondence), published in Moscow in the major languages of the world. In 1925, he received his law degree and began his non-member attachment to the Communist Party.

But Ozaki did not sequester himself in some dank corner of the political netherworld. At the university, he also lived the pleasant, rich life of a student. He was liked and admired; he made many friends. Unconsciously, he was investing in his later success as a Soviet spy. In the Intelligence Report prepared by General Headquarters, Far East Command, on the Sorge ring — the so-called Willoughby Report — the importance of Ozaki's college friendships is summed up:

Any graduate of the [Tokyo Imperial University] could know that his classmates would become leaders of Japan's business, professional, and governmental world. The men of the class of 1925 . . . while not yet at the top by 1940 would be holding positions of great responsibility throughout Japan, especially in the bureaus and ministries of the Imperial Government. Any young man with the brilliance of Ozaki Hozumi was bound to make and keep many close friends who would know almost everything there was to know and who would be glad to share their knowledge with their trusted confidant. If such a man turned traitor, his country's secrets would flow in a steady stream to the enemy.

Ozaki continued to walk the shady groves for another year. Then, in 1926, he terminated his studies and joined the staff of the *Asahi Shimbun,* the Tokyo newspaper. Clandestinely, he joined the Kanto Publication Workers' Union under the name of Genkichi Kusano, the first of his aliases. The "Genkichi" he picked up from Merisaki Genkichi, the Japanese agrarian leader who was arrested, along with his whole family, during Ozaki's student days. In 1927, he was transferred by the *Asahi Shimbun* to the *Osaka Asahi.* The following year he was sent to Shanghai as a special correspondent. This was the real turning point in his life.

China was in crisis. The Sun Yat-sen revolution had overthrown the Manchu dynasty in 1911, but the vast country had not moved into a modern era of representative government as Chinese idealists had hoped. War lords and regional leaders split up the once-unified nation into warring groups vying for control. The first party to achieve any sort of dominance was the Kuomintang (KMT), led by Dr. Sun, which adopted his moderate, step-by-step plan for China's rehabilitation. Sun's Three Stages became the KMT's official program — and remain so to this day.

They were:

(1) Unification of China under a military dictatorship.

(2) A period of "political tutelage" in which the unified country was educated in the ways of representative government.

(3) When the people had learned to exercise their political rights, a full-fledged constitutional government.

The guiding principles of Sun Yat-sen's revolution were embodied in the *San Min Chu-I,* the Three Principles of the People. Boiled down, they called for a strong Chinese political and cultural nationalism, for a government in which the central organization would hold quasi-dictatorial power (tempered by the people's right to suffrage, recall, initiative, and referendum), and for a form of Keynesian socialism to regulate capital, equalize land-holdings, and bar any outbreak of Marxist class struggle. On this last point, Sun made it bluntly clear that the proletarian dictatorship and the war of class against class should not and need not come to China.

Unfortunately, the KMT remained a loosely jointed party. In order to tighten up the organization, Sun Yat-sen made one of the great mistakes of history. Sun joined in an alliance with the Chinese Communists and the Third International. In order to strengthen KMT party organization, the Communists were to supply organizers and technicians. A solemn agreement was entered into between Sun Yat-sen, representing the Kuomintang, and Adolph Joffe, representing the Comintern, whereby it was agreed that Chinese Communists would be allowed to join the KMT as "individuals" who would "obey Kuomintang discipline." This "united front" between the KMT and the three-year-old Chinese Communist Party, formalized in 1924, was China's doom.

Michael Borodin, a Comintern representative, moved into Canton, bringing with him a host of agents, organizers, underground activists — all Moscow-trained. General Bluecher left his post with the Siberian Red Army to train the Chinese military forces and to help Chiang Kai-shek set up the Whampoa Academy, China's West Point. Under Borodin, the KMT was reorganized along soviet lines of centralized control reaching into the smallest subdivision.

While the Chinese Reds carefully infiltrated key KMT posts,

Li Ta-chao, one of the Communist leaders, stated solemnly: "In joining the Kuomintang, Communists . . . have not the slightest intention of turning [it] into a Communist party. Those Communists who joined the Kuomintang do so as individuals and not on a party basis." Even as the words were being spoken, the Comintern was plotting against the KMT and continuing its steady encroachment on Chinese national integrity.

The Soviet tactics moved on a double level of hypocrisy. In 1919, Lenin had renounced all Tsarist claims to Chinese territory and economic concessions. The historian Harold M. Vinacke outlines the immediate betrayal.[1] "The methods employed by Joffe, and his successor Leo Karakhan, were (1) to play upon the chord of Western capitalistic imperialism as contrasted by the non-imperialistic aims of the new [sic] Russia. . . . (2) to play off China against Japan in negotiations with both; (3) to cultivate the Chinese intelligentsia, securing its support, and utilizing this support to bring pressure on the Chinese government; and (4) to establish contact with Canton, the KMT seat of power, and use this as a lever with which to move [the government in] Peking."

By the time of Sun Yat-sen's death in March 1925, the Communists had been able to infiltrate thoroughly the central party machinery of the KMT. The only force against them was General Chiang Kai-shek, who had won the backing of non-Communist labor unions, the powerful overseas Chinese, and the modern middle class in the cities. In 1926 by a *coup d'état,* Chiang was able to break the Red power on the KMT, though maintaining a surface cordiality with Borodin. At this point the top-level Soviet strategy in China suddenly shifted. Until that time, the Russians had opposed the "northern expedition," a campaign against the militarists in North China to extend the influence of the KMT and hasten the unification of China.

The Russians had feared that if the Canton government became

[1] *A History of the Far East in Modern Times* (New York, 1941).

too powerful before it was outrightly Communist, it might escape
their control. After Chiang's *coup,* Borodin urged the "northern
expedition"—Sun Yat-sen's dream since 1917. Chiang played right
into Bluecher's hands. While Chiang, following a campaign mapped
out by Bluecher, began the subjugation of the northern war lords,
Borodin and the Communists reconsolidated their power at Canton.
In Chiang's absence, he was ousted as commander in chief of the
KMT armies and as chairman of the Standing Committee which
ran the party.

Victorious in his military adventures, Chiang returned to cross
his Rubicon. There was a split in the KMT, and Chiang resolved
it by driving the Communists out of power. He moved on Shanghai,
seized the city, and began the ruthless extermination of the Communists who had attempted to knife him. By 1928, Chiang had
virtually completed the unification of China, established its capital
at Nanking, and resigned both his military and civil posts. But
the Communists remained the one great threat to unity and to
the development of a peaceful China. Driven out of the cities, they
reorganized in the rural areas, giving their Leninism an agrarian
twist. Mao Tse-tung emerged as the dominant Communist and
Li Li-san, who had urged an attack on the urban centers, returned to
Moscow.

This was the China which welcomed Ozaki Hozumi. Shanghai
was still quivering from Chiang's purge, and to the confirmed Marxist like Ozaki, the new Chinese state was an abomination. In the
face of Chiang's triumphs he could write: "The so-called People's
Revolution had just occurred, giving birth to the Nationalist government in Nanking, but carrying in its wake in Shanghai a mighty
wave of Communist sentiment." From all accounts, this sentiment
resided in the sanctuary of the International Settlements, already
crawling with Soviet agents. Ozaki could also write of the waning
Western influence: "The notorious sign in the Park in Shanghai's

Bund, 'No Dogs or Chinese Allowed,'[2] had been taken down, but Englishmen remained the real masters."

Working as a correspondent in Shanghai, Ozaki made contact with the city's leftist groups — the students of the Ch'uang-Tsao-Sheh group — and the clandestine Communists. From time to time, he contributed pseudonymously to the magazine of the left-wing literary group, the Creation Society (Sozo Sha), and associated with the Communist-minded Japanese students in the East Asia Common Script School. He also visited on occasion the Zeitgeist Bookshop in the French Settlement. This front for Communist activity was run by a Mrs. Irene Wiedemeyer. Late in 1929, Mrs. Wiedemeyer introduced Ozaki to Agnes Smedley, then representing the *Frankfurter Zeitung* in the Far East.

The two became close friends and confessed their Communist sympathies. At first on a journalistic basis, and then with the understanding that there was a recipient beyond this, Ozaki gave Miss Smedley information that he picked up in the course of his work. There was much that his *Asahi* connections babbled unguardedly which Agnes Smedley wished to know.

In 1930, Kito Ginichi, a Japanese member of the American Communist Party assigned to Shanghai, suddenly called on Ozaki at his office. Kito asked Ozaki if he would like to meet an American journalist named "Johnson." Ozaki knew that Kito was a Communist agent; he realized that he was being invited to something more than a social meeting. Putting Kito off, he consulted Agnes Smedley. Sharply, and with a slight edge of fear to her manner, Miss Smedley cautioned him never to mention "Johnson" again.[3]

[2] The signs at the entrance to parks in the Shanghai International Settlement read: "The parks are reserved for the use of the foreign community. Dogs may not be brought into the parks." Propaganda convinced most of the world that the signs read: "No Dogs or Chinese Allowed."

[3] When, at Alger Hiss's suggestion, Whittaker Chambers mentioned Noel Field to Colonel Boris Bykov, head of Soviet Intelligence in the United States, as a likely espionage prospect, Bykov similarly warned Chambers never to mention the name again.

Several days later, Agnes Smedley brought up the subject of "Johnson" herself. She would introduce him, she told Ozaki. A dinner meeting was arranged at a restaurant on Nanking Road. At the appointed time, Ozaki was at the restaurant. A few minutes later, Agnes Smedley appeared and joined him. After a short wait, a tall, thickset man walked in, looked around casually, and then wandered over to their table. When he greeted them, it was in an English roughed over by a European accent. Ozaki had met Richard Sorge.

IV

Comintern to Fourth Bureau

It is interesting to note the sudden thinness of Richard Sorge's confession as he moves into the 1925–1929 period of his espionage activities. It was not a desire to be relevant which inhibited him — he had been expansive in describing his early years. Sorge knew, however, that this era — the touchiest in the Comintern's history — was one in which the heresy hunters could find evidence of his ideological weaknesses, no matter what position he took. The Japanese were not out to trace back Sorge's life to its European indiscretions. They did not press him for more facts, and he allowed himself merely the luxury of several paragraphs to give his life's account continuity.

After a discussion of Comintern organization, Sorge brushed aside this rich period of his life:

With the passing of time, it grew increasingly necessary to supplement previously acquired basic data with firsthand information obtained by special Intelligence Division espionage agents operating in all countries at all times [Sorge wrote]. It had long been a practice to send special emissaries from the Organization Division of Comintern headquarters to assist local parties with organization problems, and it was decided that such functions would have to be expanded to include intelligence work.

In accordance with that policy, I was sent to the Scandinavian countries in 1927 to engage in intelligence activities concerning their Communist parties, their political problems, and any important military issues which might arise. I began operations in Denmark, complying with instructions by assuming a position of active leadership alongside the other party heads, attending meetings and conferences and visiting the main party organizations of the country. [In short, he was that all-powerful individual, the Comintern Rep, who ruled and terrorized local Communist parties, much as Gerhart Eisler ruled the American Party in the 1930s and 1940s.]

Insofar as time permitted, I also did intelligence work on Denmark's economic and political problems, discussing my observations and findings with party representatives and incorporating their opinions in my reports to Moscow. I then went from Denmark to Sweden to study problems there in the same manner.

[Returning to Moscow] in 1928, I participated in the work of the political committee of the Comintern's second world conference,[1] after which I went again to Scandinavia, this time primarily because of the difficult party situation in Norway. . . . Party problems of various descriptions seriously impeded intelligence work in the fields of economics and politics. Orders came for me to go to England to collect information prior to my return, i.e., to study the labor movement, the status of the Communist Party and political and economic conditions in Britain in 1929. My instructions to remain strictly aloof from intra-party disputes accorded perfectly with my personal inclinations and enabled me to devote more attention to political and economic intelligence work than had been possible in Scandinavia.

This beautifully disingenuous account may have satisfied the Japanese authorities, but it is not much more than language. Between 1924 and 1927, when Sorge worked in the busy Comintern center in Moscow, a titanic struggle was rocking the Soviet Union and every Communist party on the face of the earth. Stalin was combining with Zinoviev, the Comintern chief, to destroy Trotsky. When Trotsky had been pushed out of the way — exiled to Alma Ata — Stalin combined with Bukharin to oust Zinoviev. The stage for the Moscow trials was being set. In the Hotel Lux, where Comintern leaders from other countries were kept segregated in Moscow, there were hushed consultations among the "pure" foreign Com-

---

[1] This is an error. Sorge meant the Sixth World Conference.

munists while the "impure" — those in disgrace for supporting the anti-Stalin factions — waited in misery and fear, hoping to return to grace.

On Moscow's streets, there was rioting over Trotsky. Thousands of semi-clandestine meetings, known to the secret police who feared to act, were rallying support to Trotsky. In the other principal cities, there were grave disorders as Russian Communists tried to fend off the ultimate dictatorship of Lenin's ideological successor, Stalin. Delegates to Comintern congresses, and leaders of non-Russian Communist parties, were flowing in and out of Moscow — complaining, wheedling, attempting to get Stalin's support for their faction. Left Oppositionists, not quite for Trotsky but fighting Stalin, were attempting to maintain control of the Comintern apparatus, of their local Communist parties. Even where they had a majority of votes, Stalin's steamroller tactics, his grip on the party machinery, defeated them.

As a Comintern bureaucrat, Sorge was able to view the struggle for mastery in Russia. He was unimportant enough to remain out of the line of fire between Stalin and the Old Bolsheviks. But he must have maneuvered pretty carefully and skillfully. Many minor officials were being punished for small heresies. Sorge, like most of the German Communists, tended to side with the Left Opposition and Trotsky. But he was astute enough to adopt a chameleon-like disguise. He was a soldier who had accepted Communist discipline. He hid his true sympathies in Moscow, just as he was able to hide them later in Tokyo.

When he was sent to Scandinavia and England, it was as much to purge the Left Oppositionists and to purify the party as it was to gather military, political, and economic intelligence. In England, he had a tougher job as well, to rehabilitate the British party. Torn by left–right factionalism, it had been further hurt in May 1927 by the raid on Arcos Ltd., a Russian trading company in London. British police had turned up damaging information proving that

Soviet agents were attempting to steal military secrets. The Soviet officials in England were also shown to have devoted more time to stirring up trouble for Great Britain and her colonies than to stimulating trade between the two countries. British labor leaders who had opposed the break in diplomatic relations changed their minds when they discovered, and denounced, Soviet interference in their trade unions.

Assigned to put the pieces together, Sorge did what he could. But 1927 was a bad year for the Soviet Union. Everywhere, Communists were being caught engaged in everything except the liberation of mankind from the golden chains of capitalism. In France, municipal councilors and members of the party secretariat were caught at espionage. Jacques Doriot, later to become a Nazi, was imprisoned for revolutionary activity in the French colonies.

The worst blow to the Comintern and to Stalin was the news from China. A week after the Russian leader had publicly praised Chiang Kai-shek and exchanged portraits with him, Chiang began the purge of Communists in the Kuomintang. Thousands were slaughtered in Shanghai. At Wuhan, other thousands were killed. When, at Stalin's order, the Chinese Communists set up the Canton Commune and defied Chiang, they were cut down. So terrible was the news reaching Moscow that for a while it seemed as if Stalin's political house would collapse. Only the lack of co-ordination among the Trotskyist group and the other Left Oppositionists saved Stalin from defeat. In full retreat, he could have been cut off and cut up by his political enemies. The Chinese Communist Revolution was destroyed — and would have remained finished but for the genius of Mao Tse-tung and the other Red leaders in China. In Moscow, Communists merely saw the bleeding remains of their promised victory.

These were the times that Sorge lived through, but described so casually. Instead, he carefully included in his "confession" praise for the Comintern functionaries — Lozovsky, Manuilsky, Piatnitsky, and Kuusinen — who continued to run the dwindling Comintern while the makers of the Revolution destroyed each other. These were the men who protected Sorge while the Central Control Commission — the thought-control and terror committee — took advantage of Trotskyist miscalculations and began to weed out the ranks of the Left Opposition by bribes, by blackmail, and by prolonged and deadly interrogations which destroyed the will and capacity to fight.

There is one slight indication that Sorge had no stomach for the factionalism rife in the Comintern. Reporting after his English mission to Ottomar Kuusinen, head of the Comintern's Intelligence and Organization Bureau, he complained that his espionage activities were seriously hampered by having to intervene in the squabbles of local parties.

"I submitted the following fundamental propositions," Sorge wrote in his confession, "that any basic and comprehensive intelligence program should be kept apart from the internal quarrels controlling local parties. . . . This separation, I said, was also imperative because of the frequent need of the intelligence operative for secrecy. . . . At the Moscow end, such espionage agents in foreign countries would have to be more definitely divorced than in the past from the over-all Comintern organization." He had seen the weaknesses of the Comintern apparatus during his missions to Scandinavia and England. To transmit his information, he had been forced then to turn it over to the local parties and their own courier service. Often, with particularly important material, he had had to return to Berlin in order to ensure completely reliable transmission. He realized that only an exclusively espionage apparatus, operated along military lines, was the solution.

He had another, shrewder, reason for demanding the separation of Comintern and strictly espionage activities. Sitting in Moscow, watching the Stalin machine take over more and more power, Sorge realized that the Comintern as an independent coalition of Communist parties was doomed. "The shifting of the leadership of the revolutionary labor movement from the . . . Comintern to the Russian Communist Party can be traced in my career," he was to write retrospectively. ". . . Formerly the Guidance Section of the Comintern was independent in every respect. It consulted the leaders of the Russian Communist Party. . . . Today it is no longer possible for the leaders of the Comintern to act independently of the Russian Communist Party . . . as they once did under the leadership of Zinoviev." And the Russian party, as Sorge well knew, was the Russian government and the Soviet Union.

The Comintern neither liked nor approved of Sorge's suggestions for a separation of powers. But it was no longer in control of the situation. The Red Army's Fourth Bureau (Intelligence) was immediately attracted to the idea. In China, it had put some of its best men at the disposal of the Comintern — and in the rout these men had been destroyed. Now it wanted men who would have no contact with Communist functionaries, who would hide behind false credentials and occupations, who would be full-time spies, and who could weather any changes in popular feeling toward the Communists — who could weather anything, in fact, except exposure.

When Sorge's proposals were transmitted to the Red Army, the Fourth Bureau immediately transferred him to its jurisdiction. He himself never knew whether he was technically a member of the bureau, whether he was an NKVD operative, or whether he was merely a member of the Soviet Communist Party on loan to the Red Army. However, from the moment in 1929 that he transferred to the Fourth Bureau, he was cut off from all contacts with "official" Communists. In Moscow, he secretly visited Piatnitsky, Kuusinen, and others, but that was a social contact — and unofficial.

"I began to conduct my intelligence operations in my hotel room and at houses in various locations [rather than from local party headquarters]. . . . Technically and organizationally speaking, my reports were sent to the . . . Fourth Bureau, which furnished all the technical aids [wireless contacts, radio men] and other assistance required to carry on my work." Sorge began recruiting other espionage agents in Europe, plucked from the fellow-traveling fold, from the party sympathizers, and from a selection of highly qualified Communists. His charm and good looks gave him a strong weapon in recruiting women, the personal approach often being as effective as the ideological. It was at this time that Sorge recruited Hede Massing, then the wife of Gerhart Eisler, and introduced her to Ignace Reiss, one of the top Red Army Intelligence men in Europe.

But Sorge's interest was in the Far East. The debacle in China convinced him that here was the area in which he could most effectively operate and in which his talents were most needed. After studying the region with German thoroughness, he asked for the assignment. It was promptly granted. There were conferences with General Berzin, head of Red Army Intelligence, with members of the Russian foreign office, and with a few top-level Comintern leaders, before he was given his instructions: to gather all possible information on Japanese activities, intentions, order of battle, and operations in China. His secondary mission was to report practically anything of interest that he came across.

In January 1930, Richard Sorge turned up in Shanghai. He was shielded by the flimsiest of covers — correspondent for the German *Soziologische* magazine. But in Shanghai, crowded with spies, propagandists, adventurers, and idealists, it was enough.

V

Shanghai Gesture: Red Version

SHANGHAI in the late 1920s and early 1930s may have resembled its movie-lot counterpart of polyglot tongues, menacing shadows, beautiful adventurers, sex, politics, and midnight terror. But in the focus of this narrative, the significant events took place beyond the clatter of the native sections of the city. It was among the expensive shopfronts, the broad avenues, and the relative order of the International Settlements that the real plotters moved and transacted their business. The Communist agents who came to the populous city had checked their daggers elsewhere. The cloaks they wore were those of prosaic businessmen, busy newspapermen, and assiduous benefactors of the human race. The *mise-en-scène* may have been exotic, but the Communist agents themselves could well have been operating in Washington.

A small army of these agents had been sent by the Red Army's Fourth Bureau, by the Comintern, and by the other appendages of Soviet subversion. While the Chinese Communists and their fragmented armies, led by Mao Tse-tung, moved into the rural areas to lick their wounds and re-form for later battle, their Caucasian comrades covered the waterfront. But the Soviet agents along the coastal strip wore their Marx with a difference. They were not there to foment revolution; their mission was simply to act as the eyes and ears of the Soviet foreign ministry. Only a minor portion of their work was agitational and propagandistic — a tangential activity which led to the formation of such organizations as the Noulens

Defense Committee, Agnes Smedley's China Civil Rights League, the All-China Labor Federation, all inspired and financed by Willi Muenzenberg, creator of the Communist-front technique.

The holding company for many of the cells and parallel apparatuses which flourished in Shanghai was the Pan Pacific Trade Union Secretariat (PPTUS), a subsidiary of the Comintern. Like many Comintern adjuncts, it operated out of the parent Far Eastern Bureau, which was quartered in Berlin. Later, these staff headquarters fled the Hitler terror, splitting like an amoeba, with one half going to Vladivostok and the other to Shanghai.

The PPTUS operated on two levels in China. The first was organizational. Sorge described it as giving "the links and the codes for contact with New York, London, and Moscow." It maintained this liaison, handled Far Eastern Bureau funds earmarked for the Chinese Communists and various other *apparats* and propaganda fronts, and acted as host to visiting espionage dignitaries and other miscellaneous operatives.

The second level was political — subversion, espionage, agitation. There was no clear-cut line of demarcation between the functions of the Comintern, the Fourth Bureau, and the CPUSSR in China. In his confession, Sorge devoted pages to an attempt to delimit the operational boundaries of each, but his efforts were futile. The three worked independently and together, with the PPTUS dominant organizationally and the Red Army's Intelligence section, under General Berzin, dominant in most espionage work. Sorge himself, though under orders from the Fourth Bureau, was also "Chief, Far Eastern Group, Confidential Affairs Department, Central Committee, CPUSSR."

Founded in 1927, the PPTUS was headed by a series of top Comintern agents. The first leader, "elected" at the moment of its birth, was Earl Browder. By 1929, he had been replaced by Gerhart Eisler, sent specifically to China to root out the Trotskyism which had flowered wildly after the bloody defeat of the Chinese Stalinists. In turn, Eisler was replaced by another German, Arthur Ewert, who eventually landed in a Brazilian prison as a clandestine leader of the abortive Communist *Putsch* of 1935. Ewert's successor was Eugene Dennis, using the alias Paul Walsh. The Far Eastern Bureau poured five hundred thousand dollars a year into the PPTUS treasury, and this sum was augmented by the profits of "legitimate" businesses such as a great import-export firm which the Comintern had set up in Shanghai. A regular Comintern office was also maintained in Shanghai. Its function was as political as the Comintern itself. Representing the world Communist organization in Moscow, it sought to implement the *Theses on the Revolutionary Movement in the Colonies and Semi-Colonies,* a body of doctrine promulgated at the Sixth World Congress of the Comintern in 1928. Point Four of this bold, new program for China had called for the "overthrow of the militarists and the Kuomintang." Eisler was connected with this Comintern branch, but its operating leaders were first one Paul Ruegg (alias Hilaire Noulens, alias Vandercruysen, alias ten other names, who kept fourteen apartments and at least seven bank accounts in Shanghai), and Karl Lesse, who figures briefly in the Sorge story. The Comintern group was, in effect, the liaison between Moscow and the Chinese Communist Party.

In Shanghai, too, a Red Army group under Major General Theo (alias Froelich) had established communications with the Chinese Red Army. It had its own radio transmitter, operated by a Lieutenant Colonel Feldman. The Theo group was in close touch with a Harbin Fourth Bureau apparatus, gathering political and military intelligence, whose leader was one Gloemberg-Ott. The Harbin cell also served as a post office for other espionage groups in China and, at first, was the letter box for Richard Sorge. In time, radio communication was adopted to facilitate the quick transfer of information to Moscow.

Long before Sorge was assigned to Shanghai and the Fast East, a large and active espionage group linking the Shanghai work with the

Harbin apparatus was in existence. It was directed by an American, "Jim," and it included the American vice-consul at Harbin, Tycho Lilliestrom. The composition of the "Jim" group, however, was strictly Caucasian. It could operate easily in the coastal cities and could prey on the foreign colony, but it was useless among the Chinese and Japanese.

In April 1929, less than a year before Sorge arrived in Shanghai, this apparatus had been joined by Max Klausen, a big, heavy-set German whose contribution was neither great intellect nor guile. Klausen, however, knew all about radios. He could transmit, he could build sets, and he could take them apart. So great was his skill that, in the Tokyo years, he was able to build a set small enough to fit in a briefcase yet so powerful that it could transmit to Siberia. In most respects, Klausen differed radically from Sorge and Ozaki. He was the son of a poor shopkeeper, with a minimum of schooling obtained on the little island off Schleswig-Holstein where he was born. An apprenticeship with the local blacksmith had followed. In the evenings, he attended a trade school, where he demonstrated a real mechanical aptitude. Drafted in 1917, he was assigned to a radio unit of the German Signal Corps on the Western Front.

"During my early youth," Klausen confessed later, "I had no interest in political affairs, but after my enlistment in the army I met many soldiers, particularly among my immediate superiors, who were imbued with communistic thought and were engaged in communistic propaganda. Army life . . . was favorable to the spread of the doctrine." A second influence, the blacksmith to whose shop Klausen returned after the war, made him become a Communist sympathizer. Drifting from job to job, Klausen made his way to Hamburg where, in 1921, he became a sailor. The port cities were the Red centers of Germany, and in the seamen's union his indoctrination continued. Unemployment, political upheaval, and postwar despair all convinced him that Communism was the only way out, Russia the worker's paradise.

In 1927, Klausen applied for membership in the German party. To his chagrin, he testified, "my application was not accepted immediately." For six months, he was tested by the party; he agitated among the sailors and propagandized them. An "examination" by Karl Lesse, at that time head of the Communist-controlled German Seaman's Union, clinched his membership.

Within a year after he joined the German party, he was on his way to Moscow on assignment to the Fourth Bureau of the Red Army General Staff. After brief indoctrination, he got his marching orders.

General Berzin's secretary gave me $150 (American) and a ticket from Moscow to Harbin and told me to establish contact with a comrade in Shanghai. He showed me a photograph and said that I was to meet the person appearing in it who would come to the Palace Hotel in Shanghai every Thursday at 5 P.M. I was to carry a copy of the *Shanghai Evening Post* in my left hand and a pipe in my right, and when the comrade said to me: "How is Erna?" I was to answer: "She sends her regards."

In April 1929, Klausen made contact in Shanghai with the "comrade," one Constantin Mishin, who took him to No. 10 Route Doumer in the French Concession. This was home, school, and workshop for the two men. As a cover, Klausen worked in the auto repair shop of a White Russian. In his free time, he got a long and intensive briefing from Mishin. Klausen's first job was to build a powerful short-wave transmitter and to establish radio contact with another station known as "Wiesbaden," probably located in Khabarovsk. Messages sent out were written in German or English before coding.

Once he had set up the transmitter, Klausen was directed to collect the parts for another transmitter and to deliver them to a French diplomat for smuggling into Harbin. In August 1929, Klausen was sent to Harbin himself. At the Hotel Moderne, he was met by a courier who introduced him to the chief of the Soviet agents at Harbin, Gloemberg-Ott. Several days later, Gloemberg-Ott "came alone to ask me to deliver my radio to the private home of the American vice-consul, Lilliestrom — I think he is Swiss-American." At Lilliestrom's house, Klausen was introduced to the American, who then left hurriedly. "For the next ten days, I was busy installing the radio set [in two rooms of the Lilliestrom home]. I had been brought in so Gloemberg-Ott could begin to send radio reports to Moscow on the Chinese Army."

Returning to Shanghai to continue as communications man for the ring, Klausen moved out of Mishin's apartment and into a boardinghouse. Among the tenants was Mrs. Anna Wallenius, a thirty-one-year-old widow. Mrs. Wallenius had come to Shanghai with her late husband as a refugee from the Soviets. Though she was the sister-in-law of General K. Martti Wallenius of the Finnish Army General Staff, she had little money. After her husband's death, she had supported herself first as a seamstress and then as a practical nurse at the Shanghai Isolation Hospital. The treatment she had undergone at the hands of the Bolsheviks — and her reduced circumstances — made her a violent enemy of Communism.

Ironically, Anna Wallenius fell in love with Klausen. He seemed to be a good automobile mechanic who earned a very good living. And Klausen, though hardly the moon-calf type, returned Anna's affections. Though her political views were a direct menace to him and to the espionage apparatus, he lived with her, eventually married her, and withstood all pressure from his superiors to break with her. To the Japanese police, he spoke in derogatory terms of Anna. And she spoke ill of him. But she never betrayed him — in fact, she went on several dangerous missions for him. Much as she hated Communism, she showed that repugnance in only one important way. Max and Anna never had any children — and she told him flatly that she would not bring the child of a Soviet agent into the world.

In January 1930, "Jim" turned Klausen over to the recently arrived Richard Sorge. The procedure followed the usual tight-lipped mumbo-jumbo of the underground. "Jim" merely told Klausen, "A friend of yours is staying at the Anchor Hotel and wants to see you. About 10 A.M. would be convenient for him." The friend was Joseph Weingart whom Klausen had known in Germany. A week later, Weingart took Klausen to the Cathay Hotel to "meet a man who wants to see you." The man was Richard Sorge. For the first time in his espionage career, Klausen had stepped into the big time. Within a year, Sorge was in charge of operations in Shanghai and Klausen was the chief of the radio division.

VI

Sorge at Work

A GREAT wave of strikes in Shanghai had just subsided when Richard Sorge arrived to take up his assignment. The coolies in the French Concession and the International Settlements — after rioting, smashing machinery, and attempting to knock the white man's burden off their backs — had been brought to heel by Chinese manufacturers who felt the pinch of lawlessness on their pocketbooks. At first these native industrialists had encouraged the strikers, foreseeing a cheaper labor market if Caucasian business could be driven out. But this combination of greed and "patriotism" had been self-defeating, and the Chinese had finally urged the coolies to return to their jobs. Shanghai had quieted down to its normal turbulence.

Arriving in Shanghai in the wake of civil violence, Sorge was to leave shortly after military violence seized the tortured city. The Shanghai Incident, a precursor of Japan's all-out war on China, made Sorge's mission doubly important to his masters in Moscow, and eventually led him to Tokyo, success, and Sugamo Prison.

In his cut-and-dried Germanic fashion, Sorge described his new activities under the heading of "The Writer's Espionage Activities in China between January 1930 and December 1932. A. Organization of the China Group."

I came to China with two foreign co-workers ["Alex," head of the group, returned to Russia after six months, leaving Sorge in control; Weingart, the radio operator, was replaced by the more efficient Klausen] who had been despatched on orders from the Fourth

Bureau of the Red Army. The only person in China upon whom I knew that I could depend was Agnes Smedley, of whom I had first heard in Europe. I solicited her aid in establishing my group in China and particularly in selecting Chinese co-workers. I met as many as possible of her young Chinese friends, making special efforts to become acquainted with those who volunteered to co-operate and work with foreigners for Leftist [sic] causes.

Through Agnes Smedley, Sorge was also able to recruit among Caucasians and Japanese as well. She served, moreover, as a kind of liaison agent for the people whom Sorge could not, or felt he should not, make contact with personally.

Sorge's mission had been predicated on the belief that "events in the Far East would of necessity cause momentous reverberations in the great powers of Europe and the United States and might bring about a fundamental change in the existing balance of power." In 1945, J. B. Powell and Max Eastman summed this up more succinctly by stating that "the fate of the world is at stake in China." In 1951, General MacArthur jeopardized career and reputation to make this fact clear to a stubborn, politics-ridden, and Red-infiltrated Truman-Acheson State Department. Sorge realized the importance of the Far East back in 1930 — and Moscow gave him full backing. Sorge was right; he was realistic. The State Department was wrong and bemused.

While American diplomatic officers in China were beginning to make their long and energetic apologia for "agrarian reformers" and "so-called Communists," Sorge had a clear-cut and definite mandate to pry, learn, infiltrate, so that eventually Russia could destroy. His duties were clearly stated:

"Among the main things which we attempted to ascertain through our espionage activities," he wrote, "were the classes of people actively supporting the Nanking government and the true nature of the change taking place in the government's social foundation. . . . The attitudes of the intellectuals varied, but with the expansion of the government's bureaucratic structure some of them had become government officials." His voluminous reports, filed in late 1930 and mid-1932, were the basis for the careful wooing of these classes, particularly the government intelligentsia. Eventually, these very people, permanently installed in the higher echelons of the Kuomintang, proved invaluable in toppling the Nationalist government and in convincing naïve Americans that they represented an unbiased and "democratic" opposition to the Terrible Turk of public opinion, Chiank Kai-shek. When the Chinese Communists took over, these long-time subverters went over in droves to the Reds.

With the ousting of Borodin, Bluecher, and the other advisers to the Chinese Nationalist armies, the Soviet Union had lost its main sources of military information. This area, too, was turned over to Sorge. He was asked to collect

. . . all sorts of information about the various divisions maintained by the government and the reorganizations effected by the German military advisers [pre-Hitler, called in to supplant the Russians]. Moreover, we had to keep on the lookout for changes in the military high command, in the armament of fortresses and military units. . . . We gradually compiled complete information concerning the so-called Chiang Kai-shek divisions, which were equipped with the latest weapons; the divisions loyal to the Nanking government; and the divisions of dubious reliability. . . . I gathered facts of this type chiefly through the Chinese members of my group, but I had to obtain important information personally from German military advisers and businessmen engaged in importing weapons. . . .

I had [also] been ordered to gather information continuously concerning the Nanking government's foreign policy. . . . It was clear that this was one of dependence on England and the United States and that, from a practical standpoint, the policy was paying off. . . . During the Shanghai Incident of 1932, this policy of reliance on British and American support was most interesting to observe. England and the United States made desperate efforts to help the Nanking government resist Japan.

At the same time, Sorge was keeping an eye on British and Japanese dealings with anti-Chiang factions. Even in those days, Great Britain was "using Hong Kong as a base for maneuvers" against Chiang Kai-shek — a policy which came to complete fruition in 1950 when the "anti-Communist" Labor government of England recognized the Chinese Communist government with unseemly haste.

The Nanking government's projects to meet China's perpetual agricultural crises were included in Sorge's interests. So, too, were industrial developments. China was attempting to build up a textile industry — and succeeding enough to threaten the Japanese industrialists. She was also building new arsenals and renovating old ones to meet Japan's increasing military activity in China and Manchuria. "I was able to determine the exact productive capacity of the Nanking and Hankow arsenals, obtaining official diagrams, statistical reports, and other accurate documents. I also had to investigate Chinese air routes." This and other information was treasure trove to the Chinese Communist armies.

From a "young member of the American Consulate" — carefully not identified — and from Agnes Smedley, Sorge gathered information on America's role in the Pacific.

American activities in China, which consisted chiefly of large investments in radio broadcasting and aviation enterprises, were being directed systematically by American businessmen and commercial attachés at the Shanghai consulate. The United States had also become active diplomatically in connection with problems of extra-territorial rights and the cessation of hostilities in Shanghai.

In the latter sphere, the United States had the diplomatic aid of Great Britain, hopelessly watching cheap Japanese labor, mass-production methods, and greater aggressiveness force her out of the Asiatic market. On the former question, Britain was not so active a partner.

Sorge commented prophetically:

The United States will take the place of Great Britain as the dominant power in the Far East, a future development of which signs had appeared at that time; British activities in Asia were already receding. Thus, the U.S.S.R. was placed in a position where she had to give more consideration to diplomatic relations with the United States.

At the time those words were written, the Soviet Union was a "co-belligerent" of the United States, but in the period they refer to, President Roosevelt had not yet recognized Russia; the Hull-Litvinov agreement, violated by the Communists even as it was signed, was still a Kremlin dream.

What made the "considerations" more pressing was Japan's coldly imperialistic push into Manchuria in 1931, seemingly a new departure in Japanese military diplomacy. Both the United States and Russia became cognizant of the growing power center in Asia. The American Secretary of State, Henry L. Stimson, had to his great credit stressed this country's undeviating adherence to the Open Door Policy — a prime example of enlightened self-interest. Democratic administrations to come would scrap this policy, with tragic results.

"The direct effect of the Manchurian Incident on the Soviet Union," Sorge wrote, "was to bring her face to face with Japan in a vast border region hitherto more or less neglected from the standpoint of national defense. . . . It was likewise impossible to tell whether Japan would push northward toward Siberia or southward to China." If the push were toward Siberia, then Russia's policy would be one of conciliation to both the United States and China, the only possible allies. If the push were toward China, then Russia could write off Japan as a threat and attempt to cut herself as large a slice of the imperialistic pie — China — as she could. This dilemma plagued the Soviet Union until the autumn of 1941. It explained her shifts of line in regard to Chiang Kai-shek and the United States. Sorge was fully aware of this; so, too, was Stalin. But the founding fathers of American postwar chaos, in their pre-Yalta considerations, overlooked it completely.

As time went on, then, the focus of Sorge's activities in China became Japan. "I had to discover Japan's true purpose," he wrote. From the Japanese members of his apparatus, he began to probe this particular problem — at first like a student, reading history, politics, and economics. Then his agents began bringing specific information on Japanese policy, her military techniques, her aims and purposes. All this was to culminate in his Tokyo assignment.

In a wide-open city like Shanghai, Sorge had no trouble in recruiting the necessary agents for his apparatus. He remained in the background, however, until Agnes Smedley had "developed" a candidate. Then a meeting was arranged, the prospect was carefully sounded out and given his assignment. There were no slip-ups. Perhaps Smedley was ideally suited for this job. Throughout most of her life she had been in conspiratorial work. She knew courts, prisons, plots, subversion, and the shoddy "martyrdom" of devotion to even shoddier causes.

In 1918, in New York, she had joined an Indian revolutionary society financed by the Imperial German government. Recalling this incident, Miss Smedley's indignation was great that a United States at war with the Boche had considered her activities somewhat irregular and tossed her into New York's Tombs Prison for violation of the neutrality law. Soon after the armistice was signed, the charges against her were dismissed, but she never forgot and never lost a hatred for her native America. This bitterness was turned not only against her country but against mankind as a whole. It manifested itself in what she called an inability to "reconcile myself to the sex relationship." Although she had male lovers, she preferred to dress in clothes as mannish as possible — in China she adopted the uniform of the Red Army when she was in Communist territory. An early marriage resulted in almost immediate divorce.

In Berlin, she had taken up with an Indian revolutionary,

Virendranath Chattopadhyaya, later to become a Communist. For some time she lived with him despite "his little interest in women." Repeatedly, she left him but returned. For about three years, in the 1920s, "my desire to live ebbed and I lay ill. . . . For whole days I lay in a coma, unable to move or speak." Once she tried to commit suicide, but bungled the attempt. "More than death, I feared insanity," she wrote in one of her books. Psychoanalysis saved her, she believed. In 1928, she broke with Virendranath, leaving him to his Communist work, and moved on to more exciting fields. Armed with credentials from the *Frankfurter Zeitung,* she left for China, via Moscow.

The Communist movement was tailor-made for Agnes Smedley. It combined the intrigue and secret work she had learned from Virendranath with the kind of pious sentiments she loved. She was ready to believe anything that was told to her — just so long as it had the proper humanitarian heart throb — and to repeat it in a loud clear voice to the Western world. Arriving in Harbin on New Year's Day 1929, she witnessed the hoisting of the new Chinese National flag over Manchuria. This moved her much less than the story whispered in her ear that Chinese labor was forced to work twenty-four hours a day. With a straight face, she repeated this charge in her book, *Battle Hymn of China.*

China and the Chinese people made her almost physically sick; so she proceeded to love them. Not speaking the language and knowing nothing about the country or its people, she immediately began writing "authoritatively" about Chinese politics. If a Chinese treated her nicely, she suspected him of being a police spy. If he was rude to her, he was a Kuomintang fascist. In Harbin, she walked into the office of the president of the Chamber of Commerce and virtually accused him of being an opium dealer. When, with Chinese politeness, he ignored her attacks and inquired after her health, she took this as an admission of guilt and an example of duplicity. Moving almost exclusively among Communists and their supporters, she resented the fact that the police regarded her with suspicion. When cultured, upper-class Chinese invited her to dinner, she got drunk on their liquor, insulted them, and then went roistering out into the streets shouting, "Let's all get out and pull our ricksha coolies home. Let's prove there are no classes in China."

Just when Agnes Smedley joined the Communist underground is not clear. Though she wrote about other trips to Moscow in *Battle Hymn of China,* her 1928 trip barely rated a couple of sentences — a kind of reticence which afflicted her only when she had something to hide. According to Shanghai Municipal Police records of 1929, she was in the pay of the Comintern's Far Eastern Bureau. Though native Communists were deeply underground following the great Chiang purge, she quickly made contact with them, was taken to their secret meeting places, and saw their propaganda. A librarian at the Y.M.C.A. in Shanghai showed her what was ostensibly a copy of the Gospel According to St. John. After the introductory pages it became a Communist propaganda tract. She was definitely what the Communist movement calls "special."

That she was marked as an agitator and a propagandist almost from the moment she reached China was, contrary to the usual theory, not a disadvantage. The course was planned that way. For by standing out as a friend of the Chinese underdog, by being the target of systematic and virulent attack in the KMT and the European-language press, she drew to her the Chinese and Japanese whose sympathies were marked for Soviet conquest. Her job was to make friends and recruit them, to assist in the organizational work occasionally; she never herself engaged in what people normally consider espionage — the gathering of secret documents and the wheedling of information. Later on, she could point to her outspoken and overt past as proof that she had never been a spy. The disguise was perfect.

Or perhaps "disguise" is a bad word. Sorge and most of the members of his ring in Shanghai were from time to time under police surveillance. But there was seldom enough evidence to bring about an arrest which would stick. At some point between 1935 and 1945, these Shanghai files were rifled and much incriminating evidence against Sorge, Agnes Smedley, Earl Browder, Eugene Dennis, and Irene Wiedemeyer was removed. But some reports still remain and are available in United States Intelligence files.

Despite surveillance — and despite the suspicion which followed her — Agnes Smedley went about her business with considerable equanimity. She was arrested once, then released. It made no difference to her. Aliases such as Alice Bird and Mrs. Petroikos were no real shields. But she did not care. In the Zeitgeist Bookshop on Bubbling Well Road, she lingered and made friends with susceptible radicals. Her contacts with dissident Chinese were invaluable to Sorge. He made full use of them.

The first recruit she brought Sorge turned out to be the most valuable. He was Ozaki Hozumi. "Ozaki was my first and most important associate," Sorge confessed. "I met him in Shanghai through Smedley. Our relationship, both practical and personal, was perfect. His information was the most accurate and the best that I received from any Japanese source, and I formed a close personal friendship with him immediately." It was through Ozaki that Sorge recruited other Japanese to work for him. When, in 1933, Agnes Smedley was ordered to organize a spy ring in Tientsin, she called on Ozaki — then in Japan. He made the trip to Shanghai just to discuss the matter, to tell her what man could do the job, and help launch the project.

Ozaki was merely serving a kind of apprenticeship in China. His day was to come later. But there were others, mostly Chinese, ready to be handed from Smedley to Sorge to Moscow. They made up the real Shanghai ring.

VII

Ring around Shanghai

To most Americans, espionage means one thing: the theft of military and political plans. Mata Hari and Benedict Arnold are the prototypes. Lovely women seducing generals, shadowy figures meeting in dark and noisome dives, shots in the night, and rooftop chases — all these are the elements of spying to readers of thrillers and devotees of Alfred Hitchcock. But the thirteen steps of espionage are slow and plodding ones. The effective spy is the patient worker; the effective apparatus is the one which painstakingly gathers bits and pieces of information — important and unimportant — which dredges for facts like a careful researcher and then pieces them together. Like good police work, good espionage is mostly method, routine, and drudgery.

As a trained operative, Sorge knew this. He did not try to pick Chiang Kai-shek's pocket or open the safe in the Japanese consulate. Agnes Smedley had built up a large circle of Chinese friends, and these were among the first whom he carefully cultivated. "I discovered one who was very competent and decided to use him as my interpreter. . . . After associating with him for two or three months, I spoke to him briefly of my aims and asked him to work with me." Sorge called this man "Wang." Through him, Sorge was introduced to friends and relatives — including Wang's wife, who also joined the apparatus.

Wang gave me the names of his friends in Canton when I went there to spend . . . three months, and among them I found a woman, a native Cantonese, who fitted into our work extremely well. She was on close terms with Smedley and I . . . succeeded in enlisting her. . . .

Wang brought in data and information. . . . When [it] was of such a nature as to require more accurate explanations or reports, he and I talked to the persons who brought [it] in. . . . With the passing of time, it became apparent that individual agents possessed special interests and skills with respect to certain subjects . . . and we began to divide the work in Shanghai roughly according to individual specialties. Agents in Peiping, Hankow, Canton, etc., had to handle all kinds of problems. We met late at night most of the time, using crowded streets when the weather permitted. Meetings were also held in private homes. . . . I took care to change the location from time to time. I avoided using my own home as a meeting place as much as possible. . . . In the Shanghai of those days, not much risk was involved.

Sorge's relations with the Japanese members of his spy ring were not so uncomplicated. This was not because of any fear of the Shanghai Municipal Police, however. Feeling against the Japanese was running high in the city. There were frequent flare-ups — assaults by Chinese on Japanese. The Manchurian Incident had inflamed Chinese nationalism after Chiang's victory had inspired courage. The Communists, moreover, were following with their usual determination the tactic of winning support by causing unrest and stirring up violence.

Richard Sorge wrote that "my meetings with Japanese members took place at restaurants, cafés, or Smedley's home [in the French Concession]."

Since it was dangerous for Japanese to walk around the streets of Shanghai . . . for safety's sake I waited for the Japanese member at the Garden Bridge at the boundary of the Japanese Concession and put him in an automobile or escorted him myself to the meeting place. In order to avoid detection by the Japanese police, I hardly ever visited Japanese in the Japanese Concession. There were exceptions, however; I met Ozaki once or twice in a cafe in Hongkow. I felt most at ease when we met at Smedley's home, and I took Ozaki and [other Japanese members] there on many occasions. . . . The meetings . . . were usually held late at night.

I avoided unduly frequent meetings. As far as possible I tried to separate them by intervals of at least two weeks. After Ozaki was replaced by other Japanese, I changed the rendezvous to main streets in the International Settlement. . . . Meeting dates, fixed beforehand, were strictly observed to obviate the necessity of utilizing the telephone and the mails. There were times when we were at a loss as to what to do when something important happened suddenly but we decided to stick to this whenever possible. Whenever I met a Japanese I did so alone; I did not allow my foreign national assistants to accompany me. The first time I introduced a Japanese to "Paul" [an Estonian with the rank of major general in the Red Army who succeeded Sorge] was when I did so to make liaison arrangements in connection with my departure from Shanghai. We very seldom exchanged written materials when we met; we transmitted information orally [although there were exceptions].

Ozaki was an able and respected newspaperman, a firm friend of Sorge, and the most valuable member of the Shanghai — and later the Tokyo — ring. But there were others, all important enough to be returned to Tokyo by the Fourth Bureau for further work with Sorge. Some were Communists, some fellow travelers, some adventurers, and some a combination of Communist and adventurer. Kawai Teikichi fell into this last category. He had never finished his university education and had begun moving from job to job by the time he was twenty-five years old in 1925. Early in 1928, he had gone to China and found a job as a reporter with the *Shanghai Weekly;* he managed to hold it for about two years. He ran a bookshop in Tientsin, and then began roving again. In 1939, this veteran Soviet agent was "employed" by Japanese Intelligence. In 1940, he returned to Japan and picked up his work with the Sorge ring.

Kawai became a Communist soon after arriving in Shanghai in 1928. He worked with a minor Soviet ring until October 1931, when he met Ozaki, who passed him to Sorge and Agnes Smedley. Another member of the Sorge ring called Kawai a *Shina Ronin,* a

China adventurer. Though he was a good man, he was never held in high repute. His understanding of Communism was "low" and his private life "scandalous." He always needed money and kept asking Ozaki for cash. He hated work.

Funakoshi Hisao had appeared in Shanghai in 1927 as a reporter for the *Mainichi*. Soon after this he had transferred to the Rengo Tsushinsha news agency, becoming manager of their Hankow and Tientsin branches. Between 1935 and 1937, he represented the *Yomiuri Shimbun* in Tientsin. From 1938 to 1941 he was unofficial adviser to the Japanese Army headquarters in Hankow. He had become a Communist in 1929, but it was not until 1932 that he was recruited into the underground by Kawai, who delivered him to Sorge and Agnes Smedley. After Sorge left Shanghai, Funakoshi was incorporated into "Paul's" ring. His military contacts gave him an excellent opportunity to report on the Japanese order of battle, troop movements, and other strictly G–2 matters.

Another Shanghai member who later transferred to Tokyo was Mizuno Shige. A young man of good family, he had succumbed to Communist propaganda when, at twenty, he was a student at the East Asia Common Script School in Shanghai. He immediately plunged into party activities, setting up a cell in the school, leading a student strike, agitating in the streets. Expelled from the school, he continued to work for the party, shifting over to espionage. But his overt activities were too violent not to get him into trouble. In 1931, he was deported — sent back to Japan.

In 1937, he rejoined the Sorge ring in Tokyo. Though he had been frequently arrested for Communist activity, he was permitted to hold jobs which gave him access to social and political information valuable to Russia. One such job was the compilation of the Great Japan Youth Association yearbook. As a result of this work, he was able to prepare long reports for Sorge on the Great Japan Youth Party, the Black Dragon Society, and the reorganized old-line political parties. He was able, as well, to report on the equipment of two important Japanese divisions — then preparing for the South Asia campaigns.

In the Sorge espionage stable, there were also Europeans and Americans. "Meetings were held very frequently," Sorge explained. The kind of security measures employed with other members, however, was not considered necessary. The Caucasian members used the telephone to arrange rendezvous. They met at bars, restaurants, dance halls, and in the homes of friends. "We hid the materials we collected and the documents we compiled in our homes. I destroyed or returned the materials after sending my reports to Moscow, but even so, we always had a great many documents in our possession." If there was any danger, "We left very important documents with friends for safekeeping. Our friends did not know the nature of the things left in their custody." With typical Communist consideration, they merely told these friends to hold the documents.

Sorge did not rely on his co-conspirators entirely. Not satisfied by results, he "personally went out and collected all the facts and materials" that he possibly could. "There was no embassy in Shanghai, but I immediately gained an entrée into German social circles and there gathered information of various descriptions. In these circles, we revolved around the German Consulate General; I became very well-known and sought after by people who wanted favors done. I associated with German merchants, military instructors and scholars, among whom the most important were the military advisers to the Nanking government." From them, from German fliers with the Chinese air force, and from personal observation on frequent trips out of Shanghai, Sorge was able to pick up much valuable intelligence on the inner workings of the Nanking government, plans for subjugation of the war lords, political and economic policies, and military knowledge of the Japanese armies in China.

While Sorge busily pumped his agents dry of information, the daily subversive life of the Communist movement continued in Shanghai. Irene Wiedemeyer's Zeitgeist Bookshop, a branch of the

International Union of Revolutionary Writers organized at remote control by Willi Muenzenberg in Germany, continued to be the gathering place for Communists and their dupes.

Egon Erwin Kisch, a Comintern agent, organized the Society of Friends of the Soviet Union, of which Agnes Smedley was an important member. Harold Isaacs was editing the *China Forum,* attacking the imperialists, and at Smedley's suggestion publishing such unbiased writers as Ozaki Hozumi. "Hilaire Noulens" was arrested carrying telltale documents, jailed, tried, and eventually executed. Isaacs and Smedley were busy setting up the Noulens Defense Fund, weeping that the spy had been picked up out of the sheer malice of fascist police, and roping in such innocents as Albert Einstein and Oswald Garrison Villard — as well as such people as Theodore Dreiser, Lion Feuchtwanger, and Mme. Sun Yat-sen — to sponsor this early front. Max[1] and Grace Granich, two Americans, were putting out the *Voice of China,* poking at authority, and getting help from the United States Consul, John Carter Vincent, when Shanghai police tried to shut down their magazine. Molotov's brother-in-law, Leon Minster, a Russian-American with a United States passport, was running a radio shop as a front for espionage work.

It was a gay old town for Communists. Sorge must have hated to leave it when the summons came from Moscow to return to headquarters. But war was brewing in the Pacific. Japan was on the march. Shanghai was only a way station. The Fourth Bureau had a bigger, better, more dangerous, and more rewarding assignment for Sorge — Tokyo.

[1] Brother of Communist functionary and writer, Mike Gold. Both the Granichs were known as Communists to Hede Massing and others. He later edited *China Today.*

VIII

Japan Is the Focus

"On the night of September 18, 1931," Henry L. Stimson has written,[1] "the military forces of the Japanese Empire occupied strategic cities and towns in South Manchuria. . . . It needs no argument to show that the vast struggle in the Pacific which broke out at Pearl Harbor on December 7, 1941, was merely the logical result of the events which began in Manchuria."

The importance of the Manchurian Incident, followed shortly by the establishment of the Japanese puppet state of Manchukuo, was not merely that Japan had sliced off a new piece of territory. Its real significance was in the disturbed balance of power in the Far East. Both Moscow and Washington reacted immediately and with deep concern. Of the great world powers, only Great Britain remained unperturbed. Japan was her ally; and the British lion, then as now, was too concerned with developments in Europe to worry about Japan's new imperialist venture. Much as the Foreign Office hastened to recognize the Soviet conquest of China in 1950, it recognized a Japanese sphere of dominance in the Far East. British equanimity was slightly shaken after the fighting in Shanghai in 1932, but not enough to matter. Right up to Pearl Harbor, the conservative Winston Churchill was minimizing the Japanese threat while pressing President Roosevelt to keep his eyes — and American military aid — focused on Europe.

In Washington, the issues were more clearly understood. Secretary

[1] *On Active Service in Peace and War.* (New York, 1947.)

of State Stimson realized that the United States must stand by the Open Door Policy, the traditional governor of American thinking on Asia, until the Far East clique of the Roosevelt-Truman State Department liquidated it. Stimson considered the Open Door Policy "farsighted self-interest." If the Open Door were slammed in America's face, he realized, the Nipponese imperialists would eventually dominate most of Asia and threaten our position in the Pacific. President Hoover agreed with this analysis. From a moral point of view, Mr. Hoover also felt that the United States could not abandon China to partition and national self-destruction at a time when, under Chiang Kai-shek, it was slowly but at an accelerating pace becoming a modern state.

Between the thought and its concomitant act, there is a wide gap. Secretary of War Patrick J. Hurley realized the implications of Japan's action. But he stated unequivocally that protests and conferences would get nowhere. If Japan was to be stopped, it could only be by a serious threat of economic and military sanctions. In this Stimson concurred, and he urged Mr. Hoover to take a strong stand. But Hoover was adamant against any show of military strength. He did not feel that the United States should risk war; both a pacifist and a constitutionalist, he felt that his duties and powers as President ended with the defense of the country. If any steps were to be taken which might involve the nation in hostilities, it was not up to him to take them. The power and the duty rested in the hands of Congress.[2]

The United States could afford isolationism in 1932. But Russia could not. Her internal situation was rocky; collectivization of the farms had met with the stubborn opposition of the peasants;

[2] By all Marxist and liberal theory, a "reactionary" and Republican President should have seized on the opportunity to plunge the country into war as a means of relieving the great depression, ending unemployment, and guaranteeing himself another term in the White House. But in this, as in other Marxist and liberal theorizing, the facts do not fit the case. Morality, rather than economics, still determines some men's acts.

Trotsky had been eliminated, but the Old Bolsheviks were still alive and, in Stalin's mind, their mere existence was a threat to the regime; industrialization and the switch from consumer goods production to heavy production had bogged down in a morass of corruption, inefficiency, fear, and bureaucracy. On the foreign policy level, Stalin's adventures in Asia had been liquidated in bankruptcy. Suddenly the Soviet Union was faced with an aggressive imperialist power, perhaps anxious to complete the unfinished business of the Russo–Japanese war which had nearly toppled the Tsar in the early years of the century.

Unable to meet Japan head-on in armed contest, the Soviet Union's leaders decided to employ guile instead of strength. The conspiracy — if a government can be said to conspire — was logical and, as it turned out, highly effective. In China, the Russians had a Chinese Red Army. They had a high-level underground right in the Kuomintang government, and one which sabotaged Chiang's efforts until his retreat to Formosa; they had the sympathy and support of the highly articulate student and professional class. With these pawns, the Comintern and its allied apparatuses began to do their utmost to play on Chinese nationalism by calling for war with Japan.

Japanese soldiers and civilians were insulted in Shanghai. There was a tremendous agitation for sanctions against the Nipponese invaders. Boycotts, seemingly spontaneous, caused wide repercussions in Japan and led to retaliation. Behind these acts were the Communists, capitalizing on peoples' legitimate grievances to further Moscow's ends. That China was in no position to resist Japan militarily did not particularly bother the Communists. Their work toward embroiling Chiang in a shooting war built up to a crescendo and, in 1937, forced the fight. The results were tragic for China, for the cause of responsible government, and for the world.

In Japan, the Soviets had no adequate mechanism to mold public opinion and force the government's hand. There were, comparatively speaking, a fair-sized number of Communists. But their activity was clandestine, their caliber for the most part low, and avenues of public operation virtually nil. The party was illegal, and therefore, from a propaganda and agitational viewpoint, *hors de combat*. Only in a corrupt, weak, or disorganized country can an illegal party impress its will on the body politic — and Japan was none of these. The best the Comintern could hope for was to infiltrate a few men into key positions — as spies and muddlers of policy. In effect, it hoped to create a small corps which could at the very least know what the Japanese were about to do, could be forearmed, could act accordingly.

For the job of setting up the key apparatus, the logical choice was Richard Sorge. His success in China had been more than moderate. He had built up good contacts with the Germans in China. These contacts could be invaluable in Japan — moving rapidly toward a close rapprochement with the newly victorious Nazis. His best agents in Shanghai, with the possible exception of Agnes Smedley, were Japanese. Ozaki was back in Japan and moving higher and higher toward the seat of power. He could be returned to the service of the Fourth Bureau. With this in mind, Sorge was recalled to Moscow in December 1932 to report on his work in China.

"As soon as I returned from China," Sorge noted, "I contacted General Berzin, the chief of the Fourth Bureau . . . who gave me an enthusiastic welcome. I was told that my work in China had been most satisfactory and was asked to see him for details about my future activities and mission. I was not given a desk at the department or assigned any work. I was occasionally called in to discuss some matter, but most of the time Berzin or his deputy called at my hotel." As a member of the Soviet Communist Party's Central Executive Committee, he also reported to the Secret Department which controlled his relationship with the party and held his party card. This responsibility to the Secret Department was permanent, no matter how deeply involved he became in the Red Army's Intelligence apparatus. "Here, too, I was praised for my work after I had reported before a small committee and completed the processing required." Sorge was also told that he had "a very high standing in the party."

While this job of reporting, of being examined, and of demonstrating that his contact with the outside world had not corrupted him was going on, Sorge applied for an assignment that would keep him in Moscow indefinitely. This was rejected by Berzin. "Half jokingly," Sorge suggested that he might be of value in Japan. He was met by silence. But obviously, he had hit on exactly what the Fourth Bureau had in mind for him. Several weeks later, Sorge was called in and told that the top people in Moscow wished him to go to Tokyo. He was told to make preparations for this trip immediately. "The Eastern Section apparently had determined my military mission again after discussions with army leaders," Sorge was to write. "The plan was for me to observe conditions in Japan thoroughly, explore at first hand the possibilities of operating there, and, if necessary, return to Moscow for final discussions of my future work. Such preparatory work was considered necessary by the Moscow authorities, who regarded activities in Japan as most difficult and important."

His preparations for the Tokyo assignment consisted of lengthy briefings from the Comintern's experts. One of the people involved in this process was Karl Radek, a member of the Executive Committee, later to figure in the Moscow Trials. Radek, "Alex," and Sorge "engaged in lengthy discussion of general political and economic problems involving Japan and East Asia. Radek exhibited a deep interest in my trip. As I had been in China and he was a recognized expert on politics, our talks were extremely interesting. . . . I got in touch with two members of the Foreign Commissariat who had been in Tokyo and from them obtained a detailed account of life there. . . . With Berzin's approval, I also saw my old friends Piatnitsky, Manuilsky, and Kuusinen, who were 'quite proud of their protégé.' Piatnitsky, who had been told about my Japan plans by Berzin, was extremely worried about the hardships I would face but delighted by my enterprising spirit."

While Sorge talked, visited, and consulted, the Fourth Bureau was efficiently laying the groundwork for his trip, providing him with a cover, and alerting Soviet agents concerned. With breathtaking audacity, it was decided that he was to appear in the Japanese capital as a German foreign correspondent — for freedom of movement — and as a full-fledged Nazi — to establish his *bona fides*. Sorge's last days in Moscow were spent in an ironic kind of "indoctrination." According to Hede Massing, whom he had recruited into Soviet espionage, Sorge "read voluminously and all things he could find, to be prepared for discussion on Nazi doctrine. He had familiarized himself with the phrases and sentiments He had practically memorized Hitler's *Mein Kampf*." [3]

At first look, the attempt to squeeze Sorge through the Gestapo net and get him a Nazi party card seemed practically impossible. But the Fourth Bureau was prodigious in its efforts and ubiquitous in its contacts. General Walter Krivitsky was later to demonstrate that a determined apparatus can do the incredible, when his operatives broke into the Reichschancellory of Foreign Affairs and stole a copy of the Anti-Comintern Pact, secret clauses and all. In certain respects, Sorge's task was more difficult. His name was known [4] — and it was the name of a grandson of Karl Marx's secretary. He had, moreover, left a wide trail during his early Communist days. His name was in police files; he had tangled with the Weimar Republic. He had been under suspicion in Shanghai. And how many of the people he had dealt with in China belonged to the sub-netherworld of double agents? Selling information to all comers, one might well have supplied Sorge's name to German agents.

[3] *This Deception*. (New York, 1951.)

[4] There was even a dossier on him in United States Intelligence files at the time. The tip-off had come from orders he had placed with the Eastman Kodak Company through a girl friend in Germany, for photographic supplies.

Yet Sorge left for Berlin in May 1933 to establish his cover. He had little difficulty in securing his primary disguise; the *Frankfurter Zeitung,* which had employed Agnes Smedley as a foreign correspondent, was well infiltrated by Communists. Hitler's ascent to power had liquidated the ownership of what had once been continental Europe's greatest paper — but the cell remained in existence. In short order, Sorge secured correspondent's credentials from the *Zeitung,* the *Bergen Kurier,* the *Technische Rundschau,* and the *Amsterdam Handelsblatt.*

Getting into the Nazi Party turned out to be almost as easy. The Gestapo was still in its organizational throes. The checking and cross-checking with which it later guarded against sloppiness and spies had not been fully developed. More to the point, many Communists had, on Moscow's orders, joined the National Socialist Party long before its victory. These Communists had worked at their Nazi tasks with a will and risen to positions of trust throughout the Brown Shirt organization. Red-Brown *Parteigenossen* were on hand to process Sorge's application, to expedite it, and to make sure that any dossier on him was completely buried. Sorge told Mrs. Massing that his greatest ordeal was in fraternizing with enthusiastic Nazis who insisted on taking him on drinking bouts nearly every evening. He pretended to be a teetotaler so as not to get drunk and be indiscreet. "Never will I be able to drink enough to make up for this time!" he said to her. Perhaps he was exaggerating. In his Tokyo days, he drank heavily with German Embassy officials, but never betrayed himself.

Once Sorge had the precious Nazi party card, he departed for Tokyo, via the United States and Canada. As a precaution, he was not given full instructions until he was safely out of Germany. Sorge arrived in New York in August 1933. He "registered in the Hotel Lincoln, and saw a contact man who instructed me to meet a certain employe of the *Washington Post* at the Chicago World's Fair." After several days in New York and Washington, Sorge went on to Chicago. At the fair grounds, on the shore of Lake Michigan, the German agent of Soviet Russia met an American newspaperman who "informed me that a certain Japanese would soon return to Japan and told me how to get in touch with him."

Sorge arrived in Yokohama in September. The water police let him go ashore after a routine check. Going on to Tokyo, he rented a house at No. 30 Nagasaka-machi, Azabu-ku — a good neighborhood — and got down to his job of familiarizing himself with Japan and with building up his spy ring. He introduced himself at the German Club, made a call at the German Embassy, and began holding open house at his home. It was a big place, run along bohemian lines. Men, women, and spies could be found there with little need to explain why or what they were about. For Sorge — as for the Fourth Bureau — the setup was perfect.

IX

Mission to Tokyo

WHILE Richard Sorge was in leisurely transit to Tokyo, the Fourth Bureau and the Comintern were mobilizing his assistants. Ozaki Hozumi, who was to be the top man in the ring after Sorge, was already in Japan. His knowledge of China had won him a wide reputation. His friendships reached high into the government and he was considered a brilliant young man with a brilliant career before him. He was still secretly in communication with Agnes Smedley, but ironically, neither he nor Sorge knew that they were star-crossed in conspiracy and would work together again.

By the time Sorge reached Japan, however, another and key man in the ring had already arrived. He was Branko de Voukelitch, a tall, heavy-set Yugoslav. His conversion to Communism was of very recent vintage — January 1932 — but he had flirted with Marxist doctrine ever since his student days at Zagreb. He had also been active in the Croatian independence movement in the middle 1920s. Shortly after joining the Communist Party, in Paris, he was introduced to a mysterious "Baltic woman, Olga." Voukelitch never learned, or perhaps never told, who this Olga was. But it is quite clear that she was Mme. Lydia Tchekalov Stahl, a Soviet agent who had contact with virtually every important international spy ring. Her activities ranged from France to Finland, the United States, China, Germany, and the Panama Canal.[1]

[1] Cf. *Seeds of Treason*, by Ralph de Toledano and Victor Lasky, pp. 94–107. (New York, 1950.)

Olga recruited Voukelitch at a time when he was working for the Compagnie Générale d'Electricité in Paris. His work seemingly had little to recommend him as a Soviet agent. But the Fourth Bureau knew how to pick its men. Shortly thereafter, another Soviet agent —again unidentified but possibly General Walter Krivitsky—told Voukelitch that he would be assigned to Rumania or Japan. Simultaneously, he was given permission to take his wife Edith along. In October 1932, Voukelitch received orders from the espionage underground to proceed to Japan. Through contacts in the French Communist Party, this onetime law, onetime art student, employed by an electrical company, got himself appointed a correspondent for the French picture magazine *La Vue*. A similar assignment for this man who had no newspaper experience was arranged with the Yugoslav daily, *Politica*. Traveling via the Red Sea, Singapore, Shanghai, and Yokohama, Voukelitch, his wife, and their small boy arrived in Tokyo in February 1933. They were sufficiently well financed by the Fourth Bureau to move into the Bunka Apartments, one of the city's best, and then into a luxurious house where Voukelitch immediately set up an elaborate dark room and photo lab.

"Bernhardt" (alias "Bruno Wendt"), the ring's radio man, was on hand to make the proper contact. Then the two marked time until the arrival of Sorge. But in the United States, Miyagi Yotoku, an Okinawa-born Japanese, was also getting his orders. Miyagi had arrived in the United States in 1919, at the height of anti-Japanese agitation so virulent that it left a permanent scar on his psyche. He had kicked around in San Francisco, opened a restaurant to survive, and taken up painting to live. In 1926, along with his partners in the restaurant, he had joined a Marxist study group. When he got married, he and his wife boarded with a Japanese farmer whose wife, Mrs. Kitabayashi Yoshisaburo, was to be the weak link in the Sorge chain and the cause of its breakup and arrest.

Since he was an artist with radical leanings, Miyagi joined the

Proletarian Arts Society and a host of Communist-front groups organized by the party for West Coast Japanese. When, after a series of government raids, the Japanese section of the American Communist Party was reconstructed in 1931, Miyagi joined. He had been a member for little more than a year when two Comintern agents asked him to go to work for them in Tokyo. He was directed to report for full instructions to another agent, "Roy," in Los Angeles. But Miyagi was reluctant to leave his wife or to stir out of the United States. Like many Okinawans, he harbored a strong hatred of the Japanese. Month after month, he held back. He was too busy with his painting, he said.

Suddenly, in 1933, Miyagi was called in and summarily ordered to leave for Japan. A definite assignment had come up which could not be postponed. The reluctant spy-to-be was also told that he would be gone for only a short time. Miyagi was given two hundred dollars for expenses and a dollar bill. In Tokyo, his instructions were to watch for a certain ad in the *Japan Advertiser*. He was to present himself to the man who had placed the ad. His "contact" would show him an American dollar bearing a number consecutive to the one on his. Leaving his wife behind, Miyagi packed himself off for the Orient. Obviously, what had suddenly made Miyagi's trip imperative was the arrival in Tokyo of Richard Sorge.

In December 1933, Sorge said in a statement at his trial, "I called at the office of the *Japan Advertiser* and, as instructed by the American contact man, inserted an ad in the *Japan Advertiser* and the *Pan Pacific,* its weekly publication, to the effect that I was collecting Ukiyoye [prints] and books on art and wanted interested persons to reply." Sorge ran this ad from 14 to 18 December under the head, *Wanted: To Buy Ukiyoye*. Sorge had Branko de Voukelitch "arrange a meeting with our man." The two met at the Issui Sha advertising agency and compared dollar bills. Voukelitch subsequently introduced Miyagi and Sorge to each other, late in December, at the Ueno Art Gallery.

At the first meeting between the master spy and the recruit, conversation was limited to general topics. By the fifth meeting, sometime in January 1934, Sorge made it clear that the assignment was not Communist propaganda but espionage.

"It was some time before I could decide to join Sorge's group," Miyagi confessed after his arrest. "If I had been in the United States my position would have been different, but what would be the position of a Japanese working in Japan? Especially, was this not a contradiction of myself, since I had been interested in racial emancipation?" The argument used to win Miyagi over was one which Communists still use today. "I made up my mind to participate . . . when I realized the historical importance of the mission, since we were helping to avoid war between Japan and Russia." Miyagi accepted the assignment, "although I knew well that what I was doing was illegal and that in wartime I would be hanged." When war did break out, the Japanese members of the Sorge ring consoled themselves with the fact that their country was not fighting the Soviet Union. Besides, they reasoned, Soviet victory would serve the real interest of the common people of Japan. It was the kind of cockeyed syllogism which, at about the same time, Alger Hiss, Henry Julian Wadleigh, and other Soviet agents in America, were employing.

Miyagi had been assigned to Sorge as the chief Japanese agent of the ring. But he was hardly fitted for this exalted post. His contacts in Japan were new and of a low level. Most of his information came from the Official Gazette (*Kampo*), from magazines and newspapers, from common gossip. Most of his military information came from a Corporal Koshiro Yoshinobu. Sorge made good use of Miyagi in the early Tokyo days when he needed someone who could speak Japanese and interpret the news for him. Miyagi was also valuable as a contact man and for recruiting minor members. But it didn't take Sorge long to realize that he needed an agent with friends in the top levels of government and the press, as well as in business and social circles. There was one man who fitted all the specifications — Ozaki Hozumi.

In the early summer of 1934, a stranger calling himself "Minami Ryuichi" called on Ozaki at the *Osaka Asahi* offices. Minami told Ozaki that an old friend from Shanghai wanted to meet him again. Ozaki nervously cut the conversation short — there were other members of the newspaper staff about — and invited Minami to dinner at a Chinese restaurant. There Ozaki was told that his former espionage superior, "Johnson," was in Japan and that a meeting between Johnson (Sorge) and Ozaki had been arranged for the following Sunday at a deer park. Away from prying ears, Sorge welcomed his former associate and asked for his help. He explained why he had been transferred to Tokyo, why the Soviet Union considered Japan of such prime importance, and just what needed to be done. Ozaki agreed without hesitation to return to the ring.

This was the Sorge group in Tokyo — and it remained the core of the ring even after 1935, when Sorge journeyed to Moscow to get new instructions. The Ozaki-Sorge team was and remained one of the most unusual combinations in espionage history. It had its counterpart only in the Whittaker Chambers-Alger Hiss relationship, and the parallel between the two was striking. Hiss was the clean-cut American; Ozaki was an equally clean-cut Japanese. Hiss and Ozaki came of good family and were cut to the pattern of middle-class respectability — the type which makes good civil servants and career diplomats. Sorge and Chambers also came of good family, but they had plunged into the thick of the Communist movement, had lived through its sordid and bohemian phases, were activists as well as theoreticians. Both men were omnivorous readers and students.

Had the two teams been shuffled, however, they would have paired off better. Like Hiss, Sorge remained a confirmed and unrepentant Leninist through his period of arrest, travail, and trial. Like

Chambers, Ozaki became aware of the evil he had embraced. Facing death, he found his soul. Whether he would have broken of his own volition is a matter for conjecture. He was certainly the more sensitive, the more honest man in the Sorge-Ozaki team.

In the years between 1932 and 1934, between the time he left the Shanghai ring to return to Tokyo and when he joined the Tokyo ring, Ozaki had become well known as a writer and expert on Chinese affairs. His articles in the *Chuo Koron* (*Central Review*) were accepted as authoritative. Secretly and under his Shanghai pen name of "Shirakawa Jiro," he had translated Agnes Smedley's *A Daughter of Earth* into Japanese — Miss Smedley had given him the Japanese rights on all her books — and eventually published it himself. Five books on China had appeared under his by-line; the last, in 1941, was *Strength of the Great Powers in China.* Though he was passionately dedicated to the Communist cause, he had skillfully dissembled his views. So nicely did he plead his case that the Japanese thought police never once suspected him.

Sorge took with him to Japan not only his experience in the methodology of espionage but a vast interest in the country and the knowledge that the best spy is often not the craftiest but the most hard-working. Between 1932 and 1935, his mission was more to learn and assimilate than to dig up classified information. Perhaps the most unusual pages in his confession are those which recount his early studies in Tokyo.

"At the time of my arrest, the discovery of between eight hundred and one thousand books at my home proved a source of considerable annoyance to the police. Most of these works were on Japan. In building up my library, I collected every foreign language edition of an original Japanese work that I could get, the best books that foreigners had written on Japan, and the best translations of basic Japanese works." These scholarly works were systematically digested.

With this as a point of departure, it was a simple matter to grasp contemporary Japanese economic and political problems. I studied the agrarian question very closely, and from there went on to small industry, big industry, and finally heavy industry. . . . The passing political scene told the observer versed in ancient Japanese history much more than the Alien Police suspected. . . . In addition to my home library, I utilized the German Embassy library, the personal library of the German ambassador. . . .

My study of Japan was not based solely on material appearing in books and magazines. First I must mention my meetings with Ozaki and Miyagi, which were not confined to the exchange and simple discussion of information. Frequently some real and immediate problem would bring up an analogous phenomenon in some other country . . . or turn the topic to Japanese history. My meetings with Ozaki were invaluable in this respect because of his unusually extensive knowledge of Japanese and foreign history and politics. . . . I achieved a clear understanding of the singular position of the Japanese army in control of the state, as well as of the nature of the advisers to the Emperor or Genro [elder statesmen], who defy legal definition. . . . Moreover, I could never have understood Japanese art as I did without Miyagi. Our meetings often took place at exhibitions and museums, and it was nothing unusual for our intelligence and political discussions to be pushed into the background by talk on Japanese and Chinese art.

It was this Sorge who could write that "it has been my personal desire and delight to learn something about places in which I have found myself. . . . I have never considered such study purely as a means to an end; had I lived under peaceful conditions and in a peaceful environment of political development, I should perhaps have been a scholar — certainly not an espionage agent." The spy, who drank and fornicated and roistered with his Nazi "colleagues" in Tokyo, who applied all the thoroughness of his German and Marxist background to the task of gathering information for Russia, wrote with almost touching enthusiasm of his scholarly researches. He wanted it made clear to his "readers" that he was not just a "mailbox" or a cipher in a spy ring.

The pages which deal with his intensive study, with his evaluation of deep political currents rather than with the minutiae of espionage, are the most alive in the confession. They show Sorge as he might have been had the Soviet virus not seized his system.

His pride as a topnotch foreign correspondent is almost boyish in its frankness: "My research was likewise of importance to my position as a journalist since, without it, I would have found it difficult to rise above the level of the run-of-the-mill German news reporter, which was not particularly high. It enabled me to gain recognition in Germany as the best reporter in Japan. The *Frankfurter Zeitung,* for which I worked, often praised me on the ground that my articles elevated its international prestige. . . . My journalistic fame brought me innumerable requests for articles from German periodicals, and the *Frankfurter Zeitung* and the *Geopolitik* [for which Sorge wrote occasionally] pressed me for a book on Japan at the earliest possible date."

Sorge never finished that book. He had written three hundred pages of manuscript when the Japanese police knocked on his door.

X

Tokyo Marching Orders

SORGE'S instructions for his Tokyo mission were broad in scope, yet specific in aims. The most important duty assigned to him — "It would not be far wrong to say that it was the sole object," he confessed — was "to observe most closely Japan's policy toward the U.S.S.R. . . . and at the same time, to give very careful study to the question of whether or not Japan was planning to attack the U.S.S.R." The question of a Japanese attack was such an obsession with the Soviet Union that Sorge's "frequently expressed opinions to the contrary were not always fully appreciated in Moscow." The Manchurian–Siberian border seemed to cut, like trolley tracks, right across the Kremlin.

The reorganization and augmentation of Japanese army and air units was high on the list. This "entailed the obtaining of very broad military intelligence," Sorge wrote, "because the Japanese military, in order to justify their increased budget demands, were pointing to the Soviet Union as Japan's principal enemy." Reinforcement of Manchurian garrisons was only part of the story. The Japanese armies in China could be shifted quickly to the north, so that in effect Sorge was required to turn in a running account of the growth, mechanization, and armament of Japan's war machine.

On the foreign policy level, Sorge was instructed to keep an eye on relations between the rising Swastika and the Rising Sun. Moscow remained convinced that Japan and Germany would work together in any anti-Soviet moves, both diplomatic and military. It was not until Germany's inconsiderate violation of the Hitler-Stalin Pact — and the invasion of Russia — that the Kremlin began to accept Sorge's advice that the Japanese were preparing for a move against the Western powers. The Russians also harbored a fear that Japan would join forces with Britain and the United States for an attack on the Soviet Union. This suspicion was based on no intelligence from Soviet agents — it was merely what Stalin would have done in the circumstances had he ruled the United States and Britain. In short, the suspicion was Leninist, not realist.

Japan's China policy was also of interest to Russia, particularly as Japanese military penetration became an increasingly serious threat to world peace. In a sense, the Chinese question was merely a corollary to the Soviet Union's interest in Japan vis-à-vis Germany, Britain, and the United States. Of more importance to Moscow was the role of the Japanese military in setting the course of foreign affairs. After 1931, the Russians were aware of the growing power of the Army in Tokyo. They knew that the Army's real desire was to grapple with a land power in Asia — namely, the Soviet Union. As the Japanese Navy began to rise in the ruling hierarchy, a direct result of Japan's need for petroleum, rubber, and metals, Sorge devoted himself to learning what naval leaders felt and desired. It was the Navy which eventually won out, resulting in a southward push toward the European colonies and the American Pacific frontiers.

The matter of Japanese growth in heavy industry, an index of the country's war potential, also engaged Sorge's attention. In particular, the Russians wanted to know just how much the Manchurian puppet state, Manchukuo, entered into the larger Japanese industrial picture. Mainland expansion, however, was a difficult sphere for a Japan-bound Sorge.

To ensure the safety of the Sorge ring, a careful set of precautions was developed. According to a SCAP report, it consisted of a ten-point program:

(1) All members must have rational occupation as cover. (2) Members must have no traffic with Japanese Communists or sympathizers. (3) The radio cipher must be altered by the use of different scramble numbers with each sending. (4) The transmitter must be dismantled, packed in a case, and moved after each operation. (5) Messages must be sent from different locations, never from any one house over a long period. (6) Liaison with "Moscow men" [Soviet couriers] must be carried out in the utmost secrecy with no mention of names on either side. (7) Each member must have a cover name. Real names must never be mentioned in radios or conversations [Ozaki's cover name was "Otto"; Klausen's, "Fatty"; Sorge's, "Ramsey"; Guenther Stein's, "Gustav"]. (8) Place names must be disguised in code, such as "Wiesbaden" for Vladivostok and "München" for Moscow. (9) Documents must be destroyed immediately after they have served their purpose. (10) Never under any circumstance must a Russian be admitted to the circle.

In addition to this, Ozaki worked out his own manual on how the well-disguised spy must act.

Never give the impression that you are eager to obtain news. Men who are engaged in important affairs will refuse to talk to you if they suspect that your motive is to collect information. If you give the impression that you have more information than your prospective informant, he will give with a smile. Informal dinner parties are an excellent setting for gathering of news. It is convenient to be a specialist of some kind. For my part, I am a specialist on Chinese questions, and I have always received inquiries from all quarters. I was able to gather much data from men who came to ask me questions. . . . Connections with important organizations engaged in the collection of news are vital. . . . Above all you must cultivate trust and confidence in you on the part of those you are using as informants in order to be able to pump them without seeming unnatural. . . . You cannot be a good intelligence man unless you yourself are a good source of information. You can only achieve this after constant study and wide experience.

All these rules, in point of fact, were Sorge's as well as Ozaki's. The German's first years in Japan were turned to that "constant study," to becoming a "specialist of some kind." In these years he devoted himself to the task of making himself the best-informed Occidental on Japanese politics and history. He was able to "gather much data from men who came to ask me questions" — namely the staff of the German Embassy in Tokyo, in whom he was able to "cultivate trust and confidence."

Building up contacts with the German Embassy staff, moreover, was as close as he came to espionage in the first years. His Nazi party card was enough to give him entrée to the German ambassador, Herbert von Dirksen. This in turn led to a very close friendship with Colonel Eugen Ott, an assistant military attaché who rose to ambassadorial rank by the time war had broken out in Europe. ("Close" is perhaps not the right word; when the opportunity presented itself, Sorge did not let the closeness of friendship inhibit his affair with Ott's wife.) The military attaché, the air attaché, and the Gestapo chief, Colonel Joseph Meisinger, all learned to trust Sorge and utilize his knowledge of Japan. Only the naval attaché remained slightly aloof — and not for ideological reasons. Perhaps he was a jealous husband.

Throughout this period of study, groundwork, and penetration, Sorge was also testing his communications system and slowly recruiting new members. Communication is always the most delicate and vital problem of any espionage apparatus, and in this the Sorge ring was hopelessly weak. "Bernhardt," the radio man, was a complete failure. In 1935, Sorge decided to return to Moscow in order to straighten out this aspect of his work, to get new orders, and to touch home base. In the summer of that year, he announced to his friends in the German Embassy that it was necessary for him to renew his contract with the *Frankfurter Zeitung* — and that he could do this satisfactorily only in person. Using his regular German passport, Sorge got as far as New York. Another agent called on him in his hotel room and delivered a second passport, already visaed for Moscow.

There was a new chief at the Fourth Bureau — General Uritsky, a long-time friend of Lenin, Stalin, and Voroshilov. Sorge reported to him, delivered the detailed reports he had prepared, was questioned closely, and permitted to state his case for a new radio man. Uritsky was much pleased with Sorge's successes and impressed by the need for a new communications chief. When Sorge asked for Max Klausen, his Shanghai man, the request was granted immediately. Conferences between the two China hands were arranged, and Sorge was well satisfied that his major problem was now solved.

For Klausen, the Tokyo assignment was a lifesaver. He had been recalled to Moscow in August 1933, traveling to the Soviet capital via Mukden, Harbin, and Siberia. Despite Fourth Bureau instructions, he had insisted on bringing his common-law wife, Anna Wallenius, back with him. She agreed to accompany him only in the mistaken notion that she would be permitted to go to Germany. On their first night in Moscow, they had been given the NKVD treatment; their passports and all their possessions were "stolen."

For a brief period, Klausen had remained in the Fourth Bureau's good graces, parading about the city in a Red Army officer's uniform. After six weeks of vacation, he had been assigned to a radio school for advanced training. Suddenly, the blow had fallen; the purge hit him. Klausen was yanked out of the school as "punishment for a record of inefficiency in China." He was banished to a small town on the shores of the Volga where, for two years, he mended shoes, plowed fields, and did penance by attending party propaganda lectures. Then, following Sorge's request, Klausen was ordered to Moscow by General Voroshilov.

He was perfectly pleased with the new intelligence job. "From childhood," he was to testify, "I had heard nothing but evil of Japan. . . . Therefore I gladly consented to go to work for Sorge there." The choice was not his, but his heart was in his work. In September 1935, Klausen said good-by to Anna, who was to meet him in Shanghai, and set out bearing three passports under three different names. One was Canadian, another Italian, and the third his German passport.

"There are hundreds of passports of different countries at [Fourth Bureau] Headquarters," said Klausen, describing his trip. "All are genuine. Only the names and photographs are false. Before my departure, I received instructions as to the use of the passports and was given $1800 in U. S. currency. . . . In Stockholm, I purchased an American seaman's certificate and set out for New York aboard the *Boston*. Upon my arrival I had my own German passport renewed at the German consulate and booked in at the Hotel Lincoln because I had been instructed to do so. There I received a call from a man who said his name was 'Jones.'"

Klausen was asked if he needed money; he refused it. On 28 November 1935, he arrived in Yokohama aboard the *Tatsuta Maru*. Though he had intended to go on to Shanghai for Anna Wallenius, he was short of funds. (Eight months later, he was able to proceed to Shanghai, marry her, and return with her to Japan.)

Klausen's first job in Tokyo was to make contact with Sorge and establish a legitimate cover. A meeting place had been arranged for any Tuesday evening at the Blue Ribbon Bar, but the day after Klausen hit Tokyo he met Sorge, purely by accident, at the German Club. Both men pretended that they had never seen each other before and went through the formality of an introduction. A cover, however, was a little more difficult. Klausen was not a newspaperman and could not pose as such. He tried first to set up an import-export business. It failed.

He tried again. This time, the M. Klausen Shokai (Company), with offices in the Karasumori Building, Shiba-ku, Tokyo, succeeded. The Klausen Shokai manufactured and sold printing presses for blueprints and fluorescent plates. Among its customers were some of the biggest firms in Japan: munitions plants, the Japanese Army, and the Japanese Navy. The presses he built, according to Imperial specifications, also reproduced the very blueprints which Sorge's agents stole. Within five years after he began, Klausen Shokai was able to reorganize as a joint stock company, capitalized at 100,000 yen, of which 85,000 yen was Klausen's own money. He established a branch in Mukden with a working capital of 20,000 yen. The cover was perfect. It not only gave him a legitimate income, but, since Klausen bought and sold abroad, it also gave him a perfect excuse for receiving bank drafts from New York, Shanghai, or San Francisco — cover for the Sorge ring's financial transactions.

Shortly after Sorge returned from his Moscow journey, the apparatus picked up another member. He was Guenther Stein — later to become a naturalized British subject — former Moscow correspondent for the *Berliner Tageblatt* and, during his Tokyo phase, a representative of the British *Financial News*. In 1942, Stein accepted an invitation from the Institute of Pacific Relations to become its Chungking correspondent. He wrote copiously for IPR publications — books and articles which were thoroughly circulated in Washington and helped create the myth that the Chinese Communists were a special and superlative breed of idealists. In 1944, he was one of six correspondents who penetrated to the Red Chinese capital of Yenan. In 1945, he was British delegate to the IPR's Hot Springs Conference.

Following the war, he lectured widely in the United States, propagating the idea that the Communists of China were non-Stalinist in their orientation. When, in 1949, a United States Army Intelligence report described him as "a Soviet agent," Stein hurriedly left the country. On 14 November 1950, he was arrested in France on an espionage charge, according to an official communication to SCAP from the French Embassy in Tokyo, and expelled from France.

As the Sorge ring moved into espionage high gear, its leader set aside specific tasks and areas for each member. Ozaki operated on the highest political and diplomatic levels. He was a respected and active member of the "Breakfast Group" or the "Wednesday Group," a collection of brilliant young men who served as a kind of brain trust to Prince Konoye, thrice premier of Japan. Among the members of the group was Prince Saionji Kinkazu, adopted grandson of the Genro, who had been swept liberal, left, and right into the Institute of Pacific Relations.[1]

The Breakfast Group, which met regularly to trade information and discuss the problems of the Japanese Empire, had almost semi-official status. As a member also of the China section of the Showa Kenkyo Kai, a study society sponsored by Prince Konoye, Ozaki was thrown into particularly close contact with Kazami Akira, who shortly after became chief secretary of the first Konoye Cabinet. Through Kazami, Ozaki was appointed in 1938 to the official position of Adviser to the Cabinet. He therefore had free access to state documents. He held other equally critical posts, such as adviser to the Tokyo office of the South Manchurian Railway — a kind of holding company for all business and industrial ventures in North China. The SMR, which Ozaki "served" as an intelligence officer, began trading information freely with native Japanese heavy industry, and Sorge had complete access to Japan's biggest industrial secrets.

Ozaki furnished the Sorge ring with invaluable analyses of the political affairs of the Japanese leadership. From time to time, he would borrow a particularly significant or complicated document and have it microfilmed. Often these documents were thrust upon him by high-ranking government officers who wanted him to study them as a basis for advice and discussion. Saionji, who was Consultant to the Foreign Ministry, made it a habit to lend Ozaki top secret information. Once or twice important military secrets were dropped into his lap by Japanese officers seek-

[1] Ozaki and Saionji met as delegates to the 1936 IPR Conference at Yosemite. It is not known precisely how long it took to recruit Saionji into the Sorge ring.

ing his counsel on China. "The only information of importance which I was not confident I might obtain in advance was the exact timing of a possible attack on Russia by Japan," he testified at his trial. "My activity was characterized by a total lack of special method. . . . By nature I am a sociable person. . . . Not only is my circle of friends wide, I am on intimate terms with most of them. My sources of information have been these friends."

Miyagi's job was to fill in the broad picture with bits and pieces which he got from his own circle of acquaintances. Miyagi was a longtime friend of the confidential secretary to Yabe Shu, Foreign Minister of the Konoye Cabinet, and later Premier. From this friend, Miyagi was able to obtain a great deal of pin-pointed information on the political jockeying and on military matters. He traveled about considerably and was something of an expert on mobilization; he kept Sorge well posted as to the activation of new divisions.

Some of this knowledge Miyagi got in the ancient way of spies — by hanging around bars and night clubs, and by starting conversations with soldiers on the streets. "He often complained to me about the amount he had to drink in order to obtain trivial facts," Sorge said of Miyagi. But these "trivia" often included such matters as detailed descriptions of artillery and tanks being put into use by the Japanese Army. Miyagi served another function: he was a kind of spymaster to the dozen or so Japanese agents reporting to Richard Sorge. He paid them, directed them, and often received their reports.

Branko de Voukelitch had two duties: he was the photographer for the apparatus and he collected information. It was he who prepared the many rolls of microfilm which were smuggled out of Japan. And he covered the Domei news agency. Much information which never got into the Japanese press was kicking around freely at the offices of Domei. Reporters who had seen much but could write little spoke freely there and Voukelitch gathered every bit of it in. Eventually, Voukelitch became a Havas (French) news agency correspondent. From his colleagues, he learned a good deal about the situation in Indochina, as well as the French reaction to Japan's southward push. Foreign newspapermen, including Americans, accepted Voukelitch as a fellow toiler and traded news with him.

For a time, the Yugoslav's connection with the spy ring — and the spy ring itself — was threatened. Voukelitch tired of his wife Edith and took up with a nonpolitical female, Yamazaki Yoshiko. When he made her his mistress, Edith Voukelitch took some umbrage. She left her husband but remained in Tokyo. Sorge almost literally held his breath. Would she act like the woman scorned? When Branko and Edith were divorced, the crisis passed. But Edith de Voukelitch was not permitted to step out of the Sorge ring until she had made definite pledges of silence. Sorge was authorized to pay her five thousand dollars, and he added another thousand just to make sure. Voukelitch married Yoshiko. As far as the Japanese police were able to determine, she never betrayed her marriage vows except with Richard Sorge.

Guenther Stein also served in two capacities. His contacts in the British Embassy were excellent. The Ambassador, Sir George Sansom, and the naval attaché were on friendly terms with him. He was an economist, and his studies of financial matters were of great help to Sorge. Diplomatic information, of considerable interest to the Russians, frequently fell into Stein's hands. But he also served as a courier, running microfilm to Shanghai for Sorge, and as a front for Max Klausen, who set up a radio transmitter in Stein's home. In order to prevent detection, it was necessary to have as many sites as possible available for these transmitters. Klausen was grateful to Stein.

XI

Price $40,000

THE methodology of espionage is simple and time-honored. The illicit gathering of secret information is still a handicraft, a semi-artistic enterprise in which the imponderables of temperament, skill, and rule-of-thumb dictate success or failure. It is only in the matter of communications that espionage has been at all stream-lined. The microfilm camera has placed the transmission of documents on a mass-production basis. It has also permitted the home office — the "Director" in Moscow, for example — to evaluate expertly and at leisure what in the past a hurried spy could only scan and filter through a restricted understanding. Elizabeth Bentley carried a shopping bag stuffed with rolls of microfilm in her trips between the Silvermaster home in Washington and the Soviet espionage clearinghouse in New York.

But microfilm has its limitations. It is incriminating evidence when found on the person of a foreign agent. So the apparatus falls back on the older method of code communication. Technology has invaded this field to a point, but it has also complicated it. The day of messages carried in the boot are over, and the interlineation in invisible ink of seemingly innocent letters is on the way out. Wireless telegraphy simplified the spy's job at first, until technicians with receiving sets and logarithm books learned how to apply triangulation and so locate a clandestine station. In order to meet this challenge, the spy has been forced to fall back on the human element, on cunning and versatility.

In the early days of the Sorge Tokyo apparatus, the communications problem was a minor one. Japanese secret police were, for all their notorious disregard of individual privacy, inefficient and unconcerned. They were more dedicated to stamping out political opposition and "bad thoughts'" than to digging for spies. It was only after 1939, when war punctured the map of Europe and the China Incident became more than incidental to Japan, that communication with Moscow developed hazards. Before that time the Sorge ring delivered its treason trove to couriers, or transmitted it by radio, almost at will.

"At a prearranged meeting, a courier from my group would deliver a carefully wrapped packet to a Moscow courier and receive in return a packet from Moscow," Sorge wrote. "That concluded the business; nothing more was said, except for a few general questions and answers. . . . It was permissible, however, to ask the courier if he had been to Moscow lately and, if he had, to inquire about conditions there and about old friends."

Shortly after setting up shop in Tokyo, toward the end of 1933, Sorge had his first meeting with a courier. The lack of secrecy involved in this encounter was startling. "A courier whom I did not know came from Shanghai with my name and the German Embassy as an address to contact. He telephoned the Embassy and also informed me by letter that he had arranged to have a doorman wait for me in the lobby of the Imperial Hotel on the morning of a certain day and take me to him. The meeting was carried through as planned. We arranged to go on a sightseeing visit to Nikko . . . and exchanged what we had to deliver there."

Methods of identification were traditional. Sorge told of a meeting with a courier in Hong Kong: "The courier was to enter a certain restaurant at a few minutes past three o'clock, take from his pocket a long black Manila cigar, and hold it in his hand without lighting it. When I saw the signal, I was to approach the restaurant counter, take a conspicuous pipe from my pocket and fail to light it. When the Moscow courier saw me do so, he was to light his cigar, after which I was to light my pipe. The courier would then leave the restaurant, and I would follow him slowly to a certain park where we were to hold our conversation. He would begin by saying, 'Greetings from Katcha,' and I would say, 'Greetings from Gustav.'" There were other prearranged signals — "one person would carry a yellow package and the other a red one."

After Klausen's arrival in 1935, the ring went into high gear. At the trial of the apparatus in 1942, Ozaki and Klausen were able to recall over a hundred messages of major importance transmitted to Moscow, via courier or radio. The Japanese police had recordings of many more, monitored by their radio but undecoded till Klausen confessed. The volume broadcast from Guenther Stein's home in Azabu-ku is itself noteworthy. Klausen visited him in December 1935, "examined the house . . . and decided with his consent to use the two upstairs rooms," Klausen told his questioners. "I transmitted about thirty messages from Stein's home."

In 1936 Klausen was sent to Shanghai. He had a double mission, to deliver a score of microfilm rolls and to meet and marry Anna Wallenius. The film was delivered at the Bubbling Well Road bookshop which figures so prominently in this account. When Klausen returned, Sorge was elated; the thousand frames of microfilm included the first large batch of documents he himself had photographed — at the German Embassy. This was just a beginning. Stein, his common-law wife, Klausen, and Mrs. Klausen ran what was virtually a shuttle service between Tokyo and Shanghai.

Anna Klausen made four trips alone, taking up to thirty rolls of film. In return, she was given five thousand dollars in American bills, which she deposited to the account of her husband's "company." But to Klausen's annoyance, she came back loaded down with expensive clothing and jewelry which she had bought for herself with the earnings of Klausen Shokai. She was a reluctant courier, acting under threat of punishment and exposure. Her purchases were a kind of revenge. During his first courier trip to Shanghai, Guenther Stein had been given a package for Mrs. Klausen. It contained a special dark blue shawl and a large black brooch which she was to wear on her trips to the Chinese mainland. When she appeared in Shanghai at the Bubbling Well Road bookshop, at the Sun Company department store, in the lobby of the Cathay Hotel, or strolled casually along Avenue Haig, they served to identify her to the Moscow courier.

Sorge had ironic cover for his own trips. "At the end of 1938, I myself traveled to Manila and Hong Kong as a courier for the German Embassy, at the same time carrying materials to be delivered in Moscow." The trusted friend of the German Ambassador and of Gestapo Colonel Meisinger — the "beast of Warsaw" — carried confidential Nazi documents in a pouch and microfilm copies of them under his shirt. Moscow was closer to his heart than Berlin.

Late in 1939, Richard Sorge decided that the time had come to stop courier liaison with Shanghai. The water police at Yokohama were watching the arrivals and departures of Caucasians with growing suspicion. The risk of losing a good man or, much worse, of blowing up the whole apparatus, became too great. Increasing economic pressure which the United States was exerting on the Japanese made it virtually impossible for the apparatus to use American banks. Sorge wired his superiors in Russia that liaison between his couriers and the "Moscow men" would have to be effected right in Tokyo. After much delay and grumbling, the "Director" wired back a set of cryptic instructions: "Two tickets with higher numbers for Fritz [one of Klausen's code names]. One with smaller number for liaison man."

Not long after, Max Klausen found two tickets for the Imperial Theatre in his mail box. One was for him, the other for Anna. In the darkened theatre, he was passed a small package with five thousand dollars and he turned thirty-eight microfilm rolls over to the "liaison man." Some months later, Klausen received two tickets for the All Girls Opera at the Takarazuka Theatre. Again, he and Anna attended. For thirty rolls of film, he was given three thousand dollars and twenty-five hundred yen. The man who made the trade in both cases was the Soviet Consul in Tokyo, one Vutokevitch. At a third theatre meeting, Victor S. Zaitzev, second secretary of the Embassy, made the contact. Using the cover name of "Serge," he met Klausen about ten times, usually in the Klausen Shokai's offices. In Klausen's diary these meetings are cryptically recorded as "s-tr" for "*Serge treffen*" ["met Serge"].

There were others who made contact with the ring, bringing instructions, money, or encouragement. A Dr. Woidt appeared and worked with Sorge for a while. He was a German who enjoyed the confidence of the Embassy, but he was suspected of being a double agent by the Sorge group. There was "Ingrid," an attractive American blonde whose name crops up in the Tokyo police records. Whether she was a courier is not made plain, but there are indications that her services to Sorge were more personal than political.

Courier communications were supplemented by radio messages. "Since uninterrupted radio communication with the central authorities was of the utmost importance to our work, achievement of radio contact, its constant maintenance, and precautions against detection were the most important of our illegal activities," Sorge wrote. "After Klausen arrived — his technical ability and enthusiasm for his work knew no bounds — I got permission to teach him the code and had him take over the work."

Klausen set up as many wireless stations as possible in order to ensure the success of our radio activities. At one time, he was able to send messages from four different locations. Almost always, at least three places were used. . . . We changed the places frequently in order to avoid or mislead as much as possible the surveillance, which we thought was bound to become gradually stricter. Klausen frequently endeavored to make his radio apparatus smaller so that the package which had to be carried to the place of operation each time would not be conspicuous. . . . Radio contact was used to send urgent information, our reports to the ["Director"] or organization, and Moscow's reports to us on organization and operations. . . . Klausen was always able to make excellent [radio] contact.

In the later years of the Sorge apparatus, internal communications also became a problem and a danger. There were sixteen people directly connected with Sorge's operations. Strictly speaking, they were not one ring but a series of rings within rings, all taking direction from Sorge and funneling information to him. "I myself was the only person to have direct contact with the key members [of the semi-independent rings]. . . . The direct members of the group either had no contact with one another or met on very rare occasions only." There were, of course, some exceptions.

The fact that I communicated with Klausen could hardly be kept secret over a long period of time. . . . The fact that we both belonged to the German Club, that Klausen had formerly operated a motorcycle and automobile business, and that he took very good care of me when I was severely injured in a motorcycle accident in 1938, all served to divert suspicion from our frequent meetings. Klausen visited me even when my servant was there, and occasionally other German visitors happened to meet him at my house. We telephoned to each other's homes directly, heedless of whether or not the telephone lines were tapped.

Though Sorge kept his relationship with Voukelitch secret, he allowed himself an out should they be seen together by informing the German ambassador that he maintained a tenuous association with French and Allied newspapermen for purposes of sounding them out on attitudes and picking up incidental information. Klausen, who had become paymaster of the apparatus, frequently visited Voukelitch, as did Miyagi. Guenther Stein tried to keep completely clear of Sorge. Their meetings were few and infrequent. Again, Klausen and Miyagi were the go-betweens, and the meetings were usually held in restaurants. Klausen visited Stein's home only to use it as a radio station. Ozaki and Sorge often met at out-of-the-way restaurants. Japanese sub-members rarely, if ever, visited Sorge. They reported to Miyagi, Klausen, or Ozaki.

After 1940 "I began to use my house to meet Ozaki and Miyagi. . . . I thought it would be wise to avoid public places because [they] were being asked more and more frequently who I was or who they themselves were." Special care was taken when approaching Sorge's home. Members of the apparatus resorted to the old trick of changing cabs several times to make sure they were not being trailed. When they arrived, they waited for Sorge to blink his porch light as a sign that all was clear. Another old technique was used in restaurant meetings between Klausen and Voukelitch. The two would pretend that they had run into each other accidentally. Any films, money, or papers they wished to exchange were kept in a nearly empty cigarette package. Klausen would ask for a cigarette; Voukelitch would hand him the pack. After taking a cigarette, Klausen would try to return the pack. Voukelitch would say, "Keep it. I've got another pack."

The Sorge apparatus worked steadily between 1935 and 1941. It was, in fact, one of the Soviet Union's major espionage operations. Yet, from a financial point of view, it was a shoestring operation. A General Headquarters, Far East Command, report on the apparatus in Japan carefully estimated its expenses:

The total cost of the Sorge ring was estimated at about Y3,000 a month. This was an expenditure of considerably less than U. S. $1,000 a month to pay for the extremely valuable work of nearly 20 agents. Since, with one exception, they all worked for love of the cause and not for money, their monthly pay was merely to cover living and travel costs and not to compensate them for their work. Ozaki, for example, never received a penny for himself, and was actually out of pocket since he supported some of the agents under him. Sorge, Voukelitch, and Klausen, of course, had regular incomes from their work, but still they had extra expenses. Klausen was the treasurer, and about once a year he submitted a statement of income and expenses to Sorge, who had it microfilmed and a copy sent to Russia. During Klausen's service as treasurer from 1936 till October 1941, he received U. S. $24,500 anad Y18,300 through the couriers, plus about $10,000 in bank remittances, a total of about $40,000. Certainly the information Sorge sent after 22 June 1941 was worth many millions of dollars to the Soviet Union. Since it had a profound effect on the Soviet deployment of troops, and hence on the stopping of the Germans at the most critical phase of the war, its total worth is incalculable.

The United States Intelligence report does not overestimate the value to the Soviet Union of Richard Sorge and his confederates. At every turn in Far Eastern history, the Tokyo apparatus was able to inform Moscow. When Japan became a member of the Rome-Berlin-Axis by signing the Anti-Comintern Pact of 1936, there were alarmists in the Kremlin who believed that this was the first step toward a tripartite military onslaught against Russia. But Sorge was able to report that, contrary to the foreign office handouts, the Nazis were highly dissatisfied with the Japanese. Hitler and Mussolini had pressed for a military alliance. But the Japanese had balked at going any farther than a declaration that they were against world Communism. Japan's reasons, which the German Embassy in Tokyo (and therefore Sorge) knew, were that it did not wish to arouse the Russians. The Anti-Comintern Pact, moreover, did not come as any kind of surprise to the Soviet foreign office. Two years before it was signed, Sorge had sent on to the Fourth Bureau Ambassador von Dirksen's view that German withdrawal from the League of Nations was the beginning of Nazi-Japanese rapprochement.

Again, in 1937, the Soviet Union was informed by Sorge that the China Incident could not possibly be a mopping-up operation. A carefully documented and reasoned estimate, prepared by Ozaki, noted that Japan would bog down in North China, that the struggle would be long, costly, and indecisive — and that Chinese opposition under Chiang Kai-shek would stiffen, rather than slacken, as time went by. From the vantage point of a cabinet adviser, Ozaki was able to furnish the Fourth Bureau with detailed accounts of Japan's top level plans and, more important, to make Russia privy to the thinking of Japanese leaders.

When Eugen Ott became German Ambassador in 1939, Richard Sorge moved into the post of press attaché. As such, and as a close friend and personal adviser, Sorge breakfasted with Ott every morning, saw the messages which had come in from Germany, helped prepare the replies, and got a full digest of what the ambassador had learned from the Japanese foreign office. Sorge's ties with Ott and Ozaki's ties with Prince Konoye allowed the two agents to work both sides of the street, to double-check their information, and to give Moscow an accurate synthesis.

That same summer, a clash on the Manchukuo-Mongolian border between the Red Army and the Japanese Kwantung Army — the "Nomonhan Incident" — threatened to develop into the long-awaited second act of the Russo-Japanese war of 1905. The Red Army was in no condition to fight a major war, however. Its general staff and the higher echelons of its officers' corps had been decimated in a purge which began with the liquidation of Marshal Tukhachevsky, one of the most brilliant military minds of his generation. The Polish Corridor was charged with explosives which were threatening to go off at any moment. The Soviet regime's internal difficulties were no worse than usual but they were certainly no better.

But if there was alarm in the Kremlin, Sorge was able to do much to allay it. He not only supplied vital military information — the disposition of troops, the numbers of contemplated reinforcements from Manchuria and the homeland — but he also informed Moscow that this was a feeler operation which the Japanese government was fully determined to keep on a purely local scale. The Japanese Army had no intention of provoking all-out war. It was too busy trying to lash down the Chinese dragon's tail which, feeble though it might be, was occupying the attentions of large numbers of Nipponese troops.

Nevertheless, Sorge was also forced to report that the Japanese

Army, which had always favored war against Russia, was still on the ascendant. Fortunately, he was in a position to act as a counter-force, working through Ambassador Ott and others influential in the German Embassy staff. The Army had pressed for a military alliance with Germany and Italy ever since the signing of the Anti-Comintern Pact. From Germany's point of view, such an alliance was all to the good — and Sorge was in no position to deflect this joint desire. But he was on hand when the preliminary negotiations for a tripartite pact began.

As United States Intelligence has since learned, Sorge was in effect the "primary architect" of that pact. Any military alliance is a loaded pistol. Sorge saw to it that the gun pointed at the United States rather than at Russia. Designed, as Professor Harold M. Vinacke has shown, to draw together the Sino-Japanese conflict and the new war in Europe, it provided that "if the United States should participate in either war to an extent found by the signatories to extend beyond 'short of war' action, the participants in the other war would establish a state of war with the United States. Thus, if the United States should use its fleet in the Pacific to prevent an occupation of the Netherlands Indies by Japan, Germany and Italy would be expected to declare war and wage it in the Atlantic against the United States. Or, if American aid to Britain went beyond the supply position, or threatened to become decisive, Japan would be expected to act against the United States in the Pacific."

Ambassador Ott expressed his gratitude to Sorge for the role the spy played in writing the pact by inviting him to be present at the official signing in Tokyo. At the last moment, however, Dr. Heinrich Stahmer, Hitler's personal representative who had come from China to give the treaty his blessing, objected. His motivation was not political; he just did not want a nonentity, a newspaperman, present at an occasion whose solemnity made it the exclusive property of career diplomats and high-ranking Nazis.

*   *   *

Throughout 1940, Sorge continued to transmit to Moscow, via courier and wireless, a running report of Japanese production in munitions, aircraft, and motor vehicles. He apprised the Fourth Bureau of the Japanese Army's determination to transform itself according to the German model, right down to the highly mechanized Panzer units. The friendship pact between Japan and the Soviet Union did not allay Moscow's diehard conviction that a blow from Manchukuo was inevitable and imminent.

On 20 May 1941, Sorge warned his superiors in the Fourth Bureau of another blow, more serious than any which could come from Japan. From Ott he learned that the Reichswehr was concentrating 170 to 190 divisions along the Soviet–German border in partitioned Poland. The German armies would attack all along this frontier, aiming at a quick advance on Moscow. The date of the attack, Sorge said, would be 20 June. Sorge was wrong by two days; the attack came on the morning of 22 June. Under the shattering impact of the Reichswehr, the Red Army crumpled — ostensibly because the Soviet Union had been unprepared for this violation of the Hitler–Stalin Pact which had been the signal for World War II.

Sorge's warning had come in time, however. And it had been reinforced by advices from the United States to Stalin that Hitler was preparing to obliterate his quondam ally. The early collapse of Russian resistance was due primarily to a shift in Soviet strategy. Marshal Tukhachevsky had prepared an elaborate defense in depth which conceivably might have stopped the German Panzers. Marshal Stalin, an amateur strategist, had liquidated the Tukhachevsky line along with Tukhachevsky. He had massed his troops along the frontier, deploying them so that they were most vulnerable to the German tactics of breakthrough and encirclement.

As the Red Army fell back in disorder — its best units cut to shreds — the Kremlin looked over its shoulder in terror. Would Japan take advantage of the rout and launch the long-threatened war on Russia? Or could the Red Army pull out its Far Eastern garrisons and throw them into the battle for Moscow? Sorge was ordered to drop all other intelligence work and devote himself exclusively to these questions. The Germans in Tokyo were urging a Japanese attack which would deliver the final blow to Soviet power in Europe and Asia. Sorge's objective was to keep the Russians informed on every phase of German-Japanese action. He assumed a secondary mission — to make use of Ozaki's influence in policy-making circles by having him press discreetly or openly for Japanese aggression southward.

The next phase of World War II was in the balance. The dynamism may have been history — in the Hegelian metaphor a pattern already woven which merely unrolled in the course of time. It may have been the motivated intelligence of the Sorges, the Ozakis, their allies in Washington and Chungking. What was cause, what was effect, is dialectics. The end product was Pearl Harbor.

XII

Prelude to Pearl Harbor

To most Americans, the story of Pearl Harbor is a closed book. The official historians — like Robert Sherwood and Sumner Welles — have by a judicious selection of facts and theories convinced the public that the sneak attack on Pearl Harbor and the Pacific war were inevitable. Yet nothing in history is inevitable but the claim that past events were inevitable. The facts, as they were developed in the monumental Pearl Harbor inquiry and in Japanese diplomatic documents which today are coming to light, prove conclusively that war could have been averted. A decade of history rewritten by the busy spokesmen of the Roosevelt-Truman administrations has obscured but not buried the truth. An Orwellian 1984 may be just around the corner, but it is not upon us yet.

To say that military conflict with Japan could have been prevented is not an accusation of treason or betrayal against the Roosevelt Administration. Nor is it an attempt to paint the Japanese as lily-white pacifists. The war party in the Tokyo government was powerful, determined, and ruthless. But there was also a strong pro-American party, backed by the Mikado and influential in high-level deliberations, which could have been supported and encouraged. Ambassador Joseph C. Grew, who was close to this group, repeatedly warned the State Department and the President that unless the United States was forthright and consistent in its dealings with the pro-American faction, war would come. American policy wavered between the irrational and the irascible until the die was cast. Then war — sudden, bloody, and futile — came to the Pacific. Japan was defeated; the victors were Joseph Stalin and Mao Tse-tung.

Why America blundered into war is a question of intangibles, of motives and recriminations. How the nation failed to act in its own best interests is a matter of record. When all the evidence has been blasted out of State Department files, a new generation of historians may bring it together. Yet it falls within the scope of this narrative to outline the diplomatic jockeying which preceded Pearl Harbor, if only to show where some of the responsibility for the breakdown lies. If ever a handful of men, working singly or in league, motivated by the Devil or by the mixed purposes of a tarnished liberalism, changed the course of history, this was the time.

The forces and the passions which led to the Pacific war were vast and impelling. But at the moment of crisis, when the balance could have swung toward peace, this handful of men tipped the scales for war. In Japan, Richard Sorge and Ozaki Hozumi lent their weight. In China, there was Owen Lattimore. In the United States, there were Lauchlin Currie, Edward C. Carter, and Harry Dexter White. The ties linking these groups are admittedly tenuous. Sorge, Ozaki, and White were Soviet agents. Carter, Lattimore, and Ozaki were members of the Institute of Pacific Relations. Currie has admitted close friendship with the Soviet agent, Nathan Gregory Silvermaster. Carter was the witting or unwitting tool of a Communist cell in IPR.[1] And Lattimore has been credited in various degrees with masterminding America's disastrous China policy.[2]

The importance of this three-ring circus — in Chungking, Washington, and Tokyo — becomes apparent when a log of the last days of peace is recited. Throughout the war, official historians told the United States that the mission to Washington of Admiral Nomura and Ambassador Kurusu was a blind — that an irrevocable decision

---

[1] *Cf.* Testimony of Raymond Dennett, McCarran Hearings, pp. 937ff.

[2] Lattimore has denied that he masterminded that policy, and that it was disastrous. See Appendix II.

to attack Pearl Harbor had been made early in the autumn of 1941. The opposite is the truth. The Japanese task force which steamed on Hawaii was not given the green light until 5 December when the message "Climb Mount Niitaka" was flashed by Japanese naval radio. On 21 November, Admiral Nagano Osami, chief of the Navy's general staff, instructed the Japanese commander that "if American-Japanese negotiations are successful, forces will be ordered back immediately." And as late as 2 December, Nagano was told by the highest Imperial authorities that if the Nomura-Kurusu-Hull talks were successful, the Japanese fleet would be recalled from its mission.

The pro-American group in Tokyo which pressed for a settlement of the Japanese-American differences showed an astonishing persistence. In the long months of discussions with Secretary of State Cordell Hull, they were met by rebuff after rebuff. That Hull should have been suspicious of the Japanese government was not only understandable but to his credit. Japan's history in China was not one to inspire confidence. But he should not have let this suspicion override his diplomatic perspicacity or blunt his concern for a United States already moving inexorably into the European conflict. If this is a value judgment, the following chronology may make the point more concrete.

In April 1941, two events took place which should have been of some assurance to the State Department. In Moscow, Foreign Minister Matsuoka met quietly with the American Ambassador, Laurence Steinhardt, to impress him with the importance of an improvement in relations between their two countries. The basis for the current difficulties was China, and Matsuoka suggested that Japan might offer an equitable peace to the Chinese government of Chiang Kai-shek. In return, Japan sought a promise from the United States that our good offices would be used in arriving at this peace. Should China refuse it, Japan would expect the United States to wash its hands of the China Incident. Steinhardt was impressed with Matsuoka's sincerity, and speedily sent Washington a résumé of this conversation.

On 9 April 1941, a group of private citizens of both countries presented the State Department with a plan for preserving the peace. This plan, drafted in collaboration with Nomura and having his seal of approval, was based on a Japanese guarantee of Chinese territorial and economic integrity in return for Chinese recognition of the puppet regime in Manchukuo. It involved the withdrawal of Japanese troops from China proper and the reinstitution of America's traditional and honored Open Door Policy. Japan also pledged herself to stay out of the European war unless her partners in the Tripartite Pact, Germany and Italy, were attacked by the United States. The Japanese, moreover, had long since discounted their obligations under the Tripartite Pact and had made it clear to American representatives that they would willingly make it a dead letter if they had assurances that the United States was serious in its peace negotiations.

The reaction of the State Department and Secretary Hull to these proposals was one of cynical hostility. Counterproposals were offered by the United States and the long and senseless debate began. At every turn, Nomura warned the United States that the military party in Tokyo was pushing hard for war, that delay only strengthened its hand and weakened the antiwar forces, and that if any kind of working arrangement for a negotiation of the China Incident could be arrived at, Japan would assure this country a free hand in Europe. For an administration dedicated primarily to the defeat of Hitlerism, this should have seemed like a sensible and honorable way out of the impasse. But Secretary Hull and the State Department insisted on what amounted to unconditional diplomatic surrender.

In this atmosphere of muddle and mortification, the Japanese militarists continued their ascendancy. On 24 July, a Nipponese invasion force landed in Camranh Bay, Indochina, easily overcoming the depleted and discouraged French forces. President Roosevelt called in

Nomura, and in the presence of Admiral Stark, the Chief of Naval Operations, and Acting Secretary of State Sumner Welles, he announced the full embargo of Japan — as a retaliatory move. The Japanese were not impressed by the justice of the American position. They knew that the embargo had been in the works since 2 July — long before the invasion. Sumner Welles, in his recent apologia for the Roosevelt Administration,[3] makes no mention of this fact — although he states candidly that both Admiral Stark and General Marshall had long warned that an embargo would "most probably" lead to war.

To a demand that Japan retire from Indochina, Nomura offered such a withdrawal once a Chinese settlement was effected, coupled to the proviso that no more Japanese troops would be stationed in the French territory. In return for this Nomura again asked the United States to "use its good offices for initiation of direct negotiations between the Japanese government and the Chiang Kai-shek regime for the purpose of a speedy settlement of the China Incident." None of this was pertinent, Hull replied, and it was "lacking in responsiveness to the suggestion made by the President."

More significant than the marches and countermarches of the diplomats — and of more bearing to this narrative — was the determined effort of Roosevelt's advisers to block frantic attempts by the antiwar faction to arrange a meeting between the President and Prince Konoye.[4] That Lauchlin Currie, who figures rather curiously

Seven Decisions That Shaped History (New York, 1951).

[4] On the evening of 4 August, Konoye spoke to the Ministers of War and of Navy about his plan to ask for a meeting with President Roosevelt. The Premier's words were reported verbatim and later were incorporated into his memoirs. It is interesting to note the tone of urgency with which Konoye stated his case. ". . . This conference must be held soon," he said. "The outlook of the German–Soviet war indicates that the peak will become apparent in about September. If, as people in some circles predict today, a stalemate is brought about, Germany's future cannot be viewed with optimism. If that does happen, the American attitude will stiffen and she will no longer entertain the thought of talking with Japan. . . . It is my opinion that to do everything that should be done is absolutely essential. . . ." (Pearl Harbor Hearings, pp. 3999–4000.)

later in this account, was the President's chief adviser on the Far East, is of more than passing interest. On 17 August 1941, Nomura communicated Premier Konoye's urgent request for such a meeting in mid-Pacific so that the problems which had stumped the diplomats could be thrashed out definitively "in a peaceful spirit." Twice before, this plea had been made by Nomura to the State Department — but to no avail. It took the President six days to come to a decision. Between the two dates, he received a personal appeal from Konoye. Hull was also enjoined by Ambassador Grew to urge this meeting in a letter which noted:

Not only is the proposal unprecedented in Japanese history, but it is also an indication that Japanese intransigeance is not crystallized completely owing to the fact that the proposal has the approval of the Emperor and the highest authorities in the land. The good which may flow from a meeting between Prince Konoye and President Roosevelt is incalculable.

Hull was not moved by this. Roosevelt rose to the suggestion and approved it. Several days later, his advisers had dissuaded him. Though the Japanese premier sent periodic appeals to the President for this meeting, though Konoye assented to a meeting place on American soil — in violation of all tradition — the President stalled. Grew and Eugene Dooman, a skilled and perceptive career diplomat in Tokyo, warned that failure to hold this meeting would topple the moderate Konoye government, deliver Japan into the hands of the imperialists, and convince many Japanese of America's bad faith; but the warning somehow failed to break through the wall of advisers. Both Japanese and American diplomats in Tokyo warned that time was running out, but the State Department persisted in its role as a tower of obstinacy.

On 16 October 1941, the Konoye Cabinet fell — as a direct consequence of its failure to bring about a meeting with the President. In the Ministry of Mars, the eleventh hour had almost arrived. It struck as the Japanese made one last attempt. With Japan bogged down in China and weakened by the embargo of oil and steel, with the pressure of the militarist clique growing more insistent, the moderates realized that it was now or never. Either they could come to terms with an American Secretary of State who early in the negotiations had resigned himself to war, or they could surrender their country to the war party to strike while it had the strength and the opportunity to do so.

The men who sought to halt the careening pace toward war were almost desperate, and certainly in a panic, at the State Department's refusal to come rapidly to an agreement, no matter how temporary. They were maddened by Secretary Hull's insistence on an outright disavowal by Japan of the Tripartite Pact before the American government would even discuss an alternative. They knew that the war party had already embarked on final war preparations which could only be reversed by some sort of American-Japanese understanding. Today we know that the State Department was aware of that urgency — the United States had broken the Japanese code and was privy to all its radio messages to embassies, military outposts, and diplomatic missions. Yet nothing was done.

On 20 November 1941, the Japanese made what was to be their last attempt. This was the famous offer of a *modus vivendi,* a ninety-day truce during which Japan and the United States could arrive at a Pacific settlement. Acceding to the State Department's demand, the Japanese agreed to make the Tripartite Pact a dead letter by interpreting it "freely and independently" and by disavowing all intentions of entering the European war unless they were directly attacked by one of the belligerents. Japan also accepted President Roosevelt's offer to act as a mediator in the Sino-Japanese war, and undertook to withdraw all troops from French Indochina upon the restoration of peace. In return, the economic blockade of Japan would be lifted.

From the viewpoint of American security, the *modus vivendi* was a perfect solution. It would have meant that the Japanese Army and Navy, bound by a promise to the Emperor and the Imperial Cabinet, would have been forced to call off their dogs and wait for the ninety days to end. *Those three months were vital to the United States.* General MacArthur, who had taken over the defense of the Philippines, had announced with typical optimism that he could hold them. He had qualified this sanguine appraisal, however, by setting a minimum time of three months for preparing his defenses. At the time of the truce offer, he was still two months from their projected completion.

The *modus vivendi* came within an inch of being accepted. Then, on 26 November, Hull took the step which Grew later described as "touching the button that started the war." He tossed away the truce and issued an ultimatum to the Japanese. Ten days later, the Japanese fleet, steaming on Pearl Harbor, received the message: "Climb Mount Niitaka."

The State Department did not act blindly. Stimson called Hull to question him about the *modus vivendi* on 27 November, the day after the ultimatum. For the first time, the Secretary of War learned that the truce plan had been rejected. Significantly, Hull told Stimson that he had "broken the whole matter off. I have washed my hands of it and it is now in the hands of you and [Navy Secretary Frank] Knox — the Army and Navy."

In the gingerbread edifice which then housed the State Department, war had not been declared, but it had been accepted. What had changed the minds of the President and his Secretary of State at this zero hour of history? The answer could have been found in Tokyo, Chungking, and Washington. It can be found today in the Sorge confession, in the multi-volume testimony and exhibits of the Pearl Harbor Inquiry, and in the transcript of the McCarran Committee's hearings on the Institute of Pacific Relations.

From the moment that Soviet Russia was attacked by Nazi Germany in June 1941, world Communist efforts had been devoted to the prevention of a second front in Asia. Fighting a losing battle in Europe, the Russians needed every soldier, every tank, every bullet.

Yet they could not afford to leave their Siberian borders unprotected without sound assurances that Japan would not strike them in the back as they themselves had struck Poland in 1939. Richard Sorge's job, therefore, evolved from espionage pure and simple to espionage and the influencing of policy in Japan and (through the German Embassy) in Germany.

"When the cry of war with the Soviet Union became urgent in 1941 . . . I did not restrict Ozaki's positive maneuvers within the Konoye group nor did I hesitate to work on the Germans," Sorge wrote. Ozaki began working on his friends, on Prince Saionji and Premier Konoye. He warned that Soviet strength was being underestimated and suggested that a war with the Russians would be of no value to Japan. According to Sorge, Ozaki's argument was briefly this:

The Soviet Union has no intention whatsoever of fighting Japan, and even if Japan should invade Siberia, would simply defend herself. It would be a shortsighted and mistaken move for Japan to attack Russia, since she cannot gain anything in Eastern Siberia or wrest any sizable political or economic benefits from such a war. The United States and Great Britain would very likely welcome such a Japanese embroilment with open arms and seize the opportunity to strike at the nation after her oil and iron reserves were depleted. Moreover, if Germany should succeed in defeating the Soviet Union, Siberia might fall into Japan's lap without her raising a finger. Should Japan aspire to further expansion elsewhere than in China, the Southern Area alone would be worth going into, for there Japan would find the critical resources so essential to her wartime economy, and there she would confront the true enemy [the United States] blocking her bid for a place in the sun.

Ozaki reported to Sorge the Herculean efforts of Prince Konoye to settle the China Incident and avoid any further conflict. Though Ozaki met frequently with the Premier, it is obvious that he did not seriously affect Konoye's thinking. But since the discussions sometimes took place before other Cabinet members, the views expressed by Ozaki were certainly picked up by less pacific Japanese and used by them in making the moves which eventually led to Pearl Harbor and war.

Sorge's first reports, in July, on the possibility of a Japanese attack on Russia were pessimistic. He radioed to "Wiesbaden" that Ambassador Ott, his close friend in the German Embassy, had informed him that Japan would attack Russia upon the fall of Leningrad and Moscow, and the German penetration to the Volga. But, Sorge added, Tojo was not interested in an attack on Russia. Late in July, he reported that there would be no attack on Russia. A message still later that month informed his Russian masters that the Japanese Navy had enough oil reserves for two years, the civilian population for half a year. This meant that Japan would either be forced to come to a settlement with the United States — the world's greatest oil-producing country — or to go to war with the Western powers in order to get by conquest what she lacked. For Russia, this was good news; how much oil was there in Siberia?

By the end of August, Sorge sent a message to "Wiesbaden" that Ambassador Ott had been informed that Japan would adhere strictly to its neutrality pact with Russia. The news was getting better. In September, the Fourth Bureau was informed that there would be no Japanese attack on Russia unless the Red Army collapsed suddenly. Though Sorge had let his home office know of the great summer mobilization — to be followed by an even greater one in December 1941 or January 1942 — he was able to reassure the Russians that Japanese strength in Manchuria was being held down to thirty divisions — the Kwantung Army — which were not being prepared for offensive action.

But Ozaki continued his close watch on Japanese-American negotiations. And these were enough to keep the Kremlin in a jittery state. Though Moscow knew, through Sorge, that the Japanese Cabinet had agreed on a move southward and war with the United States should the "peace" talks break down, it was also aware that the discussions might result in a temporary or permanent truce. In this case, Japan would get the oil and steel she desperately needed and, in time, turn on her ancient enemy — Russia. A long message from Sorge, when the negotiations were going well, increased the Kremlin's jitters:

Otto [Ozaki's cover name] has seen the proposals to the United States. . . . Item 4 indicates a way to solve the China problem by temporarily shelving the whole question of troop withdrawal, but suggests that Japan is prepared to withdraw troops from certain localities in Central and South China. Item 5 takes up American rights in the Far East and indicates how they can be protected. . . .

Early in October, Sorge radioed another progress report to Moscow on the course of "American–Japanese talks":

In Konoye's opinion they will end successfully if Japan decreases her forces in China and French Indochina and gives up her plan of building eight naval and air bases in French Indochina. . . . However, there will be war only if the talks break down, and *there is no doubt that Japan is doing her best to bring them to a successful conclusion, even at the expense of her German ally.* [Italics added.]

This message was sent by Sorge at a time when he was being briefed almost daily by Ambassador Ott on Japanese military and diplomatic plans — and double-checking the German information against what he learned from Konoye's adviser, Ozaki.

Also in October, Ozaki warned that "the next two or three weeks will be the most crucial with respect to Japan's advance to the south" and an attack on the Western powers. Nevertheless, Ozaki was firmly convinced that the touchy negotiations would never succeed. He saw the feverish anxiety of the Japanese militarists to launch a war against the United States and Britain. As one of the founders of the Imperial Rule Assistance Association, the most jingoist of all high-level Japanese pressure groups, Ozaki was fully cognizant of the power and the drive of the war party. He was encouraging the militarists and giving them ammunition to use against the antiwar faction. Ozaki was reading the discouraged reports of Japanese diplomats in Washington; their frustration in the face of the State Department's inability (or reluctance) to grasp the urgency of the situation made it clear that unless there was a sharp change in American thinking, war was inevitable.

In mid-October 1941, less than two months before Pearl Harbor, Sorge and Ozaki sent the Fourth Bureau a long report stating his opinion that the Japanese had given up hope of arriving at an agreement with the American government and that an attack against the United States and Britain would be launched in December or possibly in early January. The Kremlin, which had been given warning by Roosevelt of Germany's attack on Russia, returned the favor by keeping this precious military intelligence to itself. From a Soviet point of view, the reasoning was practical. A Japan at war with the United States would not venture into Siberia; and a United States plunged into war would shuck off what the Kremlin considered our lackadaisical, if not frivolous, attitude toward Lend-Lease, aircraft production, and rearmament.

With this message, Sorge felt that his mission had been accomplished. He knew, moreover, that when war came, his means of returning to Russia without breaking cover would disappear. There was no need for him to remain. He prepared a draft of a request that he be recalled to Moscow. But the wheels had already begun to turn. Though he did not know it, Sorge was marked for arrest. Ironically, the discovery of his apparatus by the Japanese secret police was purely accidental. It came through no fault or chance indiscretion of any member.[5] The arrests happened simply because

[5] Japanese Intelligence had been monitoring the Sorge ring's radio messages. But despite frantic efforts, it was able neither to decode these messages nor to locate the transmitter. After the arrests of Sorge and Klausen, when their effects were seized, the Japanese police found a copy of the *Statistisches Jahrbuch für das Deutsche Reich* among Klausen's possessions. This was the ring's codebook, and with it the Japanese were able to decipher the messages which they had been regularly recording.

no web of secrecy can be perfect; there is always one loose end, unforeseen and unpredictable, which starts unraveling it.

The instrument of betrayal was Ito Ritsu, in the postwar years a member of the Central Committee of the Japanese Communist Party and leader of the Youth Action Corps. In June 1941, Ito was arrested by the Tokkoka (the Tokyo Metropolitan Police) for Communist activities. (He was, at the time, doing confidential work for the South Manchurian Railway.) Under questioning, Ito broke down, confessed that he was a Communist. Though he held to his ideological faith, he immediately began implicating his comrades, perhaps to avoid torture. Among those he named was Kitabayashi Tomo, whom Miyagi Yotoku had lived with in the United States and then recruited into the Sorge ring when she returned to Japan. Ito had known Mrs. Kitabayashi as a Communist; when she went into the underground, she had broken off all party connections. Her sudden change made him believe that she had turned apostate. Ironically this was his revenge.

By 28 September 1941, the police had tracked down Mrs. Kitabayashi and arrested her. She had little to confess except her underground association with Miyagi, who was seized on 10 October. He was a frail, tubercular man who first tried to commit suicide by jumping out the window of the police station. After this attempt failed, his resistance collapsed quickly and he named his co-conspirators. Using his home as a trap, the police began arresting all his callers. On 14 October, Ozaki was arrested. There was no chance for one member to warn another since all meetings were by prearrangement.

On the afternoon of 15 October, Max Klausen turned up at Sorge's home to discuss transmission of the draft message requesting recall. He found Sorge very worried. "Joe [Miyagi] did not keep an appointment on the thirteenth," Sorge said, "and Otto [Ozaki] failed to meet me at the Asia Restaurant. The police may have arrested them." Impatiently, they awaited for Ozaki's arrival. He never showed up. Two days later, Klausen returned to Sorge's home. Voukelitch was there, deeply concerned over the disappearance of the two men. On the way home, Klausen ran into an officer of the Special Higher Section of the Tokkoka. Was it an accidental meeting? Klausen did not know, but his confidence was shaken. His first impulse was to burn all documents in his possession and to bury his radio transmitter. But he decided to do nothing.

The next morning, while Klausen was still asleep, the police officer he had seen walked in and arrested him. Even as Klausen was getting dressed, other police were rounding up Richard Sorge and Branko de Voukelitch. Before the day's end, all the principal members of the apparatus were in prison. (Within six months, thirty-five suspects had been arrested. Of these, sixteen were tried and the rest released as unconscious dupes or casual associates. Saionji was one of the last to be arrested. His sentence of three years was stayed, undoubtedly because of the eminence of his family background.) Ambassador Ott and Colonel Meisinger, the Gestapo chief, were not notified of Sorge's arrest. After several days, Meisinger became alarmed over the unexplained disappearance. He got in touch with the Tokkoka and learned to his amazement that Sorge had been arrested as a Soviet spy. Meisinger lashed out at the police for their stupidity and their inefficiency.

"Sorge is the only man in the German Embassy I really trust," the Gestapo chief shouted. Very politely, the Japanese outlined the evidence they had collected. Ott and Meisinger reported the arrest to Berlin, playing down its implications. Gestapo headquarters checked its files and found a full dossier on Sorge. Ott was replaced by Dr. Heinrich Stahmer and sat out the war in Peiping. After the German collapse, Meisinger was flown to Poland, where he stood trial for the atrocities he had committed in Warsaw. Ozaki was executed; Sorge's fate remains a great question. Miyagi and Voukelitch died in prison. Max and Anna Klausen, like Kawai, were in prison when the war ended. They were released by General MacArthur under the terms of the Potsdam agreement, along with all other political prisoners, and disappeared into China after receiving a sum of money from the Soviet Embassy.

When General Willoughby, MacArthur's Intelligence chief in SCAP, took the stand in August 1951 before the McCarran Internal Security Subcommittee, he made public Sorge's activities to drive Japan into a Pacific war. But he was not allowed to elaborate on the role of certain Americans in this endeavor; shortly before Willoughby testified, he was visited by a major general who gave him specific instructions as to what could be and what could not be said. The country merely heard the truth as censored by President Truman and the Pentagon. But there is evidence that pressure continued at the Tokyo end right up until the bombs fell on Pearl Harbor. Whether it came from Americans or from Communist-inspired Japanese, we still do not know. One interesting aspect of the puzzle is that Prince Saionji, a member with Ozaki of the Breakfast Group and Secretary of the Japanese Council of the Institute of Pacific Relations, amazed his friends in the government by discarding his former "liberalism" and giving comfort to the war party.

We are learning today how this co-ordinated pressure continued in Washington and Chungking. Perhaps we will never learn whether it was motivated by misguided idealism, ignorance, or Red-handed villainy. The facts are here for the reader to evaluate; the writer merely presents them.

The Japanese antiwar faction had made its last bid for peace on 20 November 1941 when it offered the United States a *modus vivendi*. This proposal was enthusiastically seconded by the Joint Chiefs of Staff who felt that the United States was not yet prepared to defend herself against attack in the Pacific. General MacArthur was not yet ready in the Philippines and the Navy was funneling much of its strength into the Atlantic.

As a matter of fact, the *modus vivendi* came as no surprise to

President Roosevelt or his Cabinet. Intercepted Japanese messages had carried the text. Secretary Hull and the President had discussed the Japanese offer at length. State Department Far East experts had prepared a draft memorandum for Hull which urged some "transitional" arrangement with Japan rather than the immediate and total settlement which certain members of the President's official family clamored for. President Roosevelt, moreover, was most anxious to accept the not-yet-offered *modus vivendi*. He, too, had prepared a draft memorandum which extended the Japanese truce proposals to six months and, in effect, recognized the Japanese position in Manchukuo by asking the Japanese government to guarantee that it would not increase its garrisons on the Manchurian border. Up to that time, in the long and anguished negotiations of those prewar years, the Japanese conquest of Manchuria was neither an issue nor a stumbling block — whatever official propagandists may have said then or write now.

At a meeting of the Cabinet, it was decided to accept the *modus vivendi*. But before this was formally done, it was felt that Chiang Kai-shek should be informed of the truce terms and of the notable advantages which the battered and weakened Chinese would derive from them. The delicate task of explaining the *modus vivendi* was assigned to Owen Lattimore, in Chungking as the President's personal representative. There seemed to be no reason why Chiang should not agree to a temporary truce which, if only for a time, would relieve China of the grinding burden of war and probably lead to a moderately equitable peace. The world will never know precisely how the truce was explained to the Generalissimo. That Chiang did not understand the terms of the *modus vivendi*, however, is a matter of record. Hull complained bitterly that Chiang had "no real idea of what the facts are."

On 25 November, moreover, Lauchlin Currie received a cable at the White House from Lattimore: ". . . I feel you should urgently advise the President of the Generalissimo's very strong reaction. . . .

Any 'modus vivendi' now arrived at with China would be disastrous to Chinese belief in America. . . . It is doubtful whether either past assistance or increasing aid would compensate for the feeling of being deserted at this hour. . . . I must warn you that even the Generalissimo questions his ability to hold the situation together if the Chinese national trust in America is undermined by *reports of Japan's escaping military defeat by diplomatic victory.*" (Italics added.) The cable was signed "Lattimore."[6]

In Washington, Assistant Secretary of the Treasury Harry Dexter White was busy lighting a fire under Secretary Hull to denounce the *modus vivendi*. A member of two Soviet spy rings, White had some years earlier demonstrated his love for China by turning over for transmission to Russia a report on Chinese finances detailed enough to permit a hostile power to wreck that nation's economy. To undercut the truce arrangements, White summoned Edward C. Carter and other leaders of the IPR to Washington.[7] He urged them to impress their friends in government with the view that a solution of the China Incident would be a "sellout." A letter by Carter, written on 29 November 1941, is extremely revealing:

"I should think that Currie probably had a terribly anxious time for the past week," Carter wrote to a friend. "For a few days, it looked as though Hull was in danger of selling China[8] and Amer-

[6] The entire cable is published in the Hearings before the Joint Committee on the Investigation of the Pearl Harbor Attack, 79th Congress, p. 4473. This historic and multi-volumed transcript is the original source for much of the material in this chapter. Other official sources are documents issued by the State Department, memoirs of the men involved, in the United States and Japan, Congressional documents, etc. The reader can find much of this material sandwiched between the covers of George Morgenstern's *Pearl Harbor; the Story of the Secret War*. (New York, 1947.)

[7] McCarran Hearings, pp. 153ff.

[8] Just three and one half years earlier, Carter had stated in a memorandum to Miriam Farley of the IPR staff that "of course I agree" with a Lattimore proposal embodied in a letter to him (18 May 1938) that IPR propagandize in favor of a partition of China by Japan, based on the military status quo. This dismemberment plan was incorporated in a memorandum by Chen Han-seng, a Chinese Communist. It went far beyond the *modus vivendi* in its generosity to Japan and its betrayal

ica and Britain down the river. Currie did not say this, but I learned it from other high sources."

Carter admitted under oath before the Senate Internal Security Subcommittee that he had gone down to Washington at White's insistence "to see if there was anything private citizens or government servants could do to make certain" the *modus vivendi* would not be consummated. "There were rumors," he added, "that Mr. Hull, who had been playing golf, I think, with Admiral Nomura . . . was being persuaded by the Japanese that by right of conquest and because Japan was so much more civilized they should really be in China as the British were in India." But Carter insisted that he had never put any pressure on Hull because the *modus vivendi* had already been rejected. This did not quite jibe with the story of Lauchlin Currie's "terribly anxious time" but the committee did not press the point.

If Carter did not personally speak to Hull, however, there were enough of the IPR's friends and supporters to do the job. There was Harry White, who always worked through the Secretary of the Treasury, Henry Morgenthau. There was Lauchlin Currie, armed with the Lattimore cable. Secretary Hull reversed himself almost overnight. On 26 November, without the knowledge of Secretary Stimson but with the approval of the President, he issued his famous "get-out-of-China-or-else" message to the Japanese. As an ultimatum, it was not as brusque as some; as a basis for further negotiation, it was a door slammed in Japan's face. "We had no serious thought that Japan would accept our proposal," Hull wrote four years later. When, on 27 November 1941 — the day after the ultimatum — the United Press reported that the "United States handed Japan a blunt statement of policy which, informed quarters

of Nationalist China. It also allowed for the free play of the Chinese Communists in their *kampf* against Chiang. Why should Lattimore and Carter feel so strongly against a temporary truce in 1941? And why should Lattimore have stated in 1938 that for IPR to press for a "settlement" ceding Manchuria would "increase its reputation"?

said, virtually ended all chances of an agreement," it was fairly
stating the case.

For the Hull ultimatum demanded that Japan withdraw from
virtually the entire Asiatic mainland — with the exception of Korea
— and returned the Japanese Empire to a *status quo* of two decades
earlier. Hull's note, embodied in a ten-point program, was sweeping to a degree unprecedented in the diplomatic relations of the
two countries. The Army Board, one of the several bodies to assess
blame for the Pearl Harbor disaster, in a gingerly fashion called
attention to the critical importance of Secretary Hull's act:

The responsibility assumed by the Secretary of State was to determine when the United States would reach an impasse with
Japan. . . . Apparently on the 26th in the morning, Mr. Hull had
made up his mind not to go through with the proposals shown the
day before to the Secretary of War [Stimson] containing the plan
for the "Three Months' Truce." . . . Evidently the action to "kick
the whole thing over" was accomplished by presenting to the Japanese the counterproposals of the "Ten Points" which they took as
an ultimatum. . . . The Japanese attacking force departed from
Tankan Bay on the 27–28 November. . . .

That the United States considered it an ultimatum was made
clear by the war warning sent to all military outposts on 27 November. It was further emphasized by President Roosevelt's statement,
when the question of the Hull note was discussed, that "we are
likely to be attacked, perhaps next Monday." He was wrong, but
only as to the date.

The Japanese government had arranged, on 19 November 1941,
to transmit the message "East Wind Rain" in the middle of its
regular short-wave news broadcast as a warning to Japanese diplomatic personnel once the war decision had been made. American
Intelligence, which had broken the Japanese code, knew that the
three words stood for the three sentences: "War with England. War
with America. Peace with Russia." The Army Pearl Harbor Board

reported that "such information [the 'winds' message] was picked up by a monitoring station. This information was received and translated on 3 December 1941, and the contents distributed to . . . high authority." The "winds" message has disappeared from Navy files. All other copies, according to the Army board, also disappeared shortly after the Pearl Harbor attack. Navy officers admitted the existence of the intercept until 1944, then suffered a progressive loss of memory. The "high authority" in the Army, Navy, and White House deny that they ever saw the message. Was it lost on the way? Did it stray? Or was it suppressed by someone of greater or lesser importance?

East Wind Rain fell on Pearl Harbor on a quiet Sunday. If some men died, other men were victorious.

XIII

Links of American Policy

No apparatus is an island of itself entire. Each serves a separate function, yet each is linked to the other. Like a vicious Underground Railroad, running in reverse from freedom to slavery, each apparatus is a station. A master switchman in the Fourth Bureau routes the trains. So, by will or necessity, the agents of the apparatuses shift from place to place till they are liquidated or arrested, or break loose to emerge in a world which uses them and rejects them.[1]

This shifting about of Soviet agents from apparatus to apparatus not only keeps many of them one jump ahead of the sheriff; it also gives them a spurious stature as soldiers of an ideal, fighting freedom's battle wherever tyranny lifts its head. The peripatetic *apparatchiks* of Communism are many (most of them write books, and the shelves are full of their "objective" accounts). Though they are tied hand and soul to the *apparat,* many of them are not ideological Communists. Hede Massing, for many years a Soviet courier, could not have explained the theory of surplus value to save her life. Harry D. White, who regularly delivered American state secrets to two Washington spy rings, was a Keynesian. Noel Field, who literally delivered his life to the Soviet Union, summed up his Communism by standing at midnight in the hushed Lincoln Memorial and singing the *Internationale* in bad Russian.

[1] The sinner who repents receives God's mercy, but liberals in New York and Washington hold to the higher morality that a man who has turned his back on Stalin is infinitely more evil than a man who refuses to turn his back on Alger Hiss.

Agnes Smedley was one of these self-styled idealists. She believed what no professional agent believes — that Communism was a rapture of the soul, that it would make all women brothers. Her books, her speeches, her interviews were all filled with this adoration of a nonexistent purpose. Though she might remark waspishly on the behavior of American — or even Russian — Communists, she clothed Communism and its "ideals" in an aura of muddled ecstasy. She had, what is more, that overwhelming and uncloying charm characteristic of a certain type of extreme neurotic. It was this charm, plus an embattled political virginity that survived the repeated rape of her Communist affiliations, which made her so dangerous. She lied with such heartrending sincerity that both she and her non-Communist friends were convinced she spoke the truth.

Agnes Smedley had taken her advanced training in Richard Sorge's Shanghai apparatus. She had gone into business for herself when Sorge moved on to Tokyo. There is reason to believe that by 1936, however, she had begun moving away from this rather primitive form of bundles to Russia and taken on the infinitely more delicate and important task of influencing that small group of Americans in Hankow who eventually became the masters of American Far Eastern policy. It would be ridiculous to credit her with sole responsibility for this indoctrination; it would be inaccurate not to give her a substantial share of the blame.

Her influence on General Joseph Stilwell, later to become one of the foremost instruments of American confusion over China, was tremendous. Though she may not have sold him the belief that the Chinese Communists were sterling democrats, she certainly showed all the proper admiration when he tried it on for size. The British Ambassador to China in the mid-late 1930s, Sir Archibald Clark-Kerr (later Lord Inverchapel) considered Agnes Smedley one of the "greatest women" on earth, and from her he accepted the myth that the Chinese Reds were dear people. Inverchapel carried these views with him when he became Ambassador to Washington. Evans Carlson, who rose to the rank of brigadier general in the United States Marines and was posthumously dubbed a party member by the Communist press, was a male Trilby to Agnes Smedley's Svengali.

Freda Utley describes Carlson as he "walked around Hankow in a dirty shirt with the sleeves cut short and unhemmed, endeavoring to look like a Communist guerrilla. His strange appearance and ecstatic praise for the Chinese Communists were ridiculed by . . . the sophisticated John Davies, then United States Consul in Hankow."[2] Yet Davies matched Carlson's assertion that the Communists were the "true Christians" by calling Agnes Smedley one of the "pure in heart." Stilwell, Carlson, and Davies — aided by writers like Edgar Snow, Guenther Stein, Owen Lattimore, T. A. Bisson — all helped sell the Chinese Communist cause to the American intellectuals and to the State Department. They were all friends of Agnes Smedley; she even conducted some of them personally to Yenan, the Red rebel capital. And through them, she influenced the group of Foreign Service officers who remained in China during World War II and helped engineer the destruction of the Nationalists.

An examination of the step-by-step abandonment of the anti-Communist forces in Asia from 1943 to the present, of the blatant deception visited upon the American people by the State Department, of the distortions and the concealments practiced by its Far East Division, of the withholding of arms and munitions from the Nationalists at a time when bullets dumped into the Pacific could have saved the day, of the high-handed tactics used by important United States diplomatic officials in attempting to force the Chinese Communists into a dominant position in the Chiang Kai-shek government — all this would require an encyclopedia. Even a cursory analysis would take up a volume. There is no better way to show

[2] *The China Story.* (Chicago, 1951.)

how Augean the State Department stable — or how Stygian its record — than to make a brief case study of John Stewart Service.

It is almost an understatement to say that John Service — along with John Carter Vincent, John P. Davies, Jr., John Emmerson,[3] and Raymond P. Ludden, career diplomats all — cooked up the stew of America's suicidal China policy and served it steaming hot to Dean Acheson. The Institute of Pacific Relations, the Foreign Policy Association, *Amerasia,* and a congeries of scholars and publicists led by Owen Lattimore, T. A. Bisson, Lawrence Rosinger, Maxwell S. Stewart, and John K. Fairbank, backed this policy enthusiastically. What has been alleged of these men in sworn testimony is entirely beside the point. In the long view, it may be unimportant to determine whether or not they are Reds. The important consideration is that they led the United States astray. At the very best, they were completely and damnably wrong — a fact which neither they nor the State Department will admit — and held to their position long after events had demonstrated the folly of their acts.

John Stewart Service is noteworthy because he remained in China throughout World War II. His reports, held proudly aloft by the Far East desk in Washington, were used to destroy Chiang and build up Mao Tse-tung. Of particular significance is the history of one such report by Service. It arrived in Washington with a covering letter from Ambassador Leighton Stuart at Chungking which discounted its information and stressed its bias. It was circulated in the State Department with a second covering note, written by John Carter Vincent, stating that Service was right, the Ambassador was wrong.

Until he was arrested under the Espionage Act in 1945, Service

[3] In May 1945, Emmerson returned from Communist-held territory in China and recommended to the State Department that Japanese prisoners in American stockades be turned over to Japanese Communists for indoctrination. (McCarran Hearings, pp. 747ff.)

was unknown to the American public. The outline of his life and career up to that point, as described by FBI representatives before a House Judiciary subcommittee investigating the puzzling circumstances of the *Amerasia* Case in 1946, reveals little:

MR. GURNEA: John Stewart Service was born in Cheng-tu, China, August 3, 1909, of American parents. . . . Since June 23, 1933, he has been employed by the State Department. . . . He has served the State Department in varying capacities from clerk to the position of second secretary at Chungking, China. . . . On July 14, 1943, he was named consul at Kunming, China. On October 10, 1943, he was placed on detached service, assigned to General Stilwell.

On November 1, 1944, he returned to the United States for a short period of time, and in January 1945 returned to China. Shortly thereafter, he accompanied the Army Intelligence Unit to the Yenan area occupied by the Chinese Communist Army, and then returned to the United States on April 12, 1945. On April 19, 1945, he was observed to meet Philip Jaffe [the leading figure in the *Amerasia* documents case] in the Statler Hotel at 6:50 P.M.

It will be recalled that following Gen. Patrick J. Hurley's return to the United States, after having served as United States Ambassador to China, he criticized Service's theories, and considered his political reporting as biased. He pointed out that Service had shown himself to be liberally disposed toward Communists, and also on occasion to be most unfriendly to the Nationalist Government of the Generalissimo Chiang Kai-shek. . . .

These are the bare bones. The flesh can be found in Service's long testimony before a State Department Loyalty Security Board, which cleared him in 1950.[4] It was before this board that Service suggested that to checkmate the Russians we must bolster the Chinese Reds. It was also before this board that he discussed his association with Guenther Stein — then but a few years away from his collaboration with Richard Sorge. "Stein was a useful source of news," Service said, "and some of my memoranda here transmit long sections of his notes of interviews he had with Communist leaders." Service

[4] See p. 169.

found Stein "a very conservative person by nature," the board was informed. Elaborating on Stein's views, Service added that "his attitude is a little bit like Agnes Smedley. . . . Guenther Stein was stricken with the sweetness and light theory about the Chinese Communists."

The best insight into Service, however, comes from the dispatches he sent while in China. On 7 April 1944, for example, he reported on the situation in Sinkiang, criticizing Chiang Kai-shek for his "reckless adventurism" and "cynical desire to destroy unity among the United Nations." Emphasizing the need for not arousing Russia's suspicions, Service recommended that the United States "avoid all appearance of unqualified diplomatic support to China . . . and limit American aid to China to direct prosecution of the war against Japan . . . soft-pedaling . . . grandiose promises of postwar aid and economic rehabilitation. . . ."

"Show a sympathetic interest in the Communist and liberal groups in China," the dispatch recommended further. "The Communists, from what little we know of them, are friendly toward America, believe that democracy must be the next step in China, and take the view that economic collaboration with the United States is the only hope for speedy postwar rehabilitation and development." The Nationalists would be forced to take any treatment we handed out, since they could turn to no country but the United States, Service continued. "American interest in the Communists will be a potent force in persuading Kuomintang China to set its house in order." Thus, he advised, we would build up a "democratic and unified China," which would "naturally gravitate" toward the United States.[5]

On 28 September 1944, John Service informed the State Department (Report No. 34), that: "Politically, any orientation which the Chinese Communists may once have had toward the Soviet Union seems to be a thing of the past. The Communists have worked to

[5] A Communist China *did* "naturally gravitate" toward the United States — on the Korean battlefields.

make their thinking and program realistically Chinese, and they are carrying out democratic policies. . . ."

In a 9 October 1944 dispatch Service drew the "important conclusion" based on reports he had received from the field, that the Communists were unbeatable, that they supported democracy; and Service advised that unless the Nationalist government aped the Red program for "economic and political reform" — which it could not do, Service noted — the Communists were likely to become the dominant force within a few years. Attempts by Chiang to eliminate the Communists, Service warned, would "mean a complete denial of democracy."

A 14 February 1945 dispatch, signed by Service and John Paton Davies, advised that "at present there exists in China a situation closely paralleling that which existed in Yugoslavia prior to Prime Minister Churchill's declaration of support of Marshal Tito." And, the report states:

Whether we like it or not, by our very presence here we have become a force in the internal politics of China and that force should be used to accomplish our primary mission [the defeat of Japan]. In spite of hero-worshiping publicity in the United States, Chiang Kai-shek is not China and by our present narrow policy of outspokenly supporting his dog-in-the-manger attitude we are needlessly cutting ourselves off from millions of useful allies; many of whom are already organized and in position to engage the enemy. These allies, let it be clear, are not confined to Communist-controlled areas of China but are to be found everywhere in the country. . . . Other important groups favor the same *program as that espoused by the so-called Communists — agrarian reform, civil rights, the establishment of democratic institutions —*[6] but the Communists

[6] Curiously enough, at the same hearing that these dispatches were read into the record, the following exchange took place between C. E. Rhetts, Service's counsel, and Service himself:

    Q. Did you ever indicate the Chinese Communist Party to be mere agrarian reformers?
    A. I never did. . . . I never used "Communists" in quotes nor said "So-called Communists."

are the only group at present having the organization and strength openly to foster such "revolutionary" ideas. [Italics added.]

Our objective is clear. . . . Support of the Generalissimo is desirable insofar as there is concrete evidence that he is willing and able to marshal the full strength of China against Japan. . . . There should be an immediate adjustment of our position in order that flexibility of approach to our primary objective may be restored.

When Service was assigned as political observer — and in effect, political adviser — to General Stilwell, he was working with a kindred spirit, yet one who did not react to subtle distinctions. The now-famous Report No. 40, written directly for Stilwell, is a completely unguarded statement of Service's views. It is a shocking document. Had it been about Russia, by a minor American diplomat in the war-beleaguered Soviet Union, he would have been recalled forthwith. Report No. 40 merits extensive quotation.[7] It is entitled, "The Need for Greater Realism in Our Relations with Chiang Kai-shek," and in its letter of transmittal Service speaks of the "frankness which I have assumed . . . regarding the stronger policy which I think it is now time to adopt."

After a cynical preamble indicating his belief that the Nationalist government was worthless and washed up militarily, Service continued: "The [Kuomintang] and Chiang will stick to us because our victory is certain and is their only hope for continued power. But our support of the Kuomintang will not stop its normally traitorous relations with the enemy and will only encourage it to continue sowing the seeds of future civil war by plotting with the present puppets for eventual consolidation of the occupied territories against the Communist-led forces of popular resistance. . . . Any new government under any other than the present reactionary control will be more co-operative and better able to mobilize the country." To aid Chiang hurts the war effort, Service added, and loses us the friendship of the Chinese Reds.

[7] See Appendix I for full text of Report No. 40.

"*We need not support the Kuomintang for international political reasons.* . . . *On the contrary, artificial inflation of Chiang's status only adds to his unreasonableness.* . . . *We need not support Chiang in the belief that he represents pro-American or pro-democratic groups.*" [8] The Communists, Service urged, were both democratic and pro-American. "*Finally, we feel no ties of gratitude to Chiang.* He has fought to have us save him — so that he can continue his conquest of his country. In the process, he has 'worked us for all we were worth.' [9] We seem to forget that Chiang is an Oriental [in contrast to Mao Tse-tung?]. . . . *We cannot hope to deal successfully with Chiang without being hardboiled.* . . . *We cannot hope to solve China's problems* . . . *without consideration of the opposition forces* — Communist, Provincial, liberal.[10]

"We should not be swayed by pleas of the danger of China's collapse. This is an old trick of Chiang's. There may be a collapse of the Kuomintang government. . . . There may be a period of some confusion, but the eventual gains of the Kuomintang's collapse will more than make up for this. . . . *The crisis is the time to push — not relax.*"

Service swore at his loyalty hearing that he had urged the sending of an American observer to Yenan only because it would gain us valuable military intelligence and thereby aid in the war against Japan. But in Report No. 40, he had said:

Public announcement that the President's representative had made a visit to the Communist capital at Yenan would have a significance that no Chinese would miss — least of all the Generalissimo. The effect would be even greater if it were only a demonstration with no real consultation. . . . The Kuomintang government could not withstand public belief that the United States was considering withdrawal of military support or recognition of the Kuomintang as the leader of Chinese resistance. More than ever we hold all the aces in Chiang's poker game. It is time we started playing them.

[8] All italics Service's.

[9] One half of one per cent of American Lend-Lease went to China.

[10] "Provincial" meant the war lords; "liberal" meant a handful of professionals with no political influence, experience, or support, and infiltrated by the Communists.

Report No. 40 referred to the Nationalist government of China —
the government which for years had stood up against the Japanese —
and to the armies which had fought and died in defense of their
country, with almost no arms, almost no food, almost no hope. It
was a plan which could only turn China over to the Communist
"agrarian reformers" and to Moscow. It was not written in 1945,
when the war with Japan was over. It was written on 10 October
1944, less than a month after the Chinese Nationalist armies, destroyed and demoralized according to political observer Service, had
launched a great offensive and captured "Tengyueh, in Yunnan
Province, the first large Chinese city to be liberated in seven years." [11]

When, in 1945, Major General Patrick J. Hurley testified before
the Senate Foreign Relations Committee that John Service and "the
professional Foreign Service men" in China had sabotaged his efforts
as Ambassador to China, he was referring specifically to Report
No. 40. [12] He elaborated on this charge by stating under oath that
Service had undercut Hurley–supervised negotiations between
Chiang and the Chinese Communists by telling Red leaders that the
Ambassador was speaking only for himself and not for the United
States government. Service denied this in 1950, along with Hurley's
further charge that the efforts of the anti-Chiang faction had been
"to destroy the Government of the Republic of China."

Yet in a 20 June 1944 dispatch, [13] Service urged that the United
States disengage herself quietly from the Nationalists. "By an apparent abandonment of China in its hour of need, we would lose
international prestige, especially in the Far East," he wrote. "On
the other hand, if we come to the rescue of the Kuomintang on its
own terms we would be buttressing — but only temporarily — a
decadent regime. . . . Weak as [Chiang] is, he is in no position . . .
to turn down or render nugatory any co-ordinated and positive

---

[11] *The World at War, 1939–1944. Prepared from Public Sources by the Military
Intelligence Division, War Department.* (An *Infantry Journal* Book.)

[12] Quoted in Tydings Exhibits, p. 1984.

[13] Tydings Exhibits, pp. 235–246 inc.

policy we may adopt toward China. The cards are all in our favor."

At the height of the Pacific war, Service implemented this by recommending a series of steps which would force Chiang to follow our direction:

Stop our present "mollycoddling" of China by: Restricting Lend-Lease, cutting down training of Chinese military cadets, discontinuing training of the Chinese army, taking a firmer stand in the financial negotiations, or stopping the shipment of gold. Any or all of these restrictive measures can be reversed as the Generalissimo and the Kuomintang become more co-operative. . . . Stop building up the Generalissimo's and the Kuomintang's prestige internationally and in the United States. . . .

He also urged a policy of encouraging "constructive criticism" of China by the OWI radio; inviting the avowedly pro-Communist Mme. Sun Yat-sen to the White House; forcing Chiang to give publicity in China to a statement by Under Secretary of State Sumner Welles which had been proscribed in Nationalist territory because it gave aid and comfort to the Reds; and "selecting men of known liberal view to represent us in OWI."

In Service's eyes, conducting an official propaganda war against Chiang was not untoward. After all, he suggested, the philosopher Lin Yu-tang, Claire Boothe Luce, Wendell Willkie, and Republican congressmen were criticizing the behavior of State Department personnel in China and pointing out the dangers inherent in the Administration's China policy.

All this proves nothing about Service. It may demonstrate a symptomatic lack of understanding, exemplified perhaps by his close association with Guenther Stein and Solomon Adler[14] (he had

[14] Testimony of Elizabeth Bentley, courier for a Soviet apparatus in Washington, before the House Un-American Activities Committee:

MR. STRIPLING: Was one Solomon Adler a member of this [espionage] group?
MISS BENTLEY: Yes; he was.
MR. STRIPLING: Was he a rather active participant?

shared quarters with Adler in China, and relied on his advice). As one case history in many, however, it becomes Exhibit A in the untold story of American diplomacy. And it has ties with the still perplexing *Amerasia* Case.

Philip Jaffe, wholesale purloiner of secret documents, was the editor of *Amerasia*. On 19 April 1945 — seven days after Service returned to the United States from China and shortly before the full emphasis of the war shifted to the Pacific — Jaffe sought him out.

Miss BENTLEY: Rather remotely, Mr. Stripling, because at the time I had charge of that group he was in China.

Adler denied categorically that he was a Communist.

XIV

Amerasia, I: 1700 Stolen Documents

To the untrained eye, the *Amerasia* Case was a bewildering glimpse of a netherworld in which top secret government documents were stolen with ease, while the Justice Department stood by or pooh-poohed the gravity of the situation. Many well-meaning people preferred it that way. It was ill-bred to make even the mildest charges against Communists: Russia was our gallant ally, and the suggestion that spies might have penetrated into the parlor of government was unthinkable. That the *Amerasia* disclosures merely scratched one surface of Communist-controlled operations in the United States never seemed to occur to anyone — or at least to anyone who counted. Only those rude and uncompromising people, the premature anti-Communists, tried to make themselves heard above the hubbub of anguished liberals. They were silenced with the ridicule and abuse which is still their lot.

Unfortunately for the security of the nation, the case was killed almost before it had begun by an administration more concerned with perpetuating itself than with protecting the welfare of the country.

In a pamphlet prepared for the Scripps-Howard newspapers, Frederick Woltman, a Pulitzer Prize winner and a careful student of the Communist movement, wrote:

Many observers believe this case — one of the weirdest in the history of American criminal jurisprudence — is the key to America's postwar diplomatic debacle in Asia. Many believe that if its prosecution had been pursued honestly and vigorously, the pro-Communists in the Far Eastern division of the State Department would have been cleaned out. That Chiang Kai-shek, instead of being hurled back to the island of Formosa, might have driven the Chinese Red Army deep into Siberia. And that China's mainland, with its 450,000,000 people, might today be ruled by a government friendly to the United States, instead of by a Soviet satellite.

For the *Amerasia* Case was not a local phenomenon. Its origins went back to Stalin's abortive attempt of 1927 to make China a Soviet appendage, to the thousands of dollars and hundreds of men spent in Nanking and Chungking and Tokyo, and to the Kremlin's two-decade gamble for Asiatic domination. America was in a blue-chip game, but America's diplomats didn't know the big boys were playing for keeps.

Amerasia, a small magazine with less than two thousand subscribers, was merely the locus of many points. It was the center of an audacious group which reached into the Army, the Navy, the Office of Strategic Services, the State Department, the Office of War Information, the Foreign Economic Administration, the Office of Censorship — virtually every agency of the Federal government or its military forces which might be concerned with vital and secret information. This information was funneled into *Amerasia's* New York office.

The *Amerasia* Case came partially to light only because of the sheer carelessness, stupidity, and cockiness of its principals. In February 1945, Kenneth E. Wells, an OSS Far East analyst, reported to the OSS security chief, Archbold van Beuren, that he had come across evidence of a leak in security. Reading the 26 January issue of *Amerasia,* he had been struck by the similarities between an article on British–American relations in Siam and a secret OSS report he himself had prepared. Comparing the two, he found that the *Amerasia* piece had lifted whole paragraphs verbatim out of the report. Obviously, the writer had not only been able to see the secret document — he must have had it before him as he wrote.

Alarmed by this indication of espionage, van Beuren flew from

Washington to New York where he presented the case to Frank Brooks Bielaski, Director of Investigations for OSS. He asked Bielaski to find out how and why the document had gotten out of OSS files. An investigation was immediately begun. An agent was assigned to keep the *Amerasia* offices on lower Fifth Avenue in New York under surveillance. Another agent was sent to the Public Library to do an analysis of past issues of the magazine. Bielaski himself made inquiries concerning Philip Jaffe, the editor. In this preliminary investigation, he learned that *Amerasia's* offices, unlike those of most magazines, worked day and night. He learned that there was an "interlocking in the way of personnel" between *Amerasia* and the Institute of Pacific Relations. He discovered that Jaffe was known as a heavy contributor to the Communist Party, had used the name J. W. Phillips in editing *China Today,* an outright Communist publication, and that he owned a (non-union) printing plant. The names of such writers on the Far East as Owen Lattimore, T. A. Bisson, Frederick Vanderbilt Field, Anna Louise Strong, Andrew Roth, and Benjamin Kizer turned up as contributors or staff members of both *Amerasia* and IPR.

Bielaski decided that the best way to crack the case open was to enter the *Amerasia* offices at night and search the premises for the OSS document which had launched the investigation. Getting together a team of men, most of them former FBI agents, he waited night after night for the lights to go out in the *Amerasia* office. Finally on Sunday night, 11 March 1945, the opportunity to enter came. An assistant superintendent of the building let them in, and the OSS team began its search.

Testifying before the Hobbs subcommittee on 10 May 1946, Bielaski said:[1]

I went myself because I did not believe in sending somebody else to do something that I would not do. . . . I personally devoted my time to looking through the office, the front office. . . .

[1] *Congressional Record,* 22 May 1950.

About the time I had come to the conclusion there was nothing in the front office of interest to me — while I was in the front office, I had sent some of my agents back through the rear part of the office . . . one of them came and said, "We think you better come back here. We found some stuff you ought to see."

I started back. Before I went back to the rooms where they were, I observed on the right side of the main corridor there was a room; to be conservative, I would say it is half as big as this. It was devoted, exclusively, to photo copy work. They had a photo copy machine, and developer pans all around on the shelves. The place was equipped to make photo copies, and make them in large quantities.

I did not know what function that was for a little magazine like *Amerasia*. There it was, and I looked it over.

I went to the end of the corridor. On the end over to the left was the room of the associate editor, who was Kate Mitchell.

On the right was a smaller office of Philip Jaffe, who was the editor. . . . I went into the office of Jaffe. He had a desk about like this.

It was covered with originals and freshly made photo copies of documents, every one of which was secret in its character. Some of them were directed, personally, to the Secretary of State. Some of them were from military attachés in China and other places, confidential. All of them were marked "Not to be shown OWI." That was evidence of the confidential nature.

Some were from Naval Intelligence. There were a good many on his desk. It would seem from the freshness of the copies that those photo copies had just been made. They accounted for the fact that the office was working so late at night. . . . The State Department documents were addressed to the Secretary for his personal attention. . . . The originals were in there, and the photostatic copies. Everybody was astounded at this stuff.

While we were looking it over, a man happened to look behind a door. Behind the door he found a suitcase and two briefcases. The suitcase was a bellows-type suitcase that was probably that thick [indicating]. . . . About 18 inches. The briefcases were very heavy with documents. I had along an expert who opened all sorts of locks. He had opened all the locks. He opened the suitcase, the briefcases. When he opened the suitcase, it seemed to be a specially constructed affair with about 10 to 15 pockets in it. . . . It was literally loaded with secret documents of all sorts from all departments of the government. These were all originals. There were no copies in the suitcase. There was one exception; in that suitcase I found an original, a typewritten original, and four copies of the particular document that I was after, that was the Office of Strategic Service document on Siam.

In addition to that, I think there were five more secret documents of the Office of Strategic Service which we had not missed, one of which was "top secret," and extremely valuable and confidential.

I took this stuff out and spread it around. It covered almost every department in the government with the exception of the Federal Bureau of Investigation. . . . There were documents from the British Intelligence, Naval Intelligence, G–2, State Department, Office of Censorship, Office of Strategic Service, and probably others. . . . There were so many we could not list them. These documents had from 3 to 4 to 150 pages. There were 300 documents.

Every one of them bore the stamp that the possession of these documents is a violation of the Espionage Act. It was stamped all over them.

About that time, one of my men who had gone into the library came in and said he found something in the library.

He had an envelope which was not sealed. It was a large manila envelope. In that envelope were, I should say, 15 or 20 documents. I could not tell whether they came mimeographed or whether they were photo copied on this machine. They were a little blurred. They were not photostats. They must have been photo copies. In between these documents, every other one, we found six top secret documents of the Navy Department. I looked at these myself. I do not recall all six of them. I am sorry I did not make more notes about them, but I remember distinctly two, probably the first two that I read. One of them was entitled, and I do not know the exact words, but one was entitled, "The bombing program for Japan." It was top secret. I read it. It showed how Japan was to be bombed progressively in the industrial centers, and it named the cities.

The second one that I read gave the location of all the ships of the Japanese fleet, subsequent to the battle of Leyte; I guess it was October 1944. It gave the ships by name, and where they were located.

We went back out into the other room. We looked over this stuff:

came to the conclusion, if I came down here to the Office of Strategic Service and told them what I had seen, they just would not believe me. I, therefore, determined to take 12 to 14 of the documents and bring them down and show them to them as proof.

I picked out all of the Office of Strategic Service documents, including the five copies of the one that I was after, and either seven or eight additional documents. I picked documents that had marks of some sort on them to indicate through whose hands they had gone.

I put those in my pocket. I felt sure that there were so many there that they could not possibly miss those documents for a week, anyhow. I put those in my pocket. We left that place. We put everything back the way we found it. We left there about 2:30 in the morning.

Repeating this story for the Senate Foreign Relations Subcommittee (the Tydings "whitewash" committee) Bielaski added several startling details: [2]

This is something I have never repeated in public or anywhere, but which I think must be told here; an envelope . . . a little bigger than this [indicating] was there. . . . The envelope was open on the table, and there were quite a few of these documents [in it].

Bielaski listed the top secret documents in this envelope. "The third document which I remember, and of which I do not remember as much as I wish I did, had to do with a new bomb, which I thought at that time was merely a . . . new piece of ordnance. I believe — I recall that it was marked 'A' bomb, but with merely a capital A with quotation marks on each side, and it didn't say 'atomic.' . . . I don't know whether it was a progress report or a plan report, or what. . . . It seemed to me it was just a bomb, an A bomb as compared to a B bomb or a C bomb." Other documents in the *Amerasia* office, Bielaski noted, dealt with the disposition of Nationalist troops — information which would have been a boon to the Chinese Red Army — and included some highly private papers concerning the "intimate" relationship between Chiang Kai-shek and

[2] Tydings Hearings, pp. 931 ff.

Mme. Chiang, as well as dispatches from Ambassador to China Christian Gauss. Every document he saw had the mail receipt stamp of the State Department and a warning that illegal possession was a violation of the Espionage Act.

A few hours later, Bielaski was back in Washington and in Archbold van Beuren's office. One by one, for dramatic effect, the Director of Investigations laid on the desk the handful of documents he had taken from the *Amerasia* offices. One dealt with the German order of battle; another was marked "For the attention of the Director of Naval Intelligence Only." A third, according to FBI records, contained one of the most highly guarded United States military secrets — that the Navy had broken the Japanese code. What the others were, van Beuren no longer recalled when he testified before the Tydings subcommittee in 1950. Of the documents as a whole, however, he said: "My opinion, and I cannot state it too strongly, is that they would have been of benefit to an enemy of the United States and a detriment to the United States. . . . I became more and more amazed as I heard [Bielaski] describe the circumstances under which he had found them and saw the documents themselves."

That same evening, van Beuren was in the office of Brigadier General William Donovan, the OSS chief, to give him the bad news. "General Donovan decided that since all the documents bore the seal of the Department of State . . . Mr. Stettinius should hear of the matter as soon as possible. It was then mid-evening and General Donovan called Mr. Stettinius at his apartment at the Wardman Park and asked whether he could come up and see him at once. He suggested to the Secretary of State that if he could get hold of him, he might ask Assistant Secretary [Julius] Holmes . . . to be present. The General, Major Monigan [an OSS legal assistant], and I went up to the Wardman Park," van Beuren has testified. This was less than twenty-four hours after Bielaski had entered the *Amerasia* offices.

"Good evening, Ed," Donovan said to Stettinius. "I've got something here that will be of great interest to you."

While the Secretary looked through the documents, Donovan explained the circumstances under which they had been found. Stettinius turned to Assistant Secretary Holmes and made one of those revealing yet cryptic remarks which raise questions as well as eyebrows:

"Good God, Julius, if we can get to the bottom of this we will stop a lot of things that have been plaguing us."

Alger Hiss and Laurence Duggan [3] were still in the State Department. So, too, was Carl Aldo Marzani [4] — later to go to jail because he denied his Communist Party membership. There were rumors of leaks in the State Department, of a strong Red cell there, of puzzling behavior on the part of certain officials. Even President Roosevelt had complained that State Department secrets had a habit of finding their way into the newspapers. What was "plaguing" Stettinius? His remark was never explained.

[3] Laurence Duggan was one of the brilliant and attractive young men who clustered about Sumner Welles. In 1935, after an abortive Communist *Putsch* in Brazil, a party lawyer appeared at the United States Embassy in Rio with a letter from Duggan urging that all facilities be placed at the disposal of this defender of the revolutionists, but warning that "the Ambassador must not be informed" of this. Duggan was later introduced to Hede Massing, then a Soviet agent, by Noel Field. As a key man in the Latin American division of the State Department, Duggan was a valuable addition to the Massing ring, and he was forthwith recruited. How long he remained, or how deeply he became involved, is not known, since Mrs. Massing turned him over to another "contact." The available evidence indicates that he pulled out shortly afterward. In 1948, when the Hiss–Chambers case filled the newspapers, Duggan was visited by the FBI. He showed such great agitation that the agents who questioned him offered to return at a later date. They were never able to complete the interview. In December of that year, Duggan "jumped or fell" from the window of his sixteenth-floor office in New York City.

[4] Carl Aldo Marzani was another brilliant young man, one who served in the hush-hush OSS during the war. His mistake was to swear, in a State Department application, that he was not and had never been a Communist. Unfortunately, a member of the "Alien" Squad, the New York City Police Department's highly efficient anti-Communist unit — organized under Mayor Fiorello LaGuardia — had infiltrated the same party unit as Marzani. After a perjury trial, Marzani was sent to jail.

The conference at Secretary Stettinius's apartment broke up when the Secretary thanked General Donovan and told him that he would take all the necessary steps as soon as he had a chance to confer with his associates the next day. Bielaski was called in by top OSS officials shortly thereafter and told that the matter was out of his hands.

"I made only one stipulation [in turning over the case to the State Department]," Bielaski said, "that was that I and my men were so apprehensive about this whole thing, that somebody must do something about it. We did not want to sit by and see this thing go on. We wanted action. We wanted it in a hurry. We thought something should be done within a week. They promised action would be taken within a week. It was only six days later that the Federal Bureau of Investigation moved in in New York."

Six days later, after consultations with Secretary of the Navy James V. Forrestal, the case was turned over to J. Edgar Hoover. Myron Gurnea was assigned to head the investigation. Some seventy-five FBI agents were put on the case and, on 16 March 1945, began a twenty-four hour surveillance of Philip Jaffe, the *Amerasia* editor. By following him, they were led to an unknown number of other people. Some were found to be merely friends or acquaintances — not implicated in the theft of government documents. Others proved to be involved in Jaffe's nefarious activities — to a greater or lesser extent. Gurnea's account of the development of the case, given at a secret session of the Hobbs subcommittee on 31 May 1946, shows how and why six people were arrested. He came armed with some seventeen hundred exhibits — the full harvest of stolen documents — and this was his story: [5]

Mr. Gurnea: Inasmuch as Philip Jaffe and Kate Mitchell were the editors and co-editors, respectively, an investigation was immediately begun of those two individuals.

[5] *Congressional Record*, 22 May 1950.

I have here a brief biography of those persons if you would like to hear them?

THE CHAIRMAN: I think we would like to hear them.

MR. GURNEA: Kate Louise Mitchell has, since 1940, been co-editor of *Amerasia* which is owned by Philip Jaffe. She lives at 127 East 54th Street, New York City. Miss Mitchell was born of American parents in Buffalo, N. Y., September 1, 1908. She is a graduate of Bryn Mawr College. . . .

After her graduation from college in 1932, she was employed by the Institute of Pacific Relations from 1933 to 1940. From 1934 to 1940, she was private secretary to Mr. Edward C. Carter, secretary general of the Institute of Pacific Relations and, in such capacity, made numerous trips with him to foreign countries.

From 1940 to 1942 she continued to do research work for the Institute of Pacific Relations on a part-time basis. She was also reported to have contributed articles to the [Communist] periodical *New Masses*. According to Miss Mitchell, *Amerasia* is now entirely owned by Philip Jaffe. It was formerly a corporation [which] was dissolved in 1943 when many of the members of the editorial board had entered the government service. At present, the publication is published, primarily, through the joint efforts of Philip Jaffe and herself. Miss Mitchell advised that she has no financial interest, whatever, in the magazine, although in 1944 she furnished $2,500 of her own money to partially meet the deficit incurred by the magazine.

Also, prior to June 1945, she had contributed $1,000 of her own money toward the deficit of that year. She made the statement that neither she nor Jaffe drew any salary for serving as editors.

In January 1943, she was listed as a guest lecturer for the School of Democracy for New York City. She was also listed as a lecturer for the Jefferson School of Social Science, the successor to the School of Democracy. She contributed to the National Council of American-Soviet Friendship.

Philip Jaffe, alias J. W. Phillips, was born March 20, 1897, in Moglive, Ukraine, Russia. He arrived in the United States in 1905 and was naturalized in New York City on May 4, 1923. He was graduated from Columbia, receiving a B.A. and M.A. degrees. On May 30 he married Agnes Newmark. He served in the United States Army from October 12 to November 28, 1918, at which time he received an honorable discharge.

He has obtained passports on at least two occasions for travel abroad, one in 1929 for travel to Europe, and the other in 1937, for travel to the Far East. . . .

Jaffe has been affiliated with a number of organizations, among which are the National League of American Writers, American Council on Soviet Relations, National Council of American-Soviet Friendship, the American League for Peace and Democracy, and the American Friends of the Chinese People.

Jaffe has been a known contact of Earl Browder, Alexander Trachtenberg, head of the Communist International Publishers, Nathan Kohn, alias Nat Ross, head of the Communist Political Association in Minnesota, and Edward Barsky, president of the Joint Anti-Fascist Refugee Committee, and others.

During the instant investigation, Jaffe was known to have contacted Earl Browder on April 16, 22, and 25, 1945.

Jaffe is also known to have visited the Soviet Consulate in New York City. Jaffe's chief source of income is Wallace Brown, Inc. [his printing company], and according to his own statement he is publishing *Amerasia* at an annual deficit of approximately $6,500 a year.

Referring, again, to the outline of the investigation, and checking into the past activities of these individuals, it was learned that Jaffe had, on previous visits to Washington, been in contact with Emmanuel Sigurd Larsen, and Lieutenant Andrew Roth. Upon receipt of this information and other matters, an intensive investigation was also begun inquiring into their past activities.

I have, also, a biography on Larsen and Roth for you.

Emmanuel Sigurd Larsen, according to available information, was born August 27, 1897, at San Raphael, Calif. His parents were both natives of Denmark and, reportedly, became naturalized citizens of the United States at San Francisco, Calif.

He was educated in China and Denmark. He received a degree from the University of Copenhagen in 1916. Thereafter, he went to China and was employed by the Chinese Postal Service.

It was reported on December 10, 1920, he married Lenore Jaffe. So far as we know, she is no relative of Philip Jaffe. She was a British subject, a native of Singapore. They had one son, James Lewis Larsen, born in Foo Chow, October 24, 1921.

According to the records of the Office of Naval Intelligence, Larsen as requested to resign from [the Chinese Postal] service in 1927 or 1928. . . .

From 1928 to March 1935, he served as traffic manager with the British-American Tobacco Co. He took care of relations between Chinese civil and military officials and the company. It is alleged he was either discharged or requested to resign from the British-American Tobacco Co. . . .

From October 1934, to February 1935, he claimed to have been employed at Pekin by the Chinese Secretary of Service as an investigator. He, allegedly, resigned from this position when the Japanese threatened his life.[6]

In a clipping taken from the *Manchuria Daily News* dated April 6, 1934, there is reported an interview given by E. Larsen, formerly of the British-American Tobacco Co., who reportedly praised, at that time, the activities of the Japanese in Manchukuo. This quoted him as saying, "That proves, conclusively, national native population of Manchukuo is overwhelmingly satisfied with the new state of affairs."

After his return to the United States, he was employed from September to October of 1935 by the American Council of Learned Societies[7] under the Rockefeller Fellowship at the Library of Congress preparing biographies on Chinese personalities.

From October 1935, to August 1944, Larsen was employed by the Office of Naval Intelligence making analyses of Chinese and Far Eastern political and economic situations and combat estimates of the above countries.

This work entailed the collection of information about enemy

[6] Under oath, Larsen told the Loyalty Board investigation of Service that his job had consisted of straight snooping on people and of reporting their activities to the police. He also stated with some relish: ". . . When I was an investigator for the Chinese in Peking I violated all the treaties and extraterritoriality and everything. I went up to Kalgan with a couple of men and pistols, took an army officer and shoved him on the train and took him down to Peking. . . ."

[7] Larsen testified at the Service Loyalty hearing: "Mr. Mortimer Graves was the one who granted me this scholarship to the Library of Congress and he was the one who recommended me for entry into the Naval Intelligence and recommended to Admiral Zacharias that I be excused from serving the rest of my scholarship on the Rockefeller project. And therefore he considered me as one of his protégés." A few days after Larsen's arrest, he testified, Graves gave him a job but told him that although a fund of $5000 had been collected "for the defense of the State Department men involved in this case . . . I was not to benefit from that fund."

troops, and it involved the handling of secret Navy documents. He was also engaged in the training of young Naval officers in Intelligence work.

On August 31, 1944, he was transferred to the Department of State at a salary of $5,600 a year as a country specialist in the Division of Territorial Studies.

I understand that, at the present time, he is unemployed and has not been successful in being employed since the time he was picked up on this case.

Lt. Andrew Roth was born in Brooklyn, April 23, 1919. His parents, Abel and Bertha, were born in Hungary. Roth's father was naturalized May 28, 1920. Roth received a degree from the City College of New York in 1939 and his M.A. from Columbia University in 1940. His thesis for his master's degree was entitled "Labor and Nationalism in China."

He enlisted in the United States Naval Reserve under the V-12 program on December 3, 1941.

During 1941 and 1942, he was enrolled in the Japanese Language School at Harvard. During this period, he married Renee Louise Knitel of Brooklyn, N. Y. He first held a rating of yeoman, second class.

On August 28, 1942, he was commissioned ensign and transferred from Cambridge, Mass., to Washington, D. C., reporting for Intelligence duties in the Office of Naval Intelligence September 12, 1942.[8]

In December of 1943, Roth was assigned to the Japanese Fleet Desk in the Office of Naval Intelligence.

On January 1, 1945, while still assigned to these duties, he was made a full lieutenant.

His former employment included that of a reading clerk, history department, City College of New York, 1939 to 1940; research worker, associated with the International Secretariat of the Institute of Pacific Relations from 1940 to March 1941 and research associate for the magazine *Amerasia* under the immediate supervision of Philip Jaffe during July and August of 1941.

---

[8] Speaking before the House of Representatives in 1946, Representative George Dondero said that Roth was placed in the key position of liaison officer between Naval Intelligence and the State Department despite "a totally unfavorable report resulting from an investigation by ONI itself when he first applied for his commission."

He also contributed articles to *Amerasia* in the months of August and November, 1940, and during June, August, and October of 1941.

On September 5, 1943, he contributed a letter to the *New York Times* in which he defended the Free German Committee in Moscow, the objectives of which he claimed to be immediate and military and not post-war and political.

Roth attended the conference of the Institute of Pacific Relations held January 3, 1945, at Hot Springs, Va., as a representative of the Office of Naval Intelligence.

The first "pertinent information" on the surveillance, Gurnea testified, was obtained on 21 March 1945, when Jaffe made one of his frequent trips to Washington. He was met in the lobby of the Statler Hotel by Larsen and Lieutenant and Mrs. Roth. Larsen and Jaffe were carrying briefcases, Roth a large Manila envelope. After lunch, Mrs. Roth left, and the three men drove away in Jaffe's car. Larsen was dropped off at his office. "Roth and Jaffe then drove by a circuitous route to a parking lot on the east side of the Library of Congress where they parked. They were observed by agents to be engaged in a discussion and an examination of papers. Later, they drove to Roth's apartment where they remained all afternoon."

After his arrest, Roth explained this unusual behavior by claiming that he had been showing Jaffe a chapter of a book he was writing. But when Mrs. Roth was asked whether Jaffe had looked over her husband's manuscript, she answered, "Absolutely not." Jaffe himself was writing a book, she added, and had no time to concern himself with Roth's work.

On the same evening, Jaffe and Larsen met again, going for an aimless walk, then returned to the hotel where they were again joined by the Roths and by Mr. and Mrs. Mark Gayn. The Gayns were a new lead for the FBI, Gurnea said. It was discovered that there were numerous contacts between Gayn and Jaffe in New York and Washington. Gayn was also in intimate contact with Kate Mitchell. The FBI dug into Gayn's past. Gurnea testified that:

Mark Julius Gayn was born April 21, 1909, at Harbin, Manchuria [of Russian parents]. In 1923, Gayn's family moved to Vladivostok, Russia, where Gayn attended a Soviet public school. In Gayn's book *Journey from the East,* he compliments the Russian educational system, the freedom of speech, and the puritanical attitude of the people. . . . In his book, Gayn also advises that in 1927 his family moved to China, where he was associated and worked with Chinese students who sought to engender the Chinese revolution.

Gayn came to the United States to attend Pomona College and Columbia School of Journalism. Between 1934 and 1939, he worked for Domei, the Japanese news agency, in China. In 1939, he emigrated to this country with his parents, becoming a citizen in 1944. Previous to his arrest, he had worked for that newspaper of leftist discombobulation, *PM,* and for the *Chicago Sun.* An issue of *Collier's* magazine, dated ten days after his arrest, published an article by Gayn entitled "Terror in Asia." An editor's note stated that it was based on information from official sources. It gave a detailed report on the bombing of Japan. Such an article is written at least eight weeks before publication. Had Gayn ever seen the document which Bielaski discovered in the *Amerasia* office?

The FBI continued its investigation of the Jaffe contacts. Roth and Larsen were meeting frequently. "Both Mr. and Mrs. Roth frequented the Institute of Pacific Relations and the Communist-front Washington Book Shop." On 12 April 1945, Mrs. Roth visited the *Amerasia* office in New York. She was observed entering Jaffe's office with a large Manila envelope under her arm. When she left, she was no longer carrying the envelope. After Roth's arrest, she denied categorically that she had been in the office at the time.[9] Roth admitted she had.

FBI agents were marking up an unusual number of meetings among those already under suspicion. At most of these meetings, one or more people would arrive with a Manila envelope and leave

[9] Hobbs Hearings, *Congressional Record,* 22 May 1950.

without it. This movement of envelopes was both to and from Jaffe. Sometimes meetings and transfers of envelopes took place several times in one day. On 19 April 1945, John Stewart Service entered the case when he met Jaffe in the lobby of the Statler.[10]

There were several meetings between Service and Jaffe. On one occasion when Service came to New York, he stayed at Gayn's home — though by his own testimony, Service barely knew Gayn. Once he visited the *Amerasia* offices. His explanation for these visits was that Roth had brought him together with Jaffe, who was "interested" in learning about the Communists in Yenan.

"Service went on to state," Gurnea testified, "that since he, Service, believed that Jaffe would ask him details on the policy of the Chinese Communists, he took with him a [classified] report he had prepared for the State Department on a long conversation with Mao Tse-tung. . . . He said Jaffe was extremely interested in it. He inquired as to whether he had other reports on Yenan which he could see. According to Service, after some hesitation, he agreed to show Jaffe other reports of his on the following day." On 20 April, Service spent the morning in Jaffe's room at the Statler. By his own admission, he gave Jaffe — a man he had never met until the previous day — copies of some of his reports on China. When questioned in 1950 on the propriety of turning over classified documents to Jaffe, Service said (1) that it was done all the time, (2) that these were not classified documents but his personal copies of classified documents, and (3) that he had been disturbed and irritated by Jaffe's demands.

There was more than physical surveillance, as the FBI prepared its case. On at least one occasion a microphone was planted in Jaffe's hotel room. On 8 May, the FBI recorded a discussion between Service and Jaffe about political, military, and policy matters, in the course of which Service warned: "Well, what I said about the military plans is, of course, very secret." A second recording: Jaffe asked

[10] *Ibid.*

Service if we would land on the shores of China; Service answered, "I don't think it has been decided. I can tell you in a couple of weeks when Stilwell gets back." A third recording was the basis for questioning by Theodore Achilles, a Loyalty Board member, during Service's 1950 hearing. It concerned a report which Jaffe wanted. "It is stated that you told Mr. Jaffe that it might be sort of hard for you to get this report because it was kept in a section where you were not assigned." Jaffe had then asked Service to mail it to him. "You told Mr. Jaffe," Achilles continued, "if you could dig up a copy of it, it would be the Far Eastern division copy and they might not be willing to part with it. But you were sure you would be able to run off a copy for him."

These recordings, naturally, could not be used as evidence in court. But the text of the conversations was made known to the State Department Loyalty Board which in 1950 cleared Service. A qualified denial was quickly accepted. Obviously, the State Department did not consider a man who revealed "very secret" military plans a bad security risk.

Simultaneous with the investigation of the six who were later arrested, the FBI dug up a number of important leads which were dropped when the Justice Department deflated the *Amerasia* Case. One of the people interviewed by the FBI as it built up its case was Miss Annette Blumenthal, an IPR typist. She told the bureau that Jaffe had brought papers for her to type, over a period of time, for which she was paid thirty cents a page. Jaffe warned her, she said, that the material was confidential. For the FBI, and later for the Loyalty Board, she identified several secret documents as among the papers which Jaffe had given her. Miss Blumenthal was an innocent victim and a valuable witness. Had the *Amerasia* defendants ever come to trial, she would have been called to the stand. It is interesting that she recalled Service's name as a member of IPR and also as a contributor of articles or material to IPR publications under the name of "John Stewart." Service denied the latter allegation.

On 5 June 1945, Roth was suddenly and inexplicably removed from active service in the Navy.

On 6 June 1945, Philip Jaffe and Kate Mitchell were arrested in the *Amerasia* offices. The charge: Violation of the Espionage Act.

Mark Gayn was arrested in his apartment in New York. Same charge.

John S. Service, Emmanuel Larsen, and Andrew Roth — now out of uniform and therefore not subject to court-martial — were arrested in Washington. Same charge.

A week before the arrests, there had been a hitch. Gurnea testified that "some of the men who were connected with the San Francisco Conference" urged a delay in prosecution for fear of "causing friction" with the Russians. (Forrestal also showed some concern, but counseled nothing.) They were overruled when an appeal was made to President Truman, who ordered them to proceed.

At the time of the arrests, over four hundred documents were found in the *Amerasia* offices. Many of them were of the highest military and diplomatic importance, from almost every sensitive agency of the government. Without re-listing them, it should be noted here that, five years later, Assistant Attorney General James McInerney told the Tydings subcommittee under oath that the *Amerasia* Case documents were unimportant — "teacup gossip." The Chinese Nationalist order of battle may have been "teacup gossip" in 1950 — but would have been invaluable to the Chinese Communists in 1945.

In Service's desk at the time of his arrest was a batch of personal correspondence. Several letters were requests to get communications to Chungking past the censorship. Most of the letters were full of vindictive references to people like Patrick J. Hurley and to the legitimate Chinese government, warm remarks about Communist leaders and individuals. Some were just plain cryptic. In the desk, too, was a code worked out for their personal use by Service, Ludden, Davies, and Emmerson. "Snow White" stood for Mme. Chiang,

"Harvard" for Communist, "asylum" for Washington. "Sophomoric perhaps," Service told the Loyalty Board.

Documents were found in Mark Gayn's possession, but he asserted that they had come from OWI, and that he had received authority to use them. In Larsen's home, the second largest batch of documents was turned up — some two hundred. But none of these other lots were really necessary. Though the FBI received utterly unfounded criticism for its work, it did a magnificent job of investigation. D. Milton Ladd, assistant to the director of the FBI, showed how this was true when he testified before the Tydings subcommittee:

MR. LADD: At the time of Jaffe's apprehension, June 6, a large number of documents were obtained from the offices of *Amerasia*. As an indication of the thoroughness of the investigation, a check was made for fingerprints on the documents recovered. Laboratory examination of material disclosed latent fingerprints of Kate Mitchell, Mark Gayn, and Emmanuel Larsen. One document contained six latent fingerprints of Mark Gayn, one latent fingerprint of Emmanuel Larsen, and one latent fingerprint of Jaffe, indicating that all three individuals had handled that one. Typewriting examinations disclosed that a number of those documents in Jaffe's possession were typed by Annette Blumenthal and several were typed on a machine belonging to Mark Gayn. Through typewriting comparisons it was further determined that two items recovered in the offices of *Amerasia* were carbon copies of items recovered in the possession of Emmanuel Larsen.

A handwriting examination disclosed three items in the known handwriting of Andrew Roth and a large number of documents which bore the handwriting of Emmanuel Larsen. . . . The subject matter of these documents included military as well as political information.

Admissions, both oral and written, made by the subjects reflected they were fully aware of the fact that they possessed confidential government documents. Such documents containing wartime secrets were recovered. . . .

SENATOR TYDINGS: Kate Mitchell?

MR. LADD: Kate Mitchell admitted that she had in her file cabinet in her office certain government documents.[11]

SENATOR TYDINGS: And Service?

MR. LADD: Service admitted that he had taken what he called copies of his official documents.

SENATOR TYDINGS: Of his own?

MR. LADD: Of his own, to Jaffe, on numerous occasions.

SENATOR TYDINGS: What excuse did he give for that, if any?

MR. LADD: . . . He considered this his own personal property. . . .

SENATOR TYDINGS: Had he given any of the classified ones to Jaffe?

MR. LADD: Yes. . . . His explanation was that he had put the classification on himself.

There was further evidence against Mark Gayn. During his surveillance, he was seen to enter the *Amerasia* offices and emerge with a full briefcase. He was followed when, with his wife, he boarded a bus. From his briefcase he took out several papers, which he read. An FBI agent, peering over his shoulder, could see enough to identify them. They were classified documents.

This was the case which the FBI, with care and energy, built up. This was the case which the Justice Department allowed to peter out until only two men received insignificant fines. But this is a story in itself. It can best be introduced by quoting an exchange between Louis B. Nichols, assistant FBI director, and Senator Tydings, during the "whitewash" investigation:

SENATOR TYDINGS: Do you have any knowledge to the effect that the bureau or anyone connected with the bureau has been approached with the purpose of bringing influence to bear in connection with the indictment or trial of the six individuals who were originally arrested?

MR. NICHOLS: I am certain no one in the bureau has been approached. . . .

SENATOR TYDINGS: Do you have any knowledge outside of the bureau?

[11] According to Representative Dondero, one of them — "Plan of Battle Operations" — was so secret that army officers who lost their copies were subject to court-martial.

MR. NICHOLS: That would be obviously a question for the department [of Justice] to answer.

SENATOR TYDINGS: Do you have any knowledge that there was any fix outside the bureau? By that I mean by the government, or whatever might be improper.

MR. NICHOLS: That is a difficult question for me to answer.

SENATOR TYDINGS: Why? Do you mean you can't answer it?

MR. NICHOLS: It is obviously for the department to answer on that.

SENATOR TYDINGS: I just don't follow you.

Senator McMahon (Dem., Conn.) quickly changed the subject.

XV

Amerasia, II: Justice in Reverse

WHEN the Case of the Six broke in the newspapers on 7 June 1945, Acting Secretary of State Joseph Grew was satisfied that a job of preliminary and necessary housecleaning had been done. Grew had been meticulous in his acts before the arrests; he had insisted on·not knowing the names of the suspects for fear that personal feelings might lead him to intervene or somehow influence the decision of the Justice Department. Now, though he was an admirer of Service's work, he pressed for quick indictments. In a statement to the press, he declared:

"Officers of the Department of State have for some time been giving special attention to the security of secret and confidential information. A few months ago it became apparent that information of a secret character was reaching unauthorized persons. . . . A comprehensive program is to be continued unrelentingly to stop this illegal and disloyal conveyance. . . . The matter is now in the hands of the Department of Justice for prosecution."

To his astonishment and horror, he was met by a barrage of abuse and vilification — as if breaking the *Amerasia* Case had been the crime. In a terrifying demonstration of ill-will, influential segments of the American press began systematically to obfuscate the issues and to belabor those who were attempting to invoke the laws of the land. Publications of varying liberalism — the *New York Post,* *PM,* the *New Republic,* and the *Nation* — echoed the *Daily Worker* cry that the defendants were innocent and the case "a trial balloon of reaction" sent up by Grew and J. Edgar Hoover in a "witch-hunt aimed essentially at the freedom of the press."

They stated, with categorical unanimity, that the arrests were a spite plot by Grew to get even with commentators and writers opposed to his policies. The *Daily Worker* asserted that Roth's arrest came after "announcement of his anti-Grew book, *Dilemma in Japan.*" The documentary evidence was casually brushed aside with the explanation that "everybody takes papers home in Washington" —a cry which was to be repeated in defense of Alger Hiss.

This tender regard for the defendants also seemed to pervade the editorial sanctums of the Republican *New York Herald Tribune.* In an editorial, "Red Baiting," this traditionally conservative daily said: "The arrests are a serious omen if they mean that anyone in the government [must] maintain a mouselike quiet if he is to the political left of the State Department. Foreign affairs are not merely the business of well-bred gentlemen in striped trousers. *The reasons behind our foreign policies* should not be concealed by a 'papa knows all' attitude." [Italics added.]

Following this *non sequitur,* the editorial continued: *"It may be that the two State Department men now under arrest developed such a feeling of urgency over the situation* that they committed offenses for which they should be punished. But the State Department's action *in calling in the FBI and bringing about arrests* which resulted in headlines concerning 'spies' and 'espionage' was *an extreme action.* It might have been better, unless the circumstances were more serious than revealed so far, to have dismissed the men concerned." [Italics added.]

The *Herald-Tribune* was giving away far more than it intended. For the hue and cry against Grew over the *Amerasia* case had little to do with the six people arrested or how "serious" their offense. Those who attacked Grew were really attacking both his Far Eastern policies and his opposition to Soviet expansionism in Asia. The publication of the Forrestal diaries and the testimony of Eugene

Dooman, veteran Far East diplomat and a close associate and supporter of Grew, have made this abundantly clear. Grew's policies
were anathema to the Communists, to the New York and Washington pinko-liberal politicos, and to the small but vociferous herd of
policy-influencers which clambered all over the New Deal and made
the United States Government its very own.

From the earliest days of the war, this motley coalition had
yammered long and mightily to oust the "reactionaries" from the
State Department. (For "reactionary" read "anti-Communist.") It
had called for "unconditional surrender" in the Far East — no matter how many lives it might cost us at the hands of a Japanese
nation driven to a last-ditch defense of its religion and its Emperor.
The cry that the Mikado must go had been long and determined.

So eager were the liberals and their chameleon friends for this
eventuality that Owen Lattimore, then Director of Pacific Operations for OWI, in 1943 violated a clear and stringent Joint Chiefs
of Staff directive — urgently seconded by the President and the
British Government as a means of saving lives — categorically
barring any propaganda attacks on the Japanese Emperor by official
American agencies. Lattimore insisted on broadcast to the Far East
of a speech by Sun Fo, pro-Communist president of the Chinese
Legislative Yuan, which ended, "The Mikado must go." When
Clay Osborne, head of the Japan and Korea desk under Lattimore,
protested, pointing out the unambiguous prohibition, he was fired
out of hand by Lattimore.

An entry made on 1 May 1945 in his diary by Forrestal[1] on
the political objectives in the Far East touched cogently on this
problem.

I raised the question as to whether or not it was time to make
a thorough study of our political objectives in the Far East and
asked these questions:

1. How far and how thoroughly do we want to beat Japan? In

[1] *The Forrestal Diaries.* (New York, 1951.)

other words, do we want to morgenthau those islands — do we want to destroy the whole industrial potential?

2. Do we want to contemplate their readmission to the society of nations after demilitarization?

3. What is our policy on Russian influence in the Far East? Do we desire a counterweight to that influence? And should it be China or should it be Japan? [2]

4. Have we given careful thought to the question of how far this country will go toward the complete defeat of Japan — the quick, costly assault versus a long, drawn-out siege? I said that it was conceivable to me that the people that desired a quick victory might turn out to be the appeasers in the case of Japan.

There was another alternative, proposed by Grew and underscored by the intercepts of Japanese communications to their diplomats which we could read by virtue of having broken their code. Japan was ready to sue for peace, but she would not do so unconditionally; she wanted a guarantee that the Emperor would remain on the throne, if only as a constitutional monarch. With such a guarantee, Grew felt, the war in the Pacific could be ended without an assault on the Japanese homeland and without the entry of the Soviet Union — eventualities which he and others in the Cabinet dreaded, and with reason. On the same day that Forrestal entered his four propositions, he also noted that:

Under Secretary Grew expanded somewhat on his impressions of the idea of the Japanese Emperor. He said his ideas had been misunderstood and misconstrued. He said he was in favor merely of deferring the decision on the question of the Japanese Emperor until we had effected a military occupation, at which time we could determine whether he was an asset or a liability. He said he was concerned only with what could save the maximum of American lives.

[2] George Kennan, one of the top State Department thinkers of the postwar period, has written that the wisest policy for the United States would have been to avoid war with Japan and permit her to be a counterweight against the Soviets. By defeating Japan we created a power vacuum. The anti-Grew faction sought to aggravate this by a total destruction of Japan.

Both Grew and Secretary Stimson were all for a statement from the United States indicating, within the unconditional surrender formula, what kind of peace we would exact from the Japanese and promising that they would be allowed to keep their Emperor and their religious institutions. The opposition to any kind of a "compromise" peace, in which the Japanese recognized that they were thoroughly beaten but which permitted them to keep a constitutional Emperor should they so desire, came from three men. They were Assistant Secretaries of State Dean Acheson and Archibald MacLeish, and OWI chief Elmer Davis. All three fulminated against it. General Marshall, to whom President Truman had strangely given the final say, agreed with them. On 29 May 1945, the formula for peace was rejected.

But a rejection of this formula was not enough for Owen Lattimore. He was determined that the United States take a categorical stand in favor of removing the Mikado as a firm condition for any Japanese–American peace. Shortly after the Grew–Stimson–Forrestal meeting and General Marshall's negative action on their proposals, the same Dean Acheson who disclaimed any role for Lattimore in high policy deliberations set up an appointment for him at the White House.[3] To the President, Lattimore "remonstrated very strongly against any position or decision taken by this government which would enable the monarchy to remain in Japan."[4]

Why Acheson, MacLeish, Lattimore, and Davis objected is a matter for conjecture. Why the Communist claque, and its liberal mouthpieces, objected is easily understood. The Yalta agreements

[3] It was at this meeting that Lattimore proposed that military aid to the Chinese National government be cut off. A year later, General Marshall had obliged. Lattimore urged a "review" of Far East policy. Within months, the men who had upheld the old policy, however badly their efforts were sabotaged — the Doomans and Grews — were out of the State Department. Lattimore's visit was about a week before Mr. Truman departed for the Potsdam conference — convinced, incidentally, that Britain and not Russia was the enemy. It is of this meeting that Lattimore testified that he got a Presidential "brushoff" after three minutes.

[4] Testimony of Eugene Dooman before the McCarran committee.

had given Russia a stranglehold on the future of China and a foothold in Japan. Should the Pacific war have ended before the Red Army could make its token contribution, that foothold would be threatened. On a broader basis, the Russians wanted no "counterweight" to their influence in the Far East. With Japan completely crushed and undergoing a "morgenthau" treatment, the Russians would have a free hand in Sovietizing the country. The necessity for removing the Emperor was also obvious; he could remain a balancing force in the defeated country and a block to rapid Soviet hegemony. The Russians wanted total demoralization, a prerequisite to their seizure of power.

Behind the scenes, the in-fighting was bitter. Eugene Dooman, who was then the chairman of the Far East subcommittee of the State, War, and Navy Co-ordinating Committee (SWINK), offered testimony on this point in September 1951:[5]

MR. DOOMAN: One of the men in the office told me that papers were going through the State Department [early in 1945] calling for the appointment of Dr. Lattimore as adviser to the China division, the papers having been initiated by the Chief of the China division.

MR. MORRIS: Who was that?

MR. DOOMAN: That was Mr. John Carter Vincent. I discussed the matter with Mr. Ballantine, who was then the Director of the Far Eastern division, and pointed out that Lattimore at that time, and for several months previously, had been using every opportunity to discredit the then Acting Secretary, Mr. Grew.

And I pointed out that it would be incongruous for a man who had expressed himself so freely on Mr. Grew to be occupying a position under Mr. Grew . . . who . . . ordered that the papers be quashed.

SENATOR EASTLAND: What did Mr. Lattimore have to say against Mr. Grew? . . . Was it because [Grew] had been opposing Communism in the Far East and he wanted a peace treaty that would prevent the Communists from getting Japan?

MR. DOOMAN: . . . The principal cause of complaint was that

[5] McCarran Hearings, pp. 704–705.

Mr. Grew had advocated an attitude on the part of the United States on noninterference with the Japanese themselves in the form of government which they wanted to institute. In other words, if they wanted to keep the Emperor, by all means let them keep it. . . .

SENATOR EASTLAND: His opposition to Grew was that Mr. Grew was favoring a policy after the war was won that would prevent the Communists from getting Japan. That is it in a nutshell, is it not?

MR. DOOMAN: . . . That is my judgment.[6]

Lattimore has disclaimed both the influence and the intent.

As the new President fumbled and stumbled, he was an easy target for a few men in key places whose ideologies, if not loyalties, were hardly stable. Grew was the obstacle. So it was decreed that Grew, too, must go. Ironically, the *Amerasia* case became the historical instrument that toppled him.

The press onslaught against the State Department for having taken essential and mandatory steps in the defense of the country obscured in the public mind the fact that the Six had been arrested for violation of the Espionage Act. Instead, it had suddenly become a question of freedom of the press, on the one hand, and Grew's policies on the other. The sole newspaperman in the case, Gayn, said that he had used the material for articles and denied that he had ever dealt with the Communists. Jaffe, released on bail, issued a statement that "the red-baiting character of this case is scandalous and often libelous." But he never sued his "libelers."

As the Case of the Six became the Case of Joseph Grew, the defendants became heroes in the leftist and liberal press. Andrew Roth, in fact, wrote a series of articles for the *New York Post* which held that "present State Department policies toward China and Japan are sowing the seeds for a third world war."[7] He described Grew

---

[6] It may be noted here that in July 1945, the Communist theoretical organ, *Political Affairs,* stated: "There are influential forces, including some in the State Department, who are seeking a compromise peace which will preserve the power of the Mikado after the war . . . directed against the Soviet Union."

[7] State Department policies *were* sowing the seeds of war. But the policies were those of the Acheson clique.

as the father of these policies. So pernicious did the charges against the Under Secretary become that he took the extraordinary course of replying publicly. Military secrets and not personalities were the basis of the case, Grew said, and *"ample evidence has been found to support the charges. . . .* We heard somebody in the chicken coop and went to see who was there." [Italics added.] The evidence against those they had found would be made public at their trial.

Kate Mitchell's uncle, James M. Mitchell, a former president of the New York Bar Association, put his law firm to work on the case. Colonel Joseph M. Hartfield, a member of the firm, visited Washington at least once to call on top officials in the Justice Department. Representative Emanuel Celler, a Democratic-American Labor Party stalwart,[8] also called on the Attorney General; his law partner, Arthur Sheinberg, acted as Jaffe's attorney. A substantial defense fund was raised for John Service, with the help of Mortimer Graves, secretary of the American Council of Learned Societies. The battle was joined.

The evidence against the *Amerasia* Six was presented to a Washington grand jury whose term was expiring. The Justice Department later claimed that, since the accused had offered to appear and waive immunity, it was decided to dismiss that jury and re-present the evidence to a newly impaneled one — the argument being that an examination of the Six would enable government attorneys to strengthen the case. According to Assistant Attorney General McInerney, the Justice Department felt that the entire business was of piddling importance since the documents were of "innocuous, very innocuous character." The special assistant to the Attorney General chosen to try the case, Robert Hitchcock of Buffalo, had decided, by McInerney's testimony, that John Stewart Service was innocent. McInerney testified before the Tydings subcommittee that Hitchcock took Service before the grand jury "but he didn't give

[8] And in 1948, let it be noted, an intransigent deprecator of the Bentley-Chambers testimony.

him the same penetrating examination that he gave Gayn and [Kate] Mitchell." [9] At no time was the jury told of Jaffe's Communist background.

How the rest of the evidence was presented is locked up in the grand jury minutes. McInerney stated that the jury believed that the documents "could be seen in almost every magazine and newspaper office in New York." This was a curious conclusion, given adequate presentation of the facts. If McInerney's analysis is to be accepted, the Justice Department also decided that Miss Mitchell's only culpability was that she shared offices with Jaffe. Somewhere along the line, the charge of conspiracy to commit espionage was dropped, and in its place was substituted conspiracy to violate the statute concerning the illegal possession of government property. Since no government documents were found in the home of Service, the shift automatically eliminated him. Twelve votes were required to indict. On 10 August the grand jury voted:

On Service—20 against indicting, none for.
On Gayn—15 against, 5 for.
On Mitchell—18 against, 2 for.
On Roth—13 for, 7 against.
On Larsen—14 for, 6 against.
On Jaffe—14 for, 6 against.

Three days later, on 13 August, J. Raymond Walsh, a radio commentator for CIO–PAC, discussed Service's release. "His arrest brought some exceedingly powerful people within the government to his defense," he said. "One can easily infer that those who began this affair wished they hadn't."

The case, which the Justice Department had announced at the time of the arrests as complete, was somehow falling apart.

Following the indictment, Larsen learned that the FBI had made a search of his home prior to the arrest. Such a search was in violation

[9] Tydings Hearings, p. 973.

of the Fourth Amendment, and according to law all evidence obtained illegally (as well as all leads secured in this manner) was inadmissible in court. Larsen's lawyers immediately moved to suppress all evidence seized in Larsen's home at the time he was taken into custody. The FBI examined the Larsen motion to quash the indictment, prepared a twenty-one-page memorandum, and submitted it several weeks later to Hitchcock and to Donald Anderson, another Justice Department attorney assigned to the case. It was Anderson's view that the Larsen motion would not stand up in court, simply because the case against him could be backed by the documents seized in the raid on *Amerasia* — documents in his handwriting or bearing his fingerprints — and by his own admissions. But Hitchcock and McInerney had already decided that their case against the remaining three defendants was "collapsing."

On 28 September, Hitchcock and McInerney moved with a rapidity virtually unknown among lawyers. Jaffe's counsel had already offered to enter a plea of guilty if he could make a deal with the government. Hitchcock and McInerney have since insisted that they were ready to accede to this request because they knew that the FBI had entered the *Amerasia* premises illegally previous to the arrests. Once Larsen's motion became public, they argued, Jaffe might make inquiries and learn of this entry, whereupon he would also move to quash the indictment.

Even for a legal mind, the Justice Department's reasoning was not particularly logical. The original lead in the *Amerasia* Case had not been tainted, it had been developed by legal surveillance; Annette Blumenthal's testimony was available. Furthermore, the FBI entry had furnished no new leads — nor had it, in the legal term, "polluted" the evidence picked up at the time of Jaffe's arrest.

Jaffe's lawyer was called in and proposed that his client would plead guilty to the illegal possession of government documents if the Justice Department would recommend a fine and no jail sentence. The lawyers agreed, and a fine of five thousand dollars was stipulated. "We asked if this was a firm commitment which under no circumstances would be withdrawn," Hitchcock told the Tydings subcommittee. "He said that it was. He also said that he insisted that our recommendation as to the fine would not be perfunctory, but made in good faith to the court, with a genuine effort on our part to have the court follow our recommendation. We gave him that assurance."

The next day was a Saturday. With no reporters present, the case was brought before Judge Proctor. In its own way, it was a classic in jurisprudence. When Albert Arent, Jaffe's lawyer, met McInerney and Hitchcock before the court went into session, he had already read in the papers of Larsen's motion to quash the indictment and suppress the evidence. Hitchcock has testified that Arent called them: "You sons of bitches."

"You're not going to back out on your word?" McInerney answered.

"No, you're not going back on yours either," Arent said.

Both Hitchcock and McInerney cited the exchange with Arent as a great victory; they had gotten him to agree to a plea before he had learned of the Larsen motion. This, however, had freed Arent from any legal or moral obligation to plead as he had promised. Yet Arent still seemed as ready to enter a guilty plea as he had been the night before.

After the legal preliminaries,[10] Arent led off with a statement on the distinguished editorial board of *Amerasia* — Owen Lattimore, William T. Stone (then in the Foreign Service), *et al.* — mentioned that Jaffe had belonged to an organization headed by Secretary Stimson, and painted his client as thoroughly scholarly and patriotic. "If Mr. Jaffe has transgressed the law, it seems he has done so from an excess of journalistic zeal," and with "no intent to jeopardize the welfare of his country." Hitchcock told the court that he agreed "in substance" with this statement. When asked how

[10] Tydings Exhibits, pp. 1933ff.

long it would take to present the government's case, he said, "Less than five minutes."

Philip Jaffe had taken the classified documents for *Amerasia* to "lend to its weight and, perhaps, its circulation," Hitchcock said. Though several hundred government documents were involved, there was no evidence that "injury or embarrassment" to the government was intended. By saying "no evidence," he might have been speaking as a careful lawyer. But he suggested also that there was evidence that the intent of taking the documents was, "quite to the contrary," innocent. So persuasive was Hitchcock — and so careful not to mention anything damaging to the defendant — that Judge Proctor characterized Jaffe's work as "evidently for a trustworthy purpose." [11]

"I accept without a doubt the assurance both of your counsel and of the government attorneys that there was no thought or act upon your part which was intended or calculated or had a tendency to injure the government. . . ." he added. "It would make quite a difference to me if I did not have that assurance and did not know, confidently, that that was true." Then he imposed a fine of twenty-five hundred dollars — one half the amount of Jaffe's annual contribution to the Communist Party.

Hitchcock told the Tydings subcommittee that Larsen's motion to quash the indictment and suppress the evidence could not stand up in court — although the prospect of a similar motion by Jaffe was given as the reason for making a deal with him. The FBI summary of the case and Justice Department legal opinions also show that Larsen had no case. Yet Hitchcock agreed, after "prolonged negotiation" with Larsen's attorney, to accept a plea of *nolo contendere* and recommend a five-hundred-dollar fine. On 2 November 1945, Hitchcock again went before Judge Proctor, advised him that "there was

[11] In 1950, Hitchcock was to assert that he did not mention Jaffe's Communist affiliations because he was certain Judge Proctor had read about the case in the newspapers.

no element of disloyalty involved," and accused the same Jaffe whom he had some weeks before exculpated, of being the "corrupter." The fine was imposed, and Larsen walked out a free man. Out of the kindness of his heart, Jaffe paid Larsen's fine and legal expenses. It was one happy family. The case against Lieutenant Roth was *nolle-prossed* because, according to the Justice Department, he was "exculpated" by Philip Jaffe.

Service went back to the State Department, reinstated by Secretary Byrnes, who congratulated him on "this happy termination of your ordeal." Gayn went abroad for the *Chicago Sun* and *PM*. Roth moved about the Orient lambasting American policy for the columns of the *Nation*. Miss Mitchell dropped out of sight, except as an occasional sponsor of a Communist front. Jaffe prospered until he came a cropper with the Communist Party in mid-1947 for his espousal of Browderism. Eventually, he became something of a Titoist. And Larsen embarked on a weird career of changing his story of the *Amerasia* Case almost with the seasons. As for *Amerasia,* it went along for a while, then collapsed. Its unfulfilled subscriptions were taken over by *Far Eastern Survey,* an IPR publication.

The hubbub over the "persecuted" *Amerasia* victims, however, had died down many weeks before. In August, Grew was forced to resign. On the twenty-fifth of that month, Dean Acheson succeeded him as Under Secretary of State — a post he did not accept until he had exacted from the President the promise of a free hand on all personnel questions. Acheson's first act was to oust Dooman and to appoint John Carter Vincent as chairman of the SWINK Far Eastern subcommittee. "Soon thereafter," Forrest Davis has written in the 5 November 1951 issue of the *Freeman,* "the Far Eastern personnel of the State Department was under Acheson's purge, new men being put on guard who have to this day engaged the solicitude of loyalty boards and Congressional committees." And within months, the Acheson-Vincent policy on Japan — a policy which Grew and Dooman had vetoed, but which Lattimore and Jaffe had advocated — was transmitted to General MacArthur.[12]

A directive on occupation policy for Japan had been drafted by Dooman. Acheson and Vincent in effect scrapped it and substituted for it one of sheer destructiveness. It aped, in most fundamentals, the type of policy imposed on her satellites by the Soviet Union, Dooman testified before the McCarran Committee. "The first thing that was to be done was to levy a capital tax of from 60 to 90 per cent on all property in excess of one thousand dollars. . . . The next thing was to expropriate all land in excess of five acres held by any one owner." This land was to be "purchased" at prewar prices — but in currency which had depreciated to 1/180th of its value.

"All holdings by any one individual in any large corporation in excess of 3 per cent were confiscated," Dooman went on. "People were removed from office on the basis of their occupation" — from executives down, "practically the whole white collar element." That war lords should be rendered harmless was part and parcel of American policy, but under Acheson and Vincent, guilt by occupation was carried right down to clerks in brokerage houses and section chiefs in factories. The effect of this, Dooman agreed, would be to create chaos in Japan and open the door to Soviet infiltration.

Acheson's personnel came close to victory and Acheson's policies came close to fruition in Japan. (MacArthur was the stumbling block, and Acheson never forgave him for it.) In China, they won hands down. We are reaping the fruits of that victory today — in

[12] Since Acheson has stated that he never met Lattimore, the connection between the two men implied here may seem like gratuitous assumption. Yet Dooman has testified before the McCarran Committee that prior to his departure from the State Department, he attended a SWINK meeting which was visited by Acheson. At the time, Dooman stated, he was "thoroughly" conversant with Lattimore's book, *Solution in Asia.* The views enunciated by Acheson at that meeting, Dooman said, were "exactly" and almost word for word Lattimore's. So, too, was Acheson's cavalier statement that "I have discovered that Far Eastern experts are a penny a dozen. . . . I prefer to be guided by experts who think more along my point of view."

Vietnam and all Southeast Asia. Certainly, the man who inadvertently gave Acheson and Vincent the lever with which to eliminate Grew and Dooman must have been well satisfied. When their *Amerasia* "trials" were over, Jaffe said to Larsen:

"Well, we've suffered a lot — but anyhow, we got Grew out."

There is a postscript to the *Amerasia* story, but one which could not be written with any degree of completeness until recently. This postscript is not an easy one to write, for it proves that the loyalty program of the State Department was steadily sabotaged for reasons best known to the saboteurs.

John Stewart Service was exonerated by the State Department after the *Amerasia* fiasco. Four times, between 1945 and 1950, he was given security clearance by various personnel and loyalty boards. Promotions came his way. After purportedly examining his record — and this included his loyalty file — the Tydings subcommittee's Democratic majority stated flatly that "We have considered the evidence and conclude that John Stewart Service is neither a disloyal person, a pro-Communist, *nor a bad security risk.*" [Italics added.]

Subsequent to the Tydings "investigation," Service was cleared two more times. On 13 December 1951, the President's Loyalty Review Board found — on the basis of what had previously been known — that there was "reasonable doubt as to his loyalty," and Service was dismissed forthwith from the State Department. Summarizing Service's relations with Philip Jaffe and quoting the wiretap evidence, the Review Board added: "To say that his course of conduct does not raise a reasonable doubt as to Service's own loyalty would, we are forced to think, stretch the mantle of charity much too far."

This ouster was, of course, a partial vindication of Senator Joe McCarthy, whose battle with Truman officialdom is discussed later in this account. But there was more to come. On 3 January 1952,

Senator McCarthy turned over to the Associated Press, International News Service, and the United Press nine closely typed pages of a Loyalty Review Board meeting, held on 13 and 14 February 1951. For several days, no newspaper carried a report of this release. When it finally appeared, it was buried in the back pages and so emasculated that its true import was lost.

For in the discussion by members of the board — all appointed by the President — it was made abundantly clear that repeated statements by Mr. Truman, by Secretary Acheson, and by other responsible officials, concerning the efficacy and reliability of the loyalty program as administered by the State Department, did not conform with the facts.

Chairman Hiram Bingham brought up one particular case. "There was only one member of the [State Department Loyalty Board] who confronted all the witnesses. After the first hearing or two, one board member in the State Department was sent abroad on a mission to Gibraltar, or some other place, and then after the next hearing, another member of the board was given some other duty. . . . In that case also [the chairman, Conrad Snow] permitted the wife of the incumbent to be present during all the hearings and to coach her husband on what he had said in the affidavit. . . . I called attention to the Secretary of State myself to the fact that 'you've got to tell the Loyalty Board members to behave themselves.' "

A member of the Review Board then noted that the State Department's practice was to call in an employe against whom there was derogatory information, warn him, and then permit him to resign without prejudice. Cases were cited in which such employes had then turned up in other sensitive government jobs. No notation had been made on their Personnel Action Sheets as to the information against them or as to their reasons for resigning.

Another member said: "What are you going to do when the attorney who is presenting the charges acts as though he were the attorney for the incumbent? I read 100 pages of a record where the three members of the board were acting as attorney for the employe. . . ."

A Review Board member interrupted: "Oh, you're talking about the State Department. They're taking the attitude that they're there to clear the employe, and not to protect the government. We've been arguing with them since the [loyalty] program started." In further discussion of this point, it was stated that "we assume some responsibility when we sit back *for three years and know that the country rests in a false sense of security. . . .* We know darn well that [the loyalty program] is *completely ineffective* in one of the most important departments of the government and I wonder whether we ought to say something about it." [Italics added.]

From Chairman Bingham some revealing statistics emphasized this complaint: "I called [the Secretary of State's] attention to the fact that his board was out of step with all other agency boards. In the Post Office Department, 10 per cent of all persons examined were found to be worthy of separation from the government. In the Commerce Department, 6.5 per cent. The average was about 6 per cent. The State Department, zero."

XVI

IPR: Carter's Pink Pill

THE Truman Administration's first noble attempt to clean house of ideologically suspicious elements established a pattern. For the *Amerasia* Case, climaxed by the cringing apologies of top government officials, was to be repeated again and again, as red herring became a staple in the President's diet. The same forces which had destroyed the *Amerasia* inquiry were later to "exculpate" Alger Hiss. They were to be defeated in this instance by the persistence and personal integrity of Richard Milhous Nixon — then a member of the House of Representatives — and the heartrending courage and self-sacrifice of Whittaker Chambers. The battle was rejoined when Senator Joe McCarthy made his still-unrefuted charges — and the forces of evil, of planned confusion, and of Micawberish judgment triumphed, at least for the time being.

The *Amerasia* Case was their school. Communists, leftists, and liberals learned that in the face of the common enemy their intramural squabbling must be forgotten. They learned that the average officeholder is quickly browbeaten, that he succumbs easily to the best of all propaganda devices, the *non sequitur*. They had in their control large segments of the press, government, and the intellectual world which later gave so generously of itself to Alger Hiss and others in the Communist network.

And yet, the *Amerasia* Case did not die — nor will it ever. It survived the ruptured findings of the Hobbs investigating subcommittee, which in 1946 sought to place the blame for the fiasco on the

FBI. It flared up briefly when Emmanuel Larsen told his story in the magazine *Plain Talk* — an account whose every line and word he had endorsed verbally and in writing, but which he later repudiated in an effort to win Administration support and return to government service. His testimony when the Tydings subcommittee reopened (and quickly closed) the case won him only what he deserved — the scorn of those whom he attempted to placate.

When the Tydings subcommittee was set up by the Senate to "conduct a full and complete study and investigation as to whether persons who are disloyal to the United States are, or have been, employed by the Department of State," there was a flicker of hope that a start might be made in cleaning out the Augean stables — and in silencing the Communist-leftist-liberal claque. But this was foredoomed by the composition of the subcommittee's Democratic majority. Senator Theodore Green of Rhode Island, an ancient wheelhorse, had little idea of what the hearings were about, but he knew that an election was coming up. Senator Brien McMahon of Connecticut was out to prove that he was a real, honest-to-Acheson liberal — even if he had to clobber every anti-Communist to do so. And Senator Millard E. Tydings of Maryland, who had once been the target of a New Deal smear campaign, was out to show that, whatever his spotty past, he could be one of the boys.

From the first day of the hearings, as Senator McCarthy took the stand to elaborate on eighty-one cases which he had outlined on the floor of the Senate, it became obvious that the Tydings-McMahon-Green coalition was determined to block all efforts to get at the bedrock of truth. If McCarthy's charges were false, as the foaming liberal press claimed, the best strategy would have been to dig down diligently for every scrap of evidence, to weigh and evaluate, and to let the facts destroy the allegations.

Instead, Tydings heckled McCarthy mercilessly, would not permit him to state his case in an orderly and sequential manner, and proclaimed to the world that he was investigating not McCarthy's charges but McCarthy. Day after day this continued, despite the protests of the Republican minority. Robert Morris, a counsel chosen to represent a non-Administration viewpoint, was appointed, but he was not permitted to question witnesses until the outcry became so great that Tydings was forced to reverse himself. During the taking of important evidence in executive session, Morris was rudely ordered out of the hearing room. Communists, perjurers, and pro-Administration witnesses were treated cordially and allowed to make the committee room their forum. Those who could offer evidence that was damaging to the State Department were treated with a hostility that often went beyond the vicious. Earl Browder was handled with deference; the most sordid insinuations against the ex-Communist Louis Budenz were exhumed from a Communist vault and spread across the record, then distilled for repetition on the Senate floor by Senator Chavez, the New Mexico Democrat, in a speech which also managed to ridicule the witness's Catholicism.

A typical exchange between Robert Morris and the Democratic members tells the story eloquently. After desperate attempts to call certain important witnesses, Morris pleaded with Tydings on the last day of the hearing:

Mr. Morris: Senator, may I mention just one case here?

Senator Tydings: Mr. Morris, we can mention cases from now until doomsday.

Mr. Morris: It is in the record, Senator. May I just finish?

Senator Tydings: Of course you are not a member of the committee. When we want counsel to speak, we will ask them. . . .

Mr. Morris: There is the case of a man named Theodore Geiger. He has been an employe of the State Department. He is now one of Paul Hoffman's top assistants [in the Economic Co-operation Administration]. He is doing work that is quasi-State Department in character. I have gone and gotten some witnesses together who will testify that he was a member of the same Communist Party unit as they were, and I think that we would be delinquent if in the face of this evidence that is now on the record — . . . .

SENATOR TYDINGS: Turn it over to the FBI or do something else with it. I would like to get a decision here. *We don't want to waste this afternoon.* [Italics added.]

Curiously enough, fourteen pages of the record — this passage included — were handily eliminated from the printed transcript of the Tydings hearings. It would never have come to light had not Senator Henry Cabot Lodge, a Republican member of the sub-committee, noted its absence from the record, called it to the attention of the Senate, and forced its reinstatement. Hurriedly, on the pretext of making an interim report, the Tydings subcommittee wound up its hearings before they had really begun. The "interim report" by parliamentary hanky-panky became the final report. It was approved, printed, and issued by the three Democratic members without the knowledge or consent of the two Republicans — Senator Lodge and Senator Bourke B. Hickenlooper.[1] Ignoring such testimony as the subcommittee had gathered, it whitewashed the State Department, attacked Senator McCarthy, and tarred what anti-Communists it could — including several who had no connection with the inquiry.

The *Amerasia* Case flickered briefly when a Federal grand jury in New York broke loose from Justice Department leadership and began hearing witnesses. Its members were aroused by evidence of widespread Communist subversion. But the Justice Department brought it under control, and the jury issued a remarkable document which tacitly admitted that something was basically wrong, that not all the facts had been made known, and then proceeded to clear the Justice Department, the FBI, OSS, and everyone concerned, of any blame. If the FBI and OSS had spoiled the case by "polluting" the evidence — as the Justice Department claimed — then they were to blame. If the FBI and OSS had acted properly,

[1] Edward Morgan, the majority counsel, claimed responsibility for the writing.

then the case had been deliberately sabotaged by the Justice Department. The grand jury never bothered to explain this contradiction.

And so, once more, the *Amerasia* Case was scuttled — along with efforts then current to clear out the Reds and their sorry friends in government. The investigation was relegated to a Davy Jones locker of torpedoed evidence and sunken causes. The public, which should have protested, merely looked on in bewilderment. For the Administration's efforts to confuse the issues, to swamp the important facts in a tidal wave of irrelevancies and half-truths, succeeded infamously. Yet the average American, though he lost track of the story line, was not lulled by the assurances of the President that all was well in the best of all possible Washingtons. Something was wrong, radically wrong, and the man with the vote wanted some straight talk to dispel his sense of unease. This the pundits of Pendergastism could not do; instead, they beat voodoo drums and chanted "McCarthyism." [2]

But the cry of "McCarthyism" did not lay the ghost. In the 1950 election, Senator Tydings was driven from office. Other candidates who campaigned on the McCarthy issue, or with his help, were elected. Right or wrong, Joe McCarthy became a symbol to many Americans of the seemingly hopeless struggle to make the Administration cognizant of the enemy within. Vitriolic though Democratic propagandists might be, they only succeeded in making the Senator from Wisconsin the country's most controversial figure. Journalistic attacks — ranging from the gutter assault of the anti-anti-Communist *New York Post* to the refined malice and studied libel of more "objective" publications — merely confirmed McCarthy's followers in the belief that he was the most maligned man in the United States. The strategy was old, they felt. It had been used

[2] This word was coined by Owen Lattimore. It was picked up by the *Daily Worker* the day after Lattimore uttered it before the Tydings Committee, and in short order had become part of liberalism's polemic vocabulary.

against every man who dared mention the Communist issue in a voice above a whisper.

The McCarthy campaign ended inconclusively. A few security risks who had comfortably weathered the President's loyalty checks were quietly fired — and word of their dismissal, ironically, came almost simultaneously with the State Department's denial of the charges against them. Yet the tumult, the shouting, and the ugly passion had one tremendous consequence. As a result of Joe McCarthy's spadework, the United States Senate set up the Internal Security subcommittee of the Judiciary Committee, under Senator Pat McCarran. Robert Morris was appointed counsel to burrow into the Institute of Pacific Relations. Careful, painstaking, and scrupulously honest — with sound insight into Communist subversion gained when he served first with the Rapp-Coudert Committee of the New York Legislature, and then as a commander in Naval Intelligence — he was a perfect choice. Benjamin Mandel quit his job as research director of the House Un-American Activities Committee to bring his encyclopedic knowledge of Communism to the McCarran group. Theirs was a difficult, a touchy, and an unrewarding job.[3] For the IPR, though it had often been tentatively accused of harboring subversives, was so loaded with eminently respectable figureheads — men of governmental prominence (like General George C. Marshall) or great wealth and social prestige — that it was virtually above reproach.

Yet the IPR was the world of affairs, of government, of endowed foundations, seen through the wrong end of the telescope. Behind the façade of imposing reputation, scholarly purpose, and professorial dignity lurked a host of Communists,[4] crypto-Communists,

[3] Morris, for instance, has been subjected to a surly and irresponsible attack by columnist Joseph Alsop, who before his wide audience virtually accused Morris of subornation of perjury — a charge he later withdrew under oath.

[4] As of this writing, fifteen people connected with IPR — at least six in key positions — have refused to testify on the grounds of self-incrimination concerning their past or present Communist connections.

pro-Communists, pinko liberals, and opportunists. IPR was the parlor — a genuine, respectable, Park Avenue drawing room — and in it sat the spies and their dupes. Wrap up IPR and you wrapped up the Ozakis, the Agnes Smedleys, the Guenther Steins, the Prince Saionjis, the Harry Dexter Whites, the Alger Hisses, and most of the *dramatis personae* of the Sorge story, the Pearl Harbor story, the *Amerasia* story [5] — as well as the architects of error and defeat in the Far East. Large chunks of Rockefeller and Carnegie money kept the plush on IPR's overstuffed chairs. Representatives of the nation's corporate wealth kicked in with their checks and their reputations, headstrong innocents who sincerely believed that the distinguishing signs of a Communist were unpressed trousers, mangy hair, and an East European accent.

IPR flourished through the years, its Communist-line dicta on the Far East widely disseminated through the government, the press, and the universities. It was a political machine, an intellectual monopoly.[6] Without its *nihil obstat* few books on the Far East could prosper. Its *imprimatur* meant scholarly and financial success. In cooperation with the State Department's Far Eastern division, it sold to the United States the policy of destroying Chiang Kai-shek and building up the Chinese Communists. It muddied the Korean

[5] Not only was most of the *Amerasia* staff connected with IPR, but the magazine was a by-blow of the Institute — designed as a vehicle for views too crudely pro-Communist for even IPR publications.

[6] Testimony before the McCarran Committee:

Mr. Morris: Mr. Dooman, do you know Lawrence Salisbury, who was editor of *Far Eastern Affairs,* which was the publication of the American Council of the Institute of Pacific Relations?

Mr. Dooman: I did.

Mr. Morris: Did he ever make any effort to change the personnel in the State Department, to your knowledge?

Mr. Dooman: Well, he is the ringleader of a group of men in the Far Eastern Division [of the State Department] who protested against the assignment of Dr. [Stanley] Hornbeck as director of the Office of Far Eastern Affairs, when Secretary of State Stettinius . . . carried out his reorganization of the State Department. . . . As a result of that rebellion, which was successful, Mr. Hornbeck was then, I believe, sent to the Netherlands as ambassador.

waters and helped launch World War 2½. It acquired semi-official status with the government. It became a sort of employment agency during the war. In a letter[7] written just before Pearl Harbor, an IPR staff member who later moved into the State Department — Robert W. Barnett — outlined its influence:

In response to your request for me to do so, I have tried to set down in this letter how the American Council of the Institute of Pacific Relations has risen to the demands of the national emergency.

From the Army, Navy, the Federal Reserve Bank, the Department of Commerce, the Administrator of Export Control, and the Office of Price Administration and Civilian Supplies have come repeated calls for assistance which have been fulfilled by our research staff. . . . We are glad that the War Department has recognized the ability of our expert on the Netherlands East Indies, Miss Ellen van Zyll de Jong, by giving her a research appointment. . . . William W. Lockwood, on temporary leave, has worked as secretary of the American Committee for International Studies, and simultaneously for General Maxwell's and for Colonel Donovan's offices in Washington, but recently has taken over the secretaryship of the American Council. Both Mr. Carter and I have been invited to serve on the staff of the office of the Co-ordinator of Information, but have remained here because the necessity for popular education and private research seemed now more urgent. . . . This is just a sample of the kind of work which the Institute is able to do and explains why the governments in this and other countries are so eager to get the services of members of the Institute staff.

Our service to governments has not, happily, lessened thus far our aid to business groups, the press, and university and secondary-school circles. The demand for Institute services from all these groups is greater than ever before. We provided indispensable information to the Fortune staff as it prepared its Far Eastern issue. We have assisted teachers' organizations to carry out their Far Eastern projects. We have set up some 13 regional conferences. Under the leadership of Catherine Porter, Miriam Farley,[8] Dorothy Borg, and Kurt Bloch,

[7] McCarran Hearings, pp. 390–391.

[8] As a political adviser to General MacArthur, sent to Japan by the State Department, Miss Farley wrote to an IPR friend: "I have been put to work doing the

a greatly enlivened Far Eastern Survey reaches a wider and more attentive audience. We broadcast weekly over CBS. We are publishing inexpensive pamphlets, among them Showdown at Singapore, Philippine Emergency, Japan Strikes South, Our Far Eastern Record, American Aid to China, and the Soviet Far East.

In the international field only in France and Holland has the work of the Institute been curtailed. The Royal Institute in London has recently augmented its studies of the Far East and the far-eastern program of the Canadian and Australian Institutes is more fundamental and better supported than at any period in the past.

You will agree with me, I feel sure, that the reasons which led to your support of the American Council last year are doubly valid now. . . . This may prove to be the year of the long-awaited Japanese–American war — or, of Japan's surrender to ABCD economic pressure. Either development will greatly increase the American Council's responsibilities to our Government and to the American public.

In a letter written by the IPR's major-domo,[9] this analysis of the organization's importance was spelled out even more clearly:

Since I last saw you, four governments have recognized the IPR's achievements and the high quality of IPR personnel by the following appointments.

You doubtless know that on President Roosevelt's nomination, Generalissimo Chiang Kai-shek invited Owen Lattimore to go to Chungking as his personal political adviser. Lattimore arrived in Chungking 10 days ago. Another member of the International Secretariat, Dr. Ch'ao-ting Chi,[10] went with our best wishes on the same plane to become general secretary of the American-British-Chinese Currency Stabilization Fund of United States, $95,000,000. Here we have a case of outstanding services of the IPR — in that of Lattimore, an American to the Chinese Government and in that of Chi, a Chi-

---

political section of MacArthur's monthly report. There will be a certain sporting interest in seeing how much I can get by with."

[9] McCarran Hearings, pp. 278–279.

[10] Chi, a Comintern agent according to the Civil Service Commission, later put aside all pretense, declared himself a Communist, and went over to Mao Tse-tung. (See Appendix II.)

nese to the American, British, and Chinese Governments. A former member of the Secretariat, Irving Friedman, for whom I secured an appointment and an opportunity to study India as an employee of the Indian Government trade commissioner in New York, has now been given an important research position in the Treasury in Washington, one for which he is highly qualified. . . . The Office of the Export Control Administration recently asked for the full-time service of all the American Council research staff for a long period. We had to persuade that office that our staff could render a greater service by continuing its work here as a well-balanced, experienced research group rather than by moving en bloc to Washington, where its services would be available only to a single government department.

Another demand of a different kind has been made upon us. Mr. Henry R. Luce, Mr. Wendell L. Willkie, and Mr. James G. Blaine have asked me to serve as chairman of the disbursements committee which is making a very thorough-going survey of China's needs and how the $5,000,000 fund, if raised, can best be spent for maximum relief and at the same time to contribute to long-range reconstruction.

All of the foregoing is for your private information, for part of it is obviously not for general circulation. . . .

While Prince Konoye has been Premier, Ushiba, the chief IPR secretary in Japan, has acted as his private secretary. While Ushiba has been helping the Premier, Saionji,[11] the grandson of the Genro, has acted as chief secretary of the IPR in Tokyo, save for the period of Matsuoka's visit to Europe. Saionji accompanied the Foreign Minister on his fantastic round of visits to Hitler, Mussolini, and Stalin.

Bruce Turner, for many years secretary of the IPR in New Zealand, has just come to Washington with a member of the New Zealand Cabinet and will shortly be going to London to help get another New Zealand Cabinet officer there.

The Royal Institute in London has recently very greatly augmented its studies of the Far East. The Far Eastern program of the Canadian and Australian Institutes is more fundamental and better supported than at any period in the past.

In view of the war emergency and the exceptional service which the Institute is asked to render at this time, I am wondering whether

[11] Member of the Sorge apparatus.

you could not consider making a special and nonrecurring gift of $250 to the American Council sometime before the 1st of September.

Sincerely yours,

EDWARD C. CARTER
Acting Secretary

Elsewhere in this narrative, members of IPR have been identified as they figured in events. The roster would take many pages were it to be anywhere near complete. For the record, it may be of value to glance at some new and some old names in this context. Among IPR's officers, contributors, and members were:

Frederick Vanderbilt Field — for years executive secretary of the American Council of IPR, who regularly made up its operating deficits to the over-all amount of $60,000; millionaire Communist, leader of the subversive American Peace Mobilization; a founder of *Amerasia,* contributor to the *New Masses* and *Daily Worker.*

Harry Dexter White — Assistant Secretary of the Treasury, author of the Morgenthau Plan, and member of two Soviet spy rings — who found a way of handling top military secrets by getting Secretary Morgenthau to arrange for a regular exchange of documents with the Army, Navy, OSS, and so on.

Lauchlin Currie — White House administrative assistant and friend of Soviet spy N. Gregory Silvermaster.

Laurence Duggan — Chief of the State Department's Latin Affairs division and, briefly, a member of the Hede Massing espionage apparatus.

Guenther Stein — IPR Chungking correspondent, member without portfolio of the Sorge spy ring; *Christian Science Monitor* correspondent and propagandist for the Chinese Communists; writer of twenty-one articles for IPR publications.

Andrew Roth — protégé of Edward C. Carter, the dominant figure in IPR; writer for IPR publications; arrested in the *Amerasia* Case.

Lawrence Rosinger [12] — State Department consultant on the Far East and recipient of two grants from IPR, one from the Rockefeller

[12] Rosinger, who still rates high in IPR circles though he took refuge in the Fifth Amendment when questioned by the McCarran Committee as to past or present membership in the Communist Party, was once the subject of complaints by scholars

Foundation, and one from the American Council of Learned Societies; salaried employe of the IPR; writer and lecturer for the Foreign Policy Association.

Joseph F. Barnes — onetime foreign editor of the *New York Herald Tribune*, and editor of the ill-fated pro-Communist *New York Star* — onetime secretary of IPR; apologist extraordinary for the Soviet Union.

Max and Grace Granich — underground Soviet agents. Both Mr. and Mrs. Granich refused to answer the McCarran Committee's questions on their Communist affiliations, standing on the Fifth Amendment.

Harriet Lucy Moore — an IPR prime-mover, named as a member of the Communist Party by one witness.[13] Harriet Moore stood on the Fifth Amendment when the McCarran Committee called her.

Maxwell S. Stewart — an editor of the *Nation* and Public Affairs Pamphlets — edited IPR's Popular Pamphlet Series; named under oath as a Communist.

Corliss Lamont — supporter of pro-Communist causes and angel of pro-Communist organizations; in 1950, a backer of the pro-Red *New York Compass*.

Alger Hiss — as a high echelon State Department official, he was one of IPR's close friends; as president of the Carnegie Endowment for International Peace, he saw to it that IPR received Carnegie money; Soviet agent, convicted of perjury for denying espionage.

Brigadier General Evans Carlson — author of IPR books, ardent supporter of the Chinese Communists, close friend of Agnes Smedley; a secret member of the Communist Party according to sworn evidence.

Israel Epstein — *New York Times* writer, author of IPR books, friend of Communism and enemy of the United States by his own writings; member of the Soviet secret police; left the United States to avoid being deported.

James S. Allen — former foreign editor of the *Daily Worker;* contributor to IPR magazines.

---

who urged that he be dropped from IPR because his writings were "non-objective" and followed the Communist line faithfully. The IPR did not heed these complaints, and, in its March 1952 *Preliminary Edition of the 1951 Annual Report*, lists Rosinger's book, *The State of Asia*, among the year's achievements.

[13] See Appendix III.

In less than a week of McCarran Committee hearings, some fifty people more or less closely associated with IPR were identified as Soviet agents, Communists, or so strongly pro-Communist that the distinction was meaningless. Phrases descriptive of the IPR were even more telling. Louis Budenz, the ex-Communist and former *Daily Worker* editor, quoted Alexander Trachtenberg, cultural commissar of the Communist Party, as having said that the IPR was "the little red schoolhouse for teaching certain people in Washington how to think with the Soviet Union in the Far East." It was "as red as a rose," spymaster Jacob Golos told his courier, Elizabeth Bentley. Alexander Barmine, a former brigadier general in the Red Army and now head of the Russian section of the Voice of America, explained it this way to the McCarran Committee:

SENATOR FERGUSON: Which was the Institute of Pacific Relations? Was it a front or one that you would penetrate?

MR. BARMINE: Of course you have sometimes what we call a cover shop. It was specially organized for the narrow military purpose. It was phony, it was a fake. There would be some import-export business or some kind of shop or some tourist office which would be built as a place for a rendezvous or a gathering and for giving the reason for legal residence in the area.

Now this [IPR] of course was a different project to the extent they had an organization that existed already that was found to be ideally suitable for not just one local place but there was a whole Pacific area that they could give movement for people and open very large possibilities for intelligence work. So it was not especially built up from an organization which should be infiltrated, taken over at the most decided place. When the question of moving people, there would be enough people there who could report to the military network, work within the organization undisturbed for their operations for collection of material,[14] for recruiting people and all.

[14] During Owen Lattimore's testimony before the McCarran Committee, there was introduced in evidence a letter to him from Edward C. Carter which touches on this point. On 11 July 1939, Carter reported:

Motylev [head of the Russian Institute of the IPR] was eager for much more intimate factual details giving both very recent economic information and also

SENATOR FERGUSON: So the Institute of Pacific Relations was the latter setup that you were going to use and were using; is that right?
MR. BARMINE: That is right.

IPR's crowning glory was Owen Lattimore. What Edward C. Carter was as administrator of the organization, Lattimore equaled as ideologue. Selfmade scholar, champion of the Moscow Trials, indefatigable propagandist for the Soviet Union and for the Chinese Communists, Lattimore could be described as the little man who was always there. In the 150,000 pieces of IPR correspondence which the Internal Security subcommittee found hidden in Frederick Vanderbilt Field's cellar and in Carter's barn at Lee, Massachusetts, the Lattimore file was overwhelming — and overwhelmingly frank.

Owen Lattimore was accused by Senator McCarthy of having been the "architect of our Far Eastern policy" — the policy which delivered China into Communist hands, attempted to subvert the sane administration of Japan, and created the causes of the present Korean strife. In the sense that the IPR's writers and correspondents made State Department policy — a fact so self-evident that no one has bothered to believe it — Lattimore was precisely what McCarthy called him. But McCarthy went beyond this. He accused Lattimore of being a "top Soviet agent."[15] There is no quick way of determining how seriously this second accusation can be taken. There is testimony from Barmine, who worked under General Berzin of the Red Army's Fourth Bureau, that Lattimore was con-

personal observations as to what is going on in China and Japan. . . . One of Motylev's most urgent requests was for information concerning Chinese internal economic and financial position. Happily this will be supplied by Chi's [see Appendix II] study for the Inquiry. . . .

[15] This charge, which Lattimore naturally denied, was made on the Senate floor, where it was privileged. At the time, there was a great clatter that McCarthy was hiding behind senatorial immunity to slander Lattimore. It is curious to note, therefore, that it was Lattimore's supporter, Drew Pearson, who first announced to the world the name of the man whom McCarthy had made a point of not identifying. (See *Ordeal by Slander*, p. 44.)

sidered "one of us" by Soviet Intelligence. Barmine also repeated a statement to this effect by General Walter Krivitzky, deceased head of Soviet Intelligence in Western Europe. And Louis Budenz, speaking on the basis of official Communist Party information given him by such men as Jack Stachel, Earl Browder, and Frederick Vanderbilt Field, testified that Lattimore was considered a member of an international Soviet apparatus. All these charges were denied by Lattimore, who even questioned the existence of General Berzin.

There is no way to evaluate this evidence. But, in a sense, it is beside the point. To grant that Owen Lattimore is merely a Johns Hopkins professor with a firm set of ideas, honestly held, and a pattern of behavior dictated by his own conscience and not the Kremlin, begs the question. Yet if any man set out to do the Soviet Union's work in the United States, he could do much worse than pattern his actions on those of the eminent professor. Lattimore's method — and the method which IPR followed — was best characterized in a letter [16] he wrote to Carter in 1938:

I think that you are pretty cagey in turning over so much of the China section of the inquiry to Asiaticus,[17] Han-seng, and Chi [Ch'ao-ting]. They will bring out the absolutely essential radical aspects, but can be depended on to do it with the right touch. [All three men were active Communist propagandists.]

For the general purposes of this inquiry, it seems to me that the good scoring position for the IPR differs with different countries. For China, my hunch is that it will pay to keep behind the official Chinese Communist position, far enough not to be covered by the same label, but enough ahead of the active Chinese liberals to be noticeable. . . . For the U.S.S.R., back their international policy in general, but without using their slogans and above all without giving them or anybody else an impression of subservience. . . .

It was this "cagey" technique of backing policies "without using

[16] McCarran Hearings, pp. 39–41.

[17] Only seven months earlier, Lattimore had written to Frederick Vanderbilt Field that Asiaticus "is regarded [by the British Council of IPR] as a representative Marxist spokesman." [McCarran Hearings, stenographic transcript p. 5123.]

their slogans" which was employed so effectively by Lattimore,[18] the IPR, and the pro-Chinese Communist cabal in the State Department and elsewhere to sell to America what are generally recognized now as the nation's enemies. This method of translating Communist propaganda into American terms was subtle, devastating, and psychologically astute. It influenced the segment of American public opinion which influences foreign policy thinking. Through such men as Under Secretary of State Sumner Welles, always in close touch with Edward C. Carter and other IPR luminaries, and John Carter Vincent, it reached directly into the State Department. IPR made its voluminous files available to government. Its publications, *Far Eastern Survey* and *Pacific Affairs* — the latter edited first by Lattimore and then by Michael Greenberg[19] — were virtually required reading among Foreign Service officers. It disseminated its propaganda cannily and persistently. In 1947, when Israel Epstein's *The Unfinished Revolution* was coming off the presses, Carter wrote a revealing letter, marked private and confidential, to Little, Brown and Company's publicity director:

This is to acknowledge Epstein's *The Unfinished Revolution in China,* which you so kindly sent me a few days ago. I have already read two-thirds of it and hope to complete it within a few days.

I think it's of the utmost importance that you devise some means of getting it read at an early date among others by Secretary of State George Marshall, Senators Vandenberg, Morse, and Ives, John Foster Dulles and John Carter Vincent of the State Department. You will know better than I how to make certain that they read it in the

[18] On 17 October 1940, Lattimore wrote to Frederick Vanderbilt Field at the Washington office of the Communist-front American Peace Mobilization:

Enclosed I am sending you an article submitted to me by "Asiaticus." For readers of *Pacific Affairs,* it would read like propaganda, and rhapsodical propaganda at that. As the article is also too long, however, we might be able to shorten it, pruning out a great many adjectives but still retaining the realistic points. . . .

[19] A member of the Bentley apparatus who became assistant to White House aide Lauchlin Currie and then moved into the State Department till he was dropped during a "reduction in force."

near future. A letter from me on the subject might lead a few of them to think that I was recommending it because I was an admirer of Epstein's and for that reason they might slightly discount my recommendation.

I have another suggestion to make. The book is *so full of profound understanding and admiration of the Chinese people* that I think it is equally important to find ways and means of getting a wide circulation in China. Have you thought of a Chinese edition? . . .

The book combines in one volume several books. It is a penetrating history of China during the war years. It is a sociological document of importance, and it is a military handbook that might have been of enormous value to the Maquis in France and even to the little handful of anti-Hitler Germans in Germany. *It might become a military and political handbook for Viet-Nam and in other Asiatic areas if the imperialist powers try to reassert their pre-Pearl Harbor domination.*

The book is not so much needed in the Communist areas in China as it is in the Kuomintang areas where *its authoritative accounts would give new hope, as well as new methods,* to the millions of Chinese who are dissatisfied with the right-wing Kuomintang domination. . . .

More than at any other time in recent years, there is a large British public both in the United Kingdom, Canada, and also in Australia and New Zealand which would find the book illuminating, not only with reference to China, but in their thinking with reference to a great many movements in the continent of Europe and elsewhere.

I congratulate Little, Brown & Co.'s *unerring wisdom* in deciding, not only to publish this book, but in leaving no stone unturned in getting a very wide circulation.

Sincerely yours,

EDWARD C. CARTER

P.S. — I have not consulted Epstein with reference to this letter. I hope, however, that it may meet with his approval and elicit further concrete suggestions from him. To that end I am taking the liberty of sending him privately a copy.

P.S.–2 — Referring to General Marshall, I wish you could find someone who would get him to read the book from start to finish and not simply the end with Epstein's analysis of Marshall. It seems to me he would need the cumulative effect of the preceding chapters *to make him reassess objectively his own role.*

I assume that *John Carter Vincent would read the book with a very open mind.* Probably he is generally acquainted with most of the material, but he has probably never seen it organized so logically. If he were sold on the book *he might persuade General Marshall to read it from cover to cover.*

Of course, many will say that Epstein is a special pleader. I think this is probably true, but *I think he is pleading for a more sound analysis of the world than many of the other current special pleaders.* I hear that the *New York Times* has asked Owen Lattimore to review the book. I hope other publications will make as wise a choice.

I imagine the Kuomintang government will put the book on the "forbidden" list for import in China. I would hope that you could get it into the hands of Ambassador Leighton Stuart and some of the American correspondents like Benjamin Welles, Christopher Rand and Arch Steele, Sun Fo, Madame Sun Yat-sen and a few others, before the bronze curtain falls. [Italics added.]

Owen Lattimore's review in the *New York Times* was rapturous. "Israel Epstein has without question established a place for himself in . . . distinguished company" by his "outspoken support of the Chinese Communists. . . ." he wrote. In the Communist *New Masses,* IPR's Frederick V. Field noted that China's "foreign oppressors are today primarily American imperialists." One of the main subjects of the praiseworthy book, Field said, was "the struggle of the Chinese people against . . . American imperialism." He drew parallels between a corrupt Chinese official and a certain American congressman. In the *Daily Worker,* Samuel Sillen placed IPR correspondent Epstein "at the top of the list." And this was the book which Carter so anxiously sought to place in General Marshall's hands so that he could be guided by it in his State Department deliberations.

In 1945, Max Eastman and J. B. Powell wrote a critical article for the *Reader's Digest* on American policy toward China. Called "The Fate of the World Is at Stake in China," it exposed the danger of pro-Chinese Communist propaganda and demonstrated how it was being used to scuttle Chiang Kai-shek, and eventually the United States. Shortly after it appeared, Carter wrote a cryptic letter to Lattimore about a visit to "One Hundred and Sixty-sixth Street," about speaking to the "son" about the "father." The son "also confirmed what I suspected, that the father likes to do his own writing. I am, however, prepared in two or three days to send the draft to him with as strong and tactful a letter as I can write on the off-chance that he might be willing to do something." This secrecy was explained by other letters in the IPR files.

Lattimore had written a draft of an answer to the *Reader's Digest,* passed it on to Carter, who hiked up to 166th Street, the home of Corliss Lamont. Lamont was to pass it on to his father, the banker Thomas W. Lamont, who was to submit it to the *New York Times* as his own. By such a stratagem, Carter may have hoped to convince *Times* readers that even conservatives were pro-Chinese Communists. Thomas Lamont's answer, though somewhat agreeing with Carter, rather neatly put him in his place:

> I, too, have been concerned over the steady drip against Russia by various commentators. . . . I have read the Readers Digest article and have gone over with care your memorandum. In effect I think you are suggesting that I write to The Times a letter urging our government to alter its apparent present policy, and to make available Lend-lease supplies to the so-called Communist armies. . . . The principle involved seems to be that I should assume knowledge of the situation . . . more adequate than our government has. . . . In your memorandum you point out that Russia has been scrupulous to send supplies to Chiang alone. Well, if that be true, why is that not additional argument for us to do the same?

Carter, who held the policies and destinies of the IPR in his hands, once wrote to a Canadian associate suggesting Earl Browder as a speaker: "He is really very well-informed and, contrary to the public view, is 100-per cent American." Among IPR's files was a batch of documents concerning another one hundred per cent American — the Communist Frederick Vanderbilt Field. In 1940, Field had submitted his resignation as executive secretary of IPR in order to assume leadership of the Communist front American Peace Mobilization which functioned during the life of the Hitler-Stalin pact. It picketed the White House, called for violent action to block aid to Britain, and agitated generally until Hitler invaded Russia. Even Carter admitted that Field's support of the APM was a tip-off to his Communist orientation. Yet Philip C. Jessup, then chairman of IPR, urged the trustees to reject Field's resignation.[20]

"We consider that it is in the best interest of the [IPR] that Mr. Field should remain as closely associated with it as possible," Jessup wrote. "We therefore should like to see him continue as secretary of the council, *exercising the maximum amount of guidance and determination of policy. . . .*" [Italics added.]

This wide tolerance was shared by the trustees, but Field insisted on going over to the Communist organization. Ten days after Field wired his resignation from IPR, "in view the inevitable criticism and misunderstanding," and asked Jessup to "reserve your own judgment until I can talk with you," Owen Lattimore recommended Field for a job with the Defense Advisory Commission. After Communists ceased considering fascism "a matter of taste" — a change which coincided with the end of the Hitler-Stalin honeymoon — Field returned to the IPR. In 1942, he decided that he

---

[20] Ambassador Philip C. Jessup was accused by Senator McCarthy of having an "affinity for Communist causes." When Jessup came up in 1951 for confirmation of his nomination as delegate to the U.N. General Assembly, he admitted membership in some Communist fronts, denied affiliation with others, admitted that in 1946 he had urged the destruction of America's atomic bombs and a cessation of military atomic production. To show how far he was from any kind of Communist sympathies, he swore that he had been a member of the isolationist organization, America First, in 1939–1941 — a strange kind of qualification for one of the key members of a strongly interventionist State Department, but one which he then shared with Ambassador to India Chester Bowles. In the teeth of overwhelming evidence, Jessup also insisted that in 1949 neither he nor the State Department had even "considered" the possibility of recognizing Red China. The Senate Foreign Relations Committee refused to confirm his appointment to the U.N. — but President Truman gave Jessup an interim appointment, thus overruling the will of Congress.

wanted a commission in the United States Army Intelligence. Carter and William T. Stone — formerly of *Amerasia* and IPR, then of the Board of Economic Warfare, and until 1951 a policy maker for the State Department's Voice of America — hastened to pull what strings they could to put an officer's uniform on Field. An FBI report on Field prevented this, much to Carter's — and Stone's — regret.

Dr. Karl A. Wittfogel, one of the outstanding scholars on the Far East, told the McCarran Committee [21] of a conversation he had in 1944 with Owen Lattimore — just returned from the Henry Wallace mission to China, Russia, and India. "We talked about possible solutions in the Far East. [Lattimore] said for Korea it would be the best solution, a good conservative solution, if the Soviet Union would take the country over, which upset me very much. I blew up properly and thought this was not the way a representative of the American government should talk. . . ."

Lattimore denied that this conversation had ever taken place. He also denied another statement attributed to him by Dr. Wittfogel. In a letter dated 20 February 1947, Lattimore wrote: "I have never argued that America should remove [the Mikado]." Wittfogel answered by quoting from Lattimore's *Solution in Asia,* published in 1945: "If the Japanese themselves decide to do without an Emperor, well and good. If not, we should show that militarism has been so catastrophically defeated that we, the victors, do not need to use the Emperor. He and all males eligible for the throne . . . should be interned preferably in China. His estates . . . should be made over to an agrarian reform program, conspicuously without his sanction. . . . New vested interests will [after his death] be able to prevent the restoration of a monarchy." [22]

[21] McCarran Hearings, pp. 305, 327.

[22] McCarran Hearings, p. 330. It may be interesting to balance Lattimore's splenetic references to Dr. Wittfogel during the hearings with Lattimore's sentiments in 1937 concerning "the bulk, quality, and really fundamental importance of the work

All of this is fragmentary. It is but a small part of the evidence on the record, which in turn is but a small part of the complete story. It shows a frame of mind and a frame of reference. From an organization set up by Elihu Root and other distinguished Americans to throw light on the complex problems of the Pacific — a sphere in which America's destiny has always moved — the Institute of Pacific Relations became a holding company of special pleaders for a Soviet Far East, and a nest of innocents. Yet innocence is an explanation, not an excuse. When Gerard Swope, the head of IPR today, goes moral bail for the Rosingers, the Epsteins, and the Fields — when he shuts his eyes to a record of malodorous achievement or refuses to recognize the consequences of IPR's hold on State Department policy, his good intentions become academic. The road to Moscow is paved with good intentions — and not all those who walk it know where they are going.

[Wittfogel] is doing. He has an organizing and executive ability that could give Henry Ford a start and a licking; and on top of the unbelievable quantity of work he and his wife have been doing, he has found time to supervise a survey of source material that I needed for my work."

XVII

Strategy of Defeat

THERE is a time lag which vitiates the power and effectiveness of exposure. Alger Hiss was caught, but long after his major evil had been done. Most of the men named by ex-Communists are long out of government; their past acts of betrayal are historic, and therefore not real. The span between a man's break with the Communist movement and his decision to speak out is a wide one — and public purpose becomes infirm in the long wait.

And history is written not by the historians, but by the men in power — by the wielders of influence and the bestowers of place. The facts which appear in the memoirs are forgotten, or they come to light when the makers of policy are at long remove from their triumphs and errors. History is official chronicle until we are dead. So Americans live on press releases. If one contradicts the other, only the scholars know.

Consider the State Department. Repeatedly its affinity for bad security risks and Communists has been demonstrated. And the Department's secretaries and assistant secretaries, without admitting their error, assert confidently that their house is now in order. Assistant Secretary John Peurifoy so stated at the time Senator McCarthy made his charges. Peurifoy was rewarded for his loyalty with the ambassadorship to Greece — and thereafter, Edward Posniak and Theodore Geiger — two of McCarthy's security-risk targets as presented to the Tydings Committee — quietly dropped out of government service. Mrs. Esther Caukin Brunauer, also on

McCarthy's not-so-little list, was suspended when her husband resigned his highly sensitive Navy post while under investigation. Others since then have been quietly eased out.

All too often the Truman Administration has put its political future ahead of the country's weal — whether in security matters or in covering up for the seamy crew of five-percenters, patronage peddlers, and Kansas City cronies. Security, in the contemporary Washington sense, means classification of all government records which might do the Administration damage and declassification of those which might aid in a political fight. When Philip Jessup testified before a Senate committee in October 1951, he was permitted to disclose the contents of documents which would help him explain his position. When General Willoughby appeared before the McCarran Committee, he was prevented by executive ukase from divulging the names of Americans who participated in Soviet underground activities in Japan.[1] Whenever a document of conse-

---

[1] On 9 August 1951:

SENATOR FERGUSON: General, are you under the same ban as other witnesses who came here, that they are unable to testify in relation to personnel files and so-called loyalty files? . . .

GENERAL WILLOUGHBY: Mr. Chairman, as a citizen, I am naturally most desirous to assist this important committee. However, as a Federal officer, I am expected to observe Army orders and Presidential directives.

I invite your attention to a Department of Army circular letter dated August 21, 1948, on the subject, Release of Personnel Records and Information. I quote:

No information of any sort relating to the employee's loyalty and no investigative data of any type, whether relating to loyalty or other aspects of the individual's record, shall be included in material submitted to a congressional committee.

Still quoting the regulation:

Any individual who may appear as a witness before a congressional committee will respectfully decline to testify concerning the loyalty of any person or as to the contents of any investigative files and will state that he is forbidden to answer such questions by pertinent directives of the Army.

SENATOR FERGUSON: . . . We have had high military officers and others quote the same in the hearings where the present Chair was chairman. In other words, you are unable to give us this information?

GENERAL WILLOUGHBY: Based on the precise wording of this.

quence is released — after public pressure — it comes too late.

When, on 2 July 1946, Assistant Secretary of State Dean Acheson told the public that charges of Communists in the State Department were "more a matter of alarm than of fact," it was accepted as an accurate statement. The public could not know that on 26 July 1946 — a matter of twenty-four days later — Secretary of State James F. Byrnes would admit in a private letter that after careful screening by a loyalty board, 284 employes had been "the subject of adverse recommendation" but only 79 had been fired. It was this letter which Senator McCarthy referred to in his Wheeling, West Virginia, speech, when he said that of the remaining 205, he had the names of 57 Communists or people loyal to the Communists but still in the State Department — which set off the fraudulent "numbers game" attack on him by the liberals. These same liberals continue to insist that there is no significance to the fact that suspected Communists remained in the employ of the Department. They maintain that the only significance lies in the fact that of the seventy-nine who were fired *only forty* were fired for suspect politics.

The public was not to know that the FBI prepared a list for the State Department which — in the words of one of its security officers: ". . . purports to show the number of 'agents,' 'Communists,' 'sympathizers,' and 'suspects' in the State Department as of May 15, 1947. The tabulation shows:

"Agents 20
Communists 13
Sympathizers 14
Suspects .... 77."

The public only had the repeated assertions of Acheson, Peurifoy, and the President that Communist infiltration was a thing of the past. The security officer's report, carefully stamped SECRET, lay hidden in the files.

Again, on 10 June 1947, a Senate Appropriations subcommittee wrote to Secretary of State Marshall warning him that "under the administration of Dean Acheson," there was "a deliberate, calculated program" to "protect Communist personnel" in the Department. Marshall did not even acknowledge receipt.[2]

So the "revisionists" of current historical appraisal are not those frustrated men who get no hearing in academic circles. The real revisionists are the official historians who accept as Gospel truth the falsifications of government public relations officers and the self-serving statements of high- or low-ranking civil servants which do not conform with the buried record. The Sorge case is a prime example. In 1949, the Pentagon issued the so-called Willoughby report on Sorge, Smedley, and others. It had been prepared by the SCAP Intelligence staff and authenticated by legal experts.

But Agnes Smedley threatened to sue General MacArthur, a palpably ridiculous threat; Harold Ickes brayed loudly in the echo valley of the liberal press; Secretary of the Army Kenneth Royall withdrew the report and retired with his tail between his legs. And in less time than it took to bury the mimeographed sheets in Pentagon files, the myth had been created that the Defense Department had "repudiated" the report, had questioned its authenticity, and had given Agnes Smedley and the others named a clean bill of health. The myth persists today, though a quick glance into the *New York Times* index demolishes it.

It has been thus with the entire history of United States policy in the Far East. Dean Acheson, testifying before the Senate Armed Services and Foreign Relations committees, meeting jointly to determine the causes of MacArthur's abrupt removal as commander of U.N. forces in Korea, reiterated two tenets of Administration propaganda on the reasons for the tremendous concessions made to Russia to lure her into the Pacific war in 1945.

Under oath, Acheson stated[3] that when the Yalta commitments

---

[2] See Appendix IV.
[3] MacArthur Hearings, p. 1845.

which destroyed Nationalist China were made, "we did not know whether we had an atomic bomb or not." Yet the clear fact, attested to by General Leslie R. Groves, was that prior to Yalta he and Secretary Stimson informed President Roosevelt that the A-bomb was a "99 per cent certainty" and that the first bomb would be exploded in a matter of months. Colonel William S. Considine of the Manhattan Project flew to Malta to intercept the American delegation to the Crimea conference in order to notify Secretary of State Stettinius that "the bomb would explode, that Groves had double-checked scientists on this, that the probable date would be August 1 [1945]."

Under oath, Acheson stated: [4] "It was the then [at the time of Yalta] military opinion, *concurred in by everyone,* that the reduction of Japan would have to be brought about by a large scale landing on the islands of Japan, and the forecast of that fighting . . . indicated that it would be a very bloody and terrible battle. It was of the utmost importance that the Russians should come into the war in the Far East." [Italics added.]

Yet seven months before Yalta, Admiral Nimitz and General MacArthur [5] had met in Honolulu to discuss Pacific strategy and had come to the agreement, according to Admiral Leahy,[6] "that Japan could be forced to accept our terms of surrender by the use of sea and air power without an invasion of the Japanese homeland." Admiral King, who was present at Yalta, told the President that "blockade and bombardment could bring about Japanese capitulation." Russian entry would "hasten that capitulation," he said, but he advised that Roosevelt concede only the southern half of Sakhalin as a "sop," since the Russians wanted to come into the war anyway. Instead, the Soviet Union was given economic and military hegemony over Manchuria, and the port of Dairen.

[4] *Ibid.*

[5] MacArthur, America's Supreme Commander in the Pacific, was not consulted by the State Department before Yalta.

[6] *I Was There.* (New York, 1950.)

There was, moreover, a report[7] by fifty War Department specialists — many of high rank — outlining the serious political and military consequences of Russian entry into the Pacific war, and strongly advising that it be prevented if at all possible. Yet the Far East was handed to Russia on a platter in order to "buy" her participation. This was the greatest blunder in American diplomatic history. "The true reason for Yalta remains an inscrutable mystery," wrote eight of the senators who took part in the MacArthur hearings. "The result of Yalta remains a triumph for Communist diplomacy."

Who pushed the hand that wielded the pen that signed the agreements at Yalta? Is there an answer in the Sorge story, the *Amerasia* Case, and the IPR? Was there a repetition of the endless attrition on policymakers which the pro-Chinese Communist lobby practiced on the State Department from 1943 on — or of the quick mobilization of strength which preceded the assault on the *modus vivendi* in 1941?

What was begun at Yalta — the great conscious and unconscious effort to deliver China to the Communists — continued at an accelerated pace in later years. In 1946, when General Marshall was preparing to go on his disastrous mission to China — disastrous, that is, to all but the Chinese Communists — a set of instructions was drawn up to guide him in negotiating an agreement between Chiang and the Reds. When he testified at the MacArthur hearings, Marshall was asked: "Do you recall who had a hand in the preparation of the directive that sent you to China?"

"At that time," said Marshall, "Mr. Byrnes was Secretary of State,

---

[7] This document, dated 21 April 1945, was requested from the Defense Department by Senator Styles Bridges during the MacArthur Hearings. Bridges was told that the document could not be located and "was probably destroyed." But Bridges had his own copy, supplied to him by one of the authors. The document stated that Russia's entry into the Asiatic war "would destroy America's position in Asia." It went on to warn that this entry, whose "military significance at this stage of the war would be relatively unimportant," would "certainly cost China her independence," and added that "the United States Army is by no means united in believing it wise to encourage the Soviet Union into the Asiatic war."

and I presume he had a hand in it; Mr. Acheson was Under Secretary of State, and I presume he had a hand in it; John Carter Vincent was the head of the China group in the State Department — *certainly he had a hand in it*. . . . I did not." [Italics added.] Acheson, however, laid all the blame at Marshall's door for a directive which ordered a "coalition" of Nationalists and Communists — or else!

All of this is preamble and commentary on the too little, too late, and too confused of America's public information. It speaks as a negative character witness for Dean Acheson — the prisoner of his Far Eastern division — for General Marshall, and for the men who have delivered most of Asia to the Communists. It speaks negatively for the host of IPR consultants, the pinko and liberal and sometimes Communist advisers of men whose stubborn policies have brought the world to the edge of war. Place the mythical average American on a witness stand today and ask him, in lawyer fashion, "What is the State Department's reputation for honesty, integrity, veracity, and loyalty?" The answer would be, "Bad."

The "average American" reads his newspapers quickly, and quickly forgets them. Place the documentation — even a small part of it — before him. Then ask: Does this make clear why the State Department has used every trick in the debater's book, every deception, to block a careful scrutiny of its personnel, its policies, and its motives? Will he answer, "It does"?

Offer Exhibit A — Dean Acheson's statement in the shockingly contrived White Paper on China. "The unfortunate but inescapable fact is that the ominous result of the civil war in China was beyond the control of the government of the United States. Nothing that this country did or could have done within the limits of its capabilities could have changed the results; nothing that was left undone by this country has contributed to it." [8]

[8] In the same letter of transmittal from which this quote is taken, Secretary Acheson says: "The Nationalist armies did not have to be defeated; they disintegrated." It is difficult to square this statement with official figures issued by the

Exhibit B — Dean Acheson's letter to Senator Connally on 5 March 1949: "The Chinese government forces have lost no battles during the past year because of lack of ammunition and equipment."

Exhibit C — General Marshall's insistence in 1946 on an armistice between the Chinese Reds and the Nationalists, at a time when Chiang was driving the Communists out of one strategic area after another. The battle was always resumed after a troop and materiel build-up by the Communists, and defeat was turned into stalemate or victory for Stalin and Mao Tse-tung. It was all reported in the American press.

Exhibit D — The half-million useless and disintegrating gas masks which we forced Chiang to buy at $8 apiece.

Exhibit E — General Marshall's embargo on the sale of arms to the Nationalists, which was not lifted until July 1947. Of this embargo, Admiral Charles M. Cooke [9] told the McCarran Committee:

SENATOR FERGUSON: Do you know anything about the supply of ammunition to the Nationalist troops?

MR. COOKE: Yes, after [General Marshall] left, around about the 1st of August 1946, the supply was cut off. . . .

SENATOR FERGUSON: Did General Marshall ever discuss this with you?

MR. COOKE: He discussed it in general without making too much comment except that he made the observation to me that we, meaning the United States, had armed the Chinese, and now we were disarming them. In other words, we had undertaken to equip 30-odd Chinese divisions, equip them with guns and things of that kind, and then we stopped the flow of ammunition and made a complete

---

Chinese Communists that their casualties at the hands of Chiang's "disintegrated" forces added up to 1,223,000.

[9] Charles Maynard Cooke, Admiral USN, retired; at the time of Pearl Harbor commander of the *Pennsylvania;* successively and/or concurrently chief of staff to Admiral King; chief strategic and policy adviser during all of World War II to Admiral King, serving with him on the Joint Chiefs of Staff and Combined Chiefs of Staff; a participant during 1945 in the formulation of United States policy toward the Far East; Commander of the Seventh Fleet; in command of all United States combat forces in China 1946–1948.

embargo, so we didn't supply it or wouldn't let them buy it for a period of about ten months, I believe. He just made that observation to me, that is all. He wasn't called on to do it, but he did it.

SENATOR FERGUSON: It amounted to disarming them because they were not getting the ammunition for the weapons we had supplied them?

MR. COOKE: That is right.

SENATOR FERGUSON: What effect would the arming of the Nationalists have had as far as the Communists were concerned?

MR. COOKE: Of course, the Communists were being very well supplied in Manchuria by the Russians from arsenals and from captured Japanese guns and ammunition. We were practically certain that was going on, and of course in our White Paper reported from our diplomatic representatives in Moscow that it was going on.

SENATOR FERGUSON: So we know that the Communists were getting arms and ammunition and also it was our policy, we put it into effect, to put an embargo on the Nationalists?

MR. COOKE: That is right.

SENATOR FERGUSON: And General Marshall had told you that of course that amounted to the disarming of the Nationalists?

MR. COOKE: Yes . . .

MR. MORRIS: During the time that [the embargo] was in force was the Chinese Government able to buy any equipment in the United States?

MR. COOKE: Not so far as I know. I am fairly sure not.

MR. MORRIS: Did the United States send any equipment to the Chinese Government during that period?

MR. COOKE: No combat equipment. Let me modify that. That is a question that comes up here about delivery of this obsolete ammunition in Tsingtao in February of 1947. . . . The number of Marines in China gradually decreased. They had ammunition there for carrying out combat operations, much more than they needed, and some of it getting old and beyond the standards acceptable to the United States. So, some of this obsolescent ammunition in Tsingtao became due for disposal. I didn't want to haul it through the town of Tsingtao in order to load it on ships, and the only other way to dispose of it was just dump it somewhere or to blow it up. Blowing up thousands of rounds of ammunition is not a very easy thing.

So when I came back in 1947 to talk to the State Department here and the Navy Department about the number of Marines in Tsingtao, the question also came up about this ammunition, as to whether to dump it or not. . . .

SENATOR FERGUSON: Why did you not give it to the Chinese Nationalists that had weapons in which to use it?

MR. COOKE: I am going into that. So then we had this conference with the State Department including General Marshall and Mr. Vincent.

SENATOR FERGUSON: That is John Carter Vincent?

MR. COOKE: John Carter Vincent.

SENATOR FERGUSON: What was his position with the State Department at that time, if you know?

MR. COOKE: He was the Assistant Secretary for Far Eastern Affairs, the same as Mr. Rusk now is.

SENATOR FERGUSON: You took it up with General Marshall. Was he then Secretary of State?

MR. COOKE: He was Secretary of State. The Secretary of Navy was there, the Chief of Naval Operations, and General Marshall, Secretary Marshall, and Mr. Vincent.

SENATOR FERGUSON: Will you tell us about the conversation you had?

MR. COOKE: Yes, I was of the view that we should take it out there and dump it and the Nationalists come and get it. They were desperately short of ammunition then. I considered it would be good for them to have it. Furthermore, I didn't think it was very practicable to dispose of it in any other way. In the discussion that ensued Mr. Vincent opposed that.

SENATOR FERGUSON: What did he say?

MR. COOKE: He just said we ought to figure out a way to destroy it.

SENATOR FERGUSON: And not give it to the Nationalists?

MR. COOKE: That is right. General Marshall recognized the problem and said he considered it was a very difficult problem to destroy it, and he approved my recommendation on it, which was carried out. . . .

MR. MORRIS: Where did that conference take place?

MR. COOKE: In the State Department.

SENATOR FERGUSON: Did Mr. Vincent assign any reason for not giving it to the Chinese Nationalists in the way you proposed?

Mr. Cooke: He just indicated it was undesirable to do so. . . . Now I could tell you, of course, there had been subsequent withholding of ammunition, for instance, in 1947 and after they moved to Formosa.

Exhibit F — The dispatches of Ambassador Leighton Stuart. In July 1947, he reported that "There are insufficient arms and ammunition to arm all combatant troops in the field." In February 1948, he said, "If American aid should materialize in adequate measure . . . the tide may turn quickly in our favor."

Exhibit G — Chiang's year-long plea to the State Department to permit him to purchase 7.42 ammunition — usable only in China — which was rewarded by a three-week supply.

Exhibit H — After the "do-nothing" 80th Congress passed a China Aid Act, it took the State Department four months — and threats of action by Senator Styles Bridges — to authorize the sale of ammunition to Nationalist China. On 15 May 1950, Vice Admiral Russell S. Berkey said, "The Chinese Reds would still be north of the Great Wall if specific items of arms authorized by Congress two years ago had reached the Nationalist forces in time. For some reason or other it took nine months to get specific items to China. Somewhere in the United States somebody slipped up, bogged down, or was interfered with."

As Freda Utley has pointed out in her best-seller, *The China Story,* it took several more months before "availability studies" were made. Then ammunition being sold as surplus to other nations at $4.55 per 1000 rounds, and list-priced at $45, was sold to Chiang for $85.

Now compare Dean Acheson's statements in Exhibits A and B, with the other exhibits. Refer to the record of Yalta. And then throw in two more exhibits — the attempts to scuttle Chiang in Formosa and to recognize the Chinese Communist government: two policy acts which ran directly counter to the will of Congress and the sentiments of the American people. Label these Exhibits I and J.

Exhibit I — On 6, 7, and 8 October 1949, the State Department held a round-table conference on American Policy Toward China. The participants were twenty-five experts on the Far East; the chairman was Philip Jessup. The public, which paid the freight, was never told of this conference nor of the makeup of the panel. Or it was not told until the summer of 1951, when Harold Stassen blasted a transcript out of the State Department's tenacious grip. Of the twenty-five participants, fifteen were connected with the Institute of Pacific Relations — either as trustees, consultants, officers, or writers. Of the fifteen, four were later to be named as members of the Communist Party in sworn testimony and one had been connected with the notorious China Aid Council. Except for Harold Stassen and Professor Kenneth Colegrove, there was no one on the panel who was known to harbor sympathies for Chiang Kai-shek. The dominant figure on the panel, although he modestly disclaims this role, was Owen Lattimore. Seated at the table as a panelist was General Marshall.[10]

The panel discussed many phases of the Chinese problem, with the weighty, chin-stroking gravity of State Department consultants. But one of the topics which aroused some fairly lively discussion was the question of recognition of Red China. They were not discussing *whether* the Communist government should be given American recognition, however, but *when* such recognition should be granted, and *how* the course of action could be made palatable to an American public which did not share the panel's tolerance for Communism.

Lawrence Rosinger proposed that "we end our ECA assistance as soon as possible to the remnants of the Chinese Nationalists." Rosinger was a little late. Secretary of State Dean Acheson had already gone beyond that, some eight months earlier, by urging a halt to all aid, economic and military, to the Chiang Kai-shek armies — a fact the public was not told.

[10] On 22 April 1950, Marshall wrote to Senator Tydings: "So far as I and my associates can recall, I never even met Mr. Lattimore."

Toward the end of one of the last sessions, at a time when Harold Stassen was not present, the panelists let their hair down

MR. JESSUP: I would like to suggest that we might have a few minutes taking up the question of the recognition of the Communist government in China. . . . I think in some of the discussion of recognition there is some confusion between the short-term and the long-term aspects. There is the question of whether you recognize the Communist government immediately on the one hand. On the other hand, there is the picture or the phantom of a duplication of the situation which existed with respect to the Soviet Union over a period of fifteen years, practically, in which we said it did not exist when it did exist and you know the complications which arose from that. . . .

ERNEST B. McNAUGHTON: Sitting in this room arguing and listening, I think I would say we had come to a state of mind where we would recognize the Communist government in China, but General Marshall has been whispering in my ear for the last few days that a lot of things we were talking about now you cannot get the American public to take right now or the Congress to take and therefore, the reasoning in a vacuum here among ourselves, facing a practical problem, I think the procedure would be to watch and wait.

MR. JESSUP: Speaking as a representative of the American public in a particular area of the country, do you think recognition would go down in your area?

MR. McNAUGHTON: I think they would blow up.

BENJAMIN KIZER: As of today, but what they will do tomorrow is another story. . . .

NATHANIEL PEFFER: I would also make it a matter of timing and I would wait. I would wait four weeks or five or six weeks. . . .

ARTHUR HOLCOMBE: I go along with those who have spoken and I guess most of us do — perhaps all — on the question of recognition and the question of timing and I take it that most of those who have spoken would also add that since to get exactly the right time is exceedingly difficult, it is best to be too early than too late. . . .

OWEN LATTIMORE: Mr. Chairman, I think I am definitely encouraged by the evident trend this morning which shows that we should proceed from facts rather than from subjective attitudes. I hope the department feels its hand strengthened but . . . it seems to me that we should come back once more, more closely to the point raised by General Marshall that timing is all important. . . . We should look little widely and take in all the rest of Asia as well. . . . Couldn't we couple recognizing the new regime in China with a number of positive steps in Asia as a whole . . . to show that the United States is . . . anxious to get the most progressive and liberal settlement possible. . . .

LAWRENCE K. ROSINGER: I'd like to associate myself with the view frequently expressed around this table that we should extend recognition. My own personal feeling is that the recognition should come as early as possible. . . . I'd like to suggest . . . preparing public opinion as a basis for early recognition. . . .

MR. JESSUP: I think this morning has been very much to the point and extremely useful. . . .

EDWIN O. REISCHAUER: We seem to be in very general agreement about the desirability of recognizing the Communist government in China and recognizing it very soon. . . .

It was to this, of course, that Ambassador Jessup was referring in the fall of 1951 when, under oath, he told the Senate Foreign Relations subcommittee considering his appointment to the U.N. General Assembly that the State Department had at no time "considered" the possibility of recognizing Red China.[11]

Exhibit J — On 23 December 1949, as the ill-armed, maligned, and betrayed armies of Chiang Kai-shek began their withdrawal to the island of Formosa, a secret set of instructions was issued to State Department information officers. Behind this document were the

[11] And during the MacArthur hearings, 2 June 1951:

SENATOR BREWSTER: You have never contemplated [recognizing Red China]?

SECRETARY ACHESON: No. We are not contemplating it; haven't contemplated it. . . .

Under oath, Brigadier General Louis J. Fortier told the McCarran Committee that 1 January 1950, Philip Jessup told him the United States would recognize Red China "in about two or three weeks."

pressures of the pro-Communist China faction,[12] the real "China lobby," which had worked long and lovingly for the collapse of the Nationalists. It did not care to see a revival of anti-Communist military strength on Formosa — nor to delay the great day of victory and recognition for the Chinese Reds. The document stated:

Formosa, politically, geographically, and strategically, is part of China in no way especially distinguished or important.

If rising public interest warrants it, gradually increasing attention may be paid Formosa, to establish publicly *the facts* indicated below. . . .

All material should be used best to counter the *false impressions* that [Formosa's] loss would seriously damage the interests of either the United States or of other countries opposing communism.

Without evidencing undue preoccupation with the subject, emphasize as appropriate any of the following main points:

. . . Formosa has no special military significance. . . .

In areas of insistent demand for United States action, particularly in the United States itself, we should occasionally make clear that seeking United States bases on Formosa, sending in troops, supplying arms, dispatching naval units, or taking any similar action would (a) accomplish no material good for China or its Nationalist regime. [Italics added.]

And, warned the State Department directive:

Avoid: References which would indicate important strategic significance or that the island is a political entity.

Just thirteen days after this order was issued, the President stated categorically: "The United States Government will not provide military aid or advice to Chinese forces on Formosa." Yet under oath,

[12] On 17 July 1949, Owen Lattimore wrote in the *New York Compass*, presumably explaining a policy to which he had given parentage, "As it became more and more obvious that Chiang Kai-shek and the Kuomintang were doomed, the conduct of American policy became increasingly delicate. The problem was how to allow them to fall without making it look as if the United States had pushed them. . . . The thing to do, therefore, is to let South Korea fall — but not let it look as though we pushed it."

during the MacArthur hearings, Acheson said just as unequivocally
of American policy toward Formosa:

First of all, it was understood and agreed that Formosa had strategic importance so far as the United States was concerned.
The second point was that that strategic importance related to
keeping Formosa out of the hands of a power which would be
hostile to the United States.

Formosa could have fallen, and the State Department would have
continued to tell the American people that it had no strategic importance — that it was outside our "defense perimeter" — just as the
State Department had, right up to the outbreak of the Korean war,
told the American people that the "dust must settle" before a strong,
Far East policy could be devised.[13] Until that far-off day, the Reds
would remain "agrarian reformers," or — as Assistant Secretary of
State Rusk said — revolutionists on the order of the American 1776
brand, with Mao Tse-tung their George Washington.

These are the exhibits, the small sampling of a vast stock. Do they
make sense? And are the poor, benighted anti-Communists — who
read an American meaning into the Sorge story, who see parallels
between Ozaki and certain men in our government, who note that
Amerasia is an unfinished chapter in a terrifying mystery story, who
wonder at IPR and its ties with the State Department — so de-
luded? For the average citizen, and the not-so-average reader, is it
easier to believe that American policy in the Far East is the result of
a widespread and deep-rooted conspiracy? Or must he ascribe it to
concentrated stupidity? And does it make much difference? For
stupidity can go only so far; and blunders which are tolerated and
extolled as genius add up to more than politics as usual.

[13] "My purpose in testifying here," Eugene Dooman told the McCarran Committee,
"was to indicate in general that policies put forward by the left-wing press, from the
Daily Worker right down the line, right down the line, were in effect substantially
translated into U. S. policies, and to indicate from personal knowledge how that
operation was carried out."

What is the verdict, then? If he is still alive — and he well ma[y] be — Richard Sorge could answer that question. Richard Sorg[e] might smile, as he smiled at his Japanese captors. "It is all accordin[g] to plan," he might say, "as the fall of China was planned." And h[e] would limp away. It is all according to plan — but not America'[s] plan, not the plan of free men who stand up for their freedom, no[r] the plan for an American destiny. Dead or alive, Sorge is winnin[g] for his masters. The Sorges of the world are winning. Time is run[-]ning short. And there is no wisdom.

Koheleth the Preacher said, "The words of the wise are as goad[s] ... And further, by these, my son, be admonished: of makin[g] many books there is no end. ... Let us hear the conclusion of th[e] whole matter. ... For God shall bring every work into judgmen[t] with every secret thing, whether it be good, or whether it be evil[.] These are not words which Communists can understand. But in th[e] day of evil victory, will they be of comfort to earthbound men?

APPENDICES

APPENDIX I

Service's Report to Stilwell

Report No. 40

U. S. ARMY OBSERVER SECTION, APO 879
October 10, 1944

Subject: The Need for Greater Realism in our Relations with Chiang Kai-shek.

To: General Stilwell, Commanding General, USAF–CBI

1. You have allowed me, as a political officer attached to your staff, to express myself freely in the past regarding the situation in China as I have seen it. Although in Yenan I am only a distant observer of recent developments in Chungking and Washington, I trust you will permit the continued frankness which I have assumed in the attached memorandum regarding the stronger policy which I think it is now time for us to adopt toward Chiang Kai-shek and the Central Government.

2. It is obvious, of course, that you cannot act independently along the lines suggested. The situation in China and the measures necessary to meet it have both military importance and far-reaching political significance; the two aspects cannot be separated. Because of this interrelation, and because of the high level on which action in China must be taken, there must be agreement and mutual support between our political and military branches. But this will be ineffective without clear decision and forceful implementation by the President.

3. It is requested that copies of this report be transmitted, as usual, to the American Ambassador at Chungking and Headquarters, USAF–CBI, for the information of Mr. Davies.

/s/ JOHN S. SERVICE

Enclosure:
Memorandum, as stated.

MEMORANDUM

Our dealings with Chiang Kai-shek apparently continue on the basis of the unrealistic assumption that he is China and that he is necessary to our cause. It is time, for the sake of the war and also for our future interests in China, that we take a more realistic line.

Kuomintang Government is in crisis. Recent defeats have exposed its military ineffectiveness and will hasten the approaching economic disaster. Passive inability to meet these crises in a constructive way, stubborn unwillingness to submerge selfish power-seeking in democratic unity, and the statements of Chiang himself to the Peoples Political Council and on October 10, are sufficient evidence of the bankruptcy of Kuomintang leadership.

With the glaring exposure of the Kuomintang's failure, dissatisfaction with Chiang is growing rapidly. The prestige of the Party was never lower, and Chiang is losing the respect he once enjoyed as a leader.

In the present circumstances, the Kuomintang is dependent on American support for survival. *But we are in no way dependent on the Kuomintang.*

We do not need it for military reasons. It has lost the southern air-bases and cannot hold any section of the seacoast. Without drastic reforms — which must have a political base — its armies cannot fight the Japanese effectively no matter how many arms we give them. But it will not permit those reforms because its war against Japan is secondary to its desire to maintain its own undemocratic power.

On the other hand, neither the Kuomintang nor any other Chinese regime, because of the sentiment of the people, can refuse American forces the use of Chinese territory against the Japanese. And the Kuomintang's attitude prevents the utilization of other forces, such as the Communist or Provincial troops, who should be more useful than the Kuomintang's demoralized armies.

We need not fear Kuomintang surrender or opposition. The Party and Chiang will stick to us because our victory is certain and it is their only hope for continued power.

But our support of the Kuomintang will not stop its normally traitorous relations with the enemy and will only encourage it to continue sowing the seeds of future civil war by plotting with the present puppets for eventual consolidation of the occupied territories against the Communist-led forces of popular resistance.

We need not fear the collapse of the Kuomintang Government. All the other groups in China want to defend themselves and fight Japan. Any new government under any other than the present reactionary control will be more cooperative and better able to mobilize the country.

Actually, by continued and exclusive support of the Kuomintang, we tend to prevent the reforms and democratic reorganization of the government which are essential for the revitalization of China's war effort. Encouraged by our support the Kuomintang will continue in its present course, progressively losing the confidence of the people and becoming more and more impotent. Ignored by us, and excluded from the Government and joint prosecution of the war, the Communists and other groups will be forced to guard their own interests by more direct opposition.

We need not support the Kuomintang for international political reasons. The day when it was expedient to inflate Chiang's status to one of the "Big Four" is past, because with the obvious certainty of defeat, Japan's Pan-Asia propaganda loses its effectiveness. We cannot hope that China under the present Kuomintang can be an effective balance to Soviet Russia, Japan, or the British Empire in the Far East.

On the contrary, artificial inflation of Chiang's status only adds to his unreasonableness. The example of a democratic, nonimperialist China will be much better counterpropaganda in Asia than the present regime, which, even in books like "China's Destiny," hypnotizes itself with ideas of consolidating minority nations (such as the "Southern Peninsula"), and protecting the "right" and at the same time national ties of its numerous emigrants (to such areas as Thailand, Malaya and the East Indies). Finally, the perpetuation in power of the present Kuomintang can only mean a weak and disunited China — a sure cause of international involvements in the Far East. The key to stability must be a strong, unified China. This can be accomplished only on a democratic foundation.

We need not support Chiang in the belief that he represents pro-American or democratic groups. All the people and all other political groups of importance in China are friendly to the United States and look to it for the salvation of the country, now and after the war.

In fact, Chiang has lost the confidence and respect of most of the American-educated, democratically-minded liberals and intellectuals. The Chen brothers, Military, and Secret police cliques which control the Party and are Chiang's main supports are the most chauvinist elements in the country. The present Party ideology, as shown in Chiang's own books "China's Destiny" and "Chinese Economic Theory," is fundamentally anti-foreign, and anti-democratic, both politically and economically.

Finally, we feel no ties of gratitude to Chiang. The men he has kept around him have proved selfish and corrupt, incapable and obstructive. Chiang's own dealings with us have been an opportunist combination of extravagant demands and unfilled promises, wheedling and bargaining, bluff and blackmail. Chiang did not resist Japan until forced by his own people. He has fought only passively — not daring to mobilize his own people. He has sought to have us save him — so that he can continue his conquest of his own country. In the process, he has "worked" us for all we were worth.

We seem to forget that Chiang is an Oriental; that his background and vision are limited; that his position is built on skill as an extremely adroit political manipulator and a stubborn, shrewd bargainer; that he mistakes kindness and flattery for weakness; and that he listens to his own instrument of force, rather than reason.

Our policy toward China should be guided by two facts. First, we cannot *hope to deal successfully with Chiang without being hard-boiled.* Second, *we cannot hope to solve China's problems* (which are now our problems) *without consideration of the opposition forces* — Communist, Provincial and liberal.

The parallel with Jugoslavia has been drawn before but is becoming more and more apt. It is as impractical to seek Chinese unity, the use of the Communist forces, and the mobilization of the population in the rapidly growing occupied areas by discussion in Chungking with the Kuomintang alone as it was to seek the solution of these problems through Mikhailovitch and King Peter's government in London, ignoring Tito.

We should not be swayed by pleas of the danger of China's collapse. This is an old trick of Chiang's.

There may be a collapse of the Kuomintang government; but it will not be the collapse of China's resistance. There may be a period of some confusion, but the eventual gains of the Kuomintang's collapse will more than make up for this. The crisis itself makes reform more urgent — and at the same time increases the weight to our influence. *The crisis is the time to push — not to relax.*

We should not let Chiang divert us from the important questions by wasting time in futile discussion as to who is to be American commander. This is an obvious subterfuge.

There is only one man qualified by experience for the job.[1] And the fact is that *no one who knows anything about China and is concerned over American rather than Chiang's interests will satisfy Chiang.* [All italics Service's.]

We should end the hollow pretense that China is unified and that we can talk only to Chiang. This puts the trump card in Chiang's hands.

Public announcement that the President's representative had made a visit to the Communist capital at Yenan would have a significance that no Chinese would miss — least of all the Generalissimo. The effect would be great even if it were only a demonstration with no real consultation. But it should be more than a mere demonstration; we must, for instance, plan on eventual use of the Communist armies and this cannot be purely on Kuomintang terms.

Finally, if these steps do not succeed, we should stop veiling our negotiations with China in complete secrecy. This shields Chiang and is the voluntary abandonment of our strongest weapon.

Chinese public opinion would swing violently against Chiang if he were shown obstructive and noncooperative with the United States. We should not be misled by the relatively very few Kuomintang die-hards; they are not the people. The Kuomintang Government could not withstand public belief that the United States was considering withdrawal of military support of recognition of the Kuomintang as the leader of Chinese resistance.

More than ever, we hold all the aces in Chiang's poker game. It is time we started playing them.

October 10, 1944   JOHN S. SERVICE

[1] See part 2 of this Appendix.

2

The above memorandum was written just a few weeks before General Stilwell was removed as American commander in China and adviser to Chiang, something which Chiang had asked long before. There was no question of whom Service, writing to his chief, Stilwell, meant by saying "There is only one man qualified by experience for the job."

Testimony of Henry Wallace, who reported Chiang's request for Stilwell's removal to President Roosevelt, and of Joseph Alsop who accompanied Wallace on his China Mission, throws rather a different light on the matter.

Before the McCarran Committee on 17 October 1951, Wallace said:

General Joseph W. Stilwell, the American commander in the China-Burma-India theater, was wholly preoccupied with the campaign in Burma. The Chinese armies being attacked by the Japanese had received no American aid to strengthen them. The Generalissimo complained to me that even the air support for them was limited by General Stilwell's policies . . . the Generalissimo said to me very frankly that he lacked confidence in General Stilwell while he had high confidence in General Chennault. His stated reason for lack of confidence in General Stilwell was Stilwell's poor understanding of political problems.

In any case it was very clear to me, from the tone and language of the Generalissimo, that he and Stilwell could not cooperate. It seemed to me further it was an unmanageable situation to have an American commander in China who did not enjoy the Generalissimo's confidence and could not achieve friendly cooperation with him. The military situation in China was already critical. In fact, Chiang Kai-shek gave me the impression . . . of hardly knowing which way to turn. [He gave] me a personal message to President Roosevelt . . . I was deeply moved by the cry of a man in great trouble and I was moved to start in to help him as soon as possible . . .

Testimony of Joseph Alsop before the McCarran Committee, 18 October 1951:

This recommendation to dismiss General Stilwell . . . was the heaviest blow to the Communist cause in China that could be struck at that time.

Basically this was true because General Stilwell was strongly gripped with certain attitudes highly favorable to the Chinese Communist cause and because with his vast authority as theater commander was able to give effect to those attitudes . . .

The germ of a military prejudice in favor of the Communists and against the Nationalists . . . became a violent infection when General Stilwell was brought into sharp collision with the Generalissimo by his wartime assignment in China.

From almost the beginning there were bitter disagreements between the two men which ultimately generated a consuming hatred of Chiang Kai-shek in General Stilwell's mind. . . . "The Manure Pile" [was] his name for the Generalissimo's wartime capital. . . . Peanut was General Stilwell's customary name for the Generalissimo . . . he was not only hostile to the Generalissimo, but very friendly to the Communists. . . . General Stilwell actually encouraged and instructed his staff to denigrate and belittle Chiang Kai-shek in the same manner . . .

APPENDIX II

Lattimore and OWI

The question of Hong Chew-sih and Chi Ch'ao-ting deserves some amplification. Hong and Chi's father were employed by Owen Lattimore during his tenure as the OWI's director of Pacific Operations. In the light of the Lattimore case, excerpts from his own testimony before the Tydings subcommittee and from certain inter-office memoranda of the United States Civil Service Commission acquire a certain significance.

From the testimony, 2 May 1950

SENATOR HICKENLOOPER: During your acquaintance with Mr. Chi, prior to the war or during the war, did you believe him to be or *did you learn him to be* a Communist at any time?

MR. LATTIMORE: No, sir; no sir.

SENATOR HICKENLOOPER: When did you first know that he was, in fact, a Communist?

MR. LATTIMORE: I do not know that he is, in fact, a Communist now, Senator.

SENATOR HICKENLOOPER: Is there any doubt in your mind that he would be here as the proposed representative of Communist China to the United Nations if he is not a Communist?

MR. LATTIMORE: It is possible, Senator. . . . [Italics added.]

And, again:

SENATOR HICKENLOOPER: Dr. Lattimore, during the time — or at any time during the time that you were the Director of Pacific Operations for the OWI did you believe, or *had you been reliably informed* that the *China Daily News,* in New York, was either a

Communist newspaper, Communist controlled, or had strong Communist leanings?

MR. LATTIMORE: No, sir; very definitely not. *My knowledge of the China Daily News, or the New China Daily News, whichever it was called in those days, in New York, came primarily from Dr. Chi, old Dr. Chi . . . whom I knew to be a staunch democrat and anti-Communist. . . .* [Italics added.]

The Civil Service Commission memoranda are a series of high-level communications concerning Hong Chew-sih, the old and the young Drs. Chi, and the *China Daily News* — all investigated by the Civil Service Commission and found to be completely Communist or so pro-Communist as to make the difference academic — and recounting official conversations with Owen Lattimore at which these findings were not only discussed at length but urged upon him. Also in the author's possession are the actual résumés of the investigator's conversations with Lattimore.[1]

The first of the memoranda, dated 12 October 1942 and written under the letterhead of the "Office of the Executive Director and Chief Examiner," recounted in considerable detail the Communist associations and activities of Hong Chew-sih and categorized the *China Daily News* as a Chinese version of the Communist *Daily Worker*. It concludes with a "finding of ineligibility" barring Hong from government employment. The second memorandum, dated 2 September 1943, is a report on discussions between CSC and three OWI representatives, including Lattimore, on the question of Hong's continued employment in the Office of War Information as a subordinate to Lattimore.

"Mr. Hong was discussed and they were fully advised regarding the substance of the derogatory information. . . ." the memorandum states. "The OWI representatives were also informed of the

[1] Perhaps not pertinent, but certainly interesting, is one statement made by the man who abhors "guilt by association" and deplores an "ordeal by slander." Explaining why he had fired a girl from OWI, Lattimore gave as one of his reasons that "there is a rumor that she used to be the girl friend of the former Chinese ambassador."

unfavorable information secured regarding Dr. Chi and his son, which included testimony to the effect that the young Dr. Chi is or was until recently a Communist and that he at one time was a delegate to the Third International in Moscow, and to the effect that the elder Dr. Chi was removed from his position as Commissioner of Education in the Shansi Province because of Communist activities." Lattimore's reaction to this is outlined: "The substance of Mr. Lattimore's statements was to the effect that he wants to retain Mr. Hong . . . *all evidence to the contrary notwithstanding*." [Italics added.] The CSC continued to rate Hong ineligible.

A third memorandum, dated 14 November 1943 and under the letterhead of the "Office of the Chief Law Officer," goes into great detail about long arguments with Lattimore over Hong and the two Drs. Chi. Lattimore is quoted verbatim:

"I know there is a law preventing the hiring of Communists. Personally and frankly, I would not be too worried if an individual Communist were in Hong's position."

The upshot of the discussions was that Hong and Dr. Chi were maintained in the OWI at Lattimore's insistence, even though the Civil Service Commission believed, but did not press its belief, that the men should be discharged. The ineligibility rating was removed "in view of Lattimore's knowledge of the complicated Chinese political situation."

With this background in mind, consider Lattimore's testimony that he never learned that Dr. Chi was a Communist, that he knew old Dr. Chi to be "a staunch democrat and anti-Communist," and that he was never "reliably informed" that the *China Daily News* had strong Communist leanings.

2

Before the McCarran Committee Owen Lattimore repeated his denials that he had ever been informed that Hong Chew-sih and the two Chis were Communists. On the last day of Lattimore's testimony, Senator McCarran made a long statement summarizing his opinions, as well as those of all members of the subcommittee, of Lattimore's performance on the stand. Before he began, he gave Lattimore a chance to make a final statement, but this opportunity was turned down. Later in the day, however, Lattimore issued a statement to the press. McCarran's summation, plus a *New York Times* report of Lattimore's press release, are appended here.

TEXT OF STATEMENT READ BY SENATOR McCARRAN ON BEHALF OF THE SENATE INTERNAL SECURITY SUBCOMMITTEE AT THE CONCLUSION OF TESTIMONY BY OWEN LATTIMORE, MARCH 21, 1952:

It has been the settled practice of this committee to reserve its conclusions, with respect to the substance of testimony that is taken, until the conclusion of the hearings on the particular matter under investigation. After careful consideration, however, this committee feels it proper at this time to make a statement with respect to the conduct of this witness, as a witness, during the time he has been before us. In doing this, the committee is not reversing its policy of reserving judgment. What the committee has to say now represents facts, not conclusions — not the findings of the committee, but its observations with respect to the deportment and conduct of Mr. Lattimore as a witness.

Mr. Lattimore came here at his own request to appear and testify. He came with a 50-page statement which was no casual document. It bore obvious indicia of careful preparation, and the witness testified he had been working on it for months, and had been assisted by his counsel. It was released to the Press before delivery, and Mr. Lattimore's invective was scattered to all parts of the country. Many times when asked if he had facts to support his insulting conclusions, the witness replied that he did not.

The committee has been confronted here with an individual so flagrantly defiant of the United States Senate, so outspoken in his discourtesy, and so persistent in his efforts to confuse and obscure the facts, that the committee feels constrained to take due notice of his conduct. The United States Senate is a constitutional institution, representing the states and the people thereof. A deliberate affront to the Senate of the United States, or to the Congress, is not necessarily an affront to the individuals who compose those bodies, but is an affront to the people of this nation, who are here represented.

The committee might have had a right to expect that a witness who claimed to be an objective scholar and a patriotic citizen would first objectively analyze the past policy of the United States in the Far East and help point the way to a determination of what has been wrong, and what corrective measures may be required. The committee might have had a right to expect that he would lend eager aid in exposing whatever communist infiltration there may have been in the Institute of Pacific Relations, or in any other organization in a position to exert influence on the thinking of our diplomats and the conduct of our foreign affairs. The committee might have had a right to expect that Mr. Lattimore's statement would be calm, temperate, and factual.

Instead, the committee was confronted with an initial fusillade of invective, and a consistently evasive, contentious, and belligerent attitude.

Suggestions have been made that the committee should seek to discipline Mr. Lattimore for his contumacious and contemptuous conduct.

Clearly, Mr. Lattimore did, on many occasions, stand in contempt of the committee. Clearly, he took that position voluntarily and intentionally. Mr. Lattimore used, toward the committee, language which was insolent, overbearing, arrogant, and disdainful. He flouted the committee, he scoffed at the committee's efforts, he impugned the committee's methods, and he slandered the committee's staff. His language was frequently such as to outrage and offend both the committee as a whole, and its members individually; and, apparently, with intent to do so.

There has been no striking-back on the part of the committee. The committee has employed no sanctions against Mr. Lattimore because, through forbearance, it has been found possible to make progress without disciplinary action. Despite Mr. Lattimore's recalcitrance at many points, the committee believes a record has been made covering his essential testimony with respect to the major matters here being investigated.

The fact remains that Mr. Lattimore was allowed to use the witness chair as a rostrum from which to attack the committee, its staff, and its hearings. He was, to use a phrase from his own prepared statement before the committee, "accorded the publicity facilities" of the committee's hearings; and the record shows in many ways that neither was he insensible of his opportunity in that regard, nor did he fail to take advantage of it. There is no other country in the world where a witness before a committee of the principal legislative body of the Nation would be granted any such latitude.

Few witnesses within the memory of the members of this committee have been permitted to use language as intemperate, provocative, and abusive of the committee, as Mr. Lattimore used in his prepared statement, which he was permitted to read. No witness, so far as any member of the Subcommittee can recall, ever before was given free rein to read, before a Senate Committee, a prepared statement so clearly contemptuous of the committee and of the Senate.

The committee is aware that in this direction lies one of the present dangers to our Democratic way of life: The fact that there are those in this country today who seek to use the right of free speech in furtherance of their efforts to set up a system within which freedom of speech will not exist. But the committee has preferred to err, if at all, on the side of allowing the witness too much latitude, rather than on the side of allowing too little. That preference does not include any predilection toward allowing a witness to escape reproof for contumacy.

Contumacy may take many forms, as Mr. Lattimore has demonstrated during his appearances here. Willful unresponsiveness is one of the forms of contumacy often resorted to by disputatious witnesses, and this witness has proved himself expert at disputation. The committee frequently found it extremely difficult to get Mr. Lattimore to give a direct answer; and on numerous occasions he was reluctant to give any responsive answer at all. This witness who had stated he was "not interested in fine or technical distinctions" proceeded throughout his testimony to split hairs with glib facility.

At times Mr. Lattimore refused to testify with respect to conclusions; at other times, he appeared eager to do so; and he did so testify on a number of occasions. In fact, in some instances he testified vehemently to conclusions which the committee found itself unable to draw from facts of record — as in the case of his testimony that he did not have any influence on United States Foreign Policy with respect to the Far East.

On this point, as on other matters of substance, the committee prefers to reserve its own conclusions. However, Mr. Lattimore's testimony is significant with respect to the facts. He testified that he wrote a letter to the President of the United States, in 1945, making certain statements with regard to conditions in the Far East, and urging a review of United States Foreign Policy with respect to the Far East, from which review then top officials of the State Department should be excluded. Mr. Lattimore testified that he saw the President personally, and left with him memoranda suggesting certain courses of action with respect to Japan and China; and that these memoranda included a recommendation for giving a larger measure of high authority to officials with China backgrounds.

Soon thereafter, according to Mr. Lattimore's own testimony, the then top officials of the State Department were replaced, including former Ambassador Grew. Further, the number and importance of top jobs in the State Department, held by persons with China backgrounds, was increased. Finally this witness testified that the policy advocated, shortly thereafter, in the so-called "Directive" of December 15, 1945, on China policy, and which our government sought to carry out in China, was substantially the same as the policy outlined in Mr. Lattimore's memoranda with respect to China; and that the policy adopted by the United States, with respect to Japan, was substantially the same as the policy with respect to Japan outlined in Mr. Lattimore's memoranda.

These facts, to which Mr. Lattimore testified before this committee, went unmentioned by him during his testimony before the Tydings Committee.

Mr. Lattimore has testified to having a type of memory with which the committee is quite familiar. With respect to some matters, he has demonstrated that his memory is extremely good. But he has testified that his memory was unreliable with respect to matters which ordinary men might be expected to remember most clearly. Very few men forget about their visits to the President of the United States, if the number of such visits is small. But Mr. Lattimore, who said he saw President Truman just once, wanted this

ommittee to believe he had forgotten the incident when he testi-
ied before the Tydings Committee with respect to his influence on
'oreign Policy.

Mr. Lattimore also has testified before this committee that all
luring that prior Senate investigation he forgot the fact that he had
. desk in the State Department Building for "four, five, or six"
nonths during the last war.

*The precise extent to which Mr. Lattimore gave untruthful testi-
nony before this committee will never be determined.* Human
imitations will prevent us from ever attaining the complete knowl-
dge of all his activities which would make it possible to assess each
tatement he has made and to catalogue fully whatever untruths he
nay have uttered. *That he has uttered untruths stands clear on the
ecord. Some of these have been so patent and so flagrant* as to merit
nention at this time, as illustrative of the conduct and attitude of
he witness. [Italics added.]

The witness testified concerning an occasion when he had lunch-
:on with the Soviet Ambassador to the United States. The date of
his luncheon was later placed as during the period when Soviet
Russia elected, for its own purposes, tc team up with the Nazi war
nachine. But in spite of the anxiety which free men throughout the
world experienced at the alliance of those two totalitarian colossi,
he witness testified that his luncheon with the Soviet Ambassador
ook place after the Soviet Union had abandoned its alliance with
he Nazis. Confronted later with evidence that the meeting took
place during the Hitler-Stalin Pact, the witness admitted he had
estified incorrectly.

In connection with that same matter, the witness testified there
nad been much publicity about his appointment as advisor to Chiang
Kai-shek, at the time of his meeting with the Soviet Ambassador,
with whom he had discussed the appointment, though the record
shows that the announcement of the appointment was not made until
eleven days after the luncheon meeting in question.

The witness testified that he never read an article by a Mr. T. A.
Bisson which had provoked considerable controversy within the
Institute of Pacific Relations in 1943. He testified further that the
expressions of opinion in that article were contrary to what he himself was writing at that time. Thereafter the witness identified a
letter over his own signature which indicated that he had not only

read the Bisson article but had agreed with it; and that the only fault he found with it was that the underlying thoughts could have been expressed more convincingly.

Mr. Lattimore has given us many plausible but differing answers as to when he realized that Frederick V. Field was pro-Communist. The witness and Field have been shown by frequent and extensive testimony to have been closely associated in the Institute of Pacific Relations. The witness initially testified that he discovered that Field was pro-Communist some time in the 1940s, and not until then. When presented with a letter which he said he received in 1939, and which clearly reflected the communist expressions of Mr. Field, the witness said that "judging from this letter my memory was in error by about two years."

Later in the hearings, the witness was shown to have recommended the same Mr. Field, at a time subsequent to 1939, as a person who could supply personnel for the Defense Advisory Commission. Thereupon Mr. Lattimore avoided admitting that he had recommended to the Defense Advisory Commission a man whom he knew to be at least pro-Communist, by reversing his preceding testimony.

In going back to his original position, he stated that at the time when he testified his "memory was in error by about two years," his admission was not accurate because he was weary from long days of examinations. This explanation took no account of the fact that the admission in question took place during the first day of examination after the witness had finished reading his statement, and apparently ignored the existence of the letter which had impelled the first change in testimony on this point.

The witness made no similar claim of being unsure of himself when he testified erroneously with respect to handling Mr. Lauchlin Currie's mail. In reply to the question "Is it your testimony that you did not, at the request of Lauchlin Currie, take care of his mail at the White House when he was away?" Mr. Lattimore replied "That certainly is my statement."

Subsequently, Mr. Lattimore identified a letter which he had written in July 1942 which included the statement: "Currie asked me to take care of his correspondence while he was away and in view of your telegram of today, I think I had better tell you that he has gone to China on a special trip. This news is absolutely confidential until released to the Press." When confronted with this letter, the witness said: "Obviously my memory was inaccurate."

When the witness was asked, in connection with discussion of a trip he had made in 1937 to Communist Headquarters in China, "Did you or anyone in your party make pre-arrangements with the Communist Party in order to get in?" he answered, "None whatever." He was then presented with the text of an article which he had written for the London *Times,* and was asked if the statements in that article were true. After he affirmed that they were, he read into the record from that article — his own article — the statement: "I sent a letter to the Red Capitol by ordinary mail and got in answer — a cordial invitation."

These are all instances of significant untruths, established as such. They all concern matters of obvious importance to this committee in trying to determine the nature of the organization, methods of operation, and influence of the Institute of Pacific Relations. The committee attempts to draw no conclusions from these matters at this time.

Aside from matters of self-contradiction, the record contains also instances of testimony by this witness concerning matters with respect to which other witnesses have testified to the exact opposite. Some of these instances concern matters which are highly relevant to the subject of the committee's inquiry and which are substantial in import.

For example: Over a period of two years, first before the Senate Foreign Relations Committee of the United States Senate, later before this committee in Executive Session, and then again before us in open session, Mr. Lattimore stated that he did not know that Dr. Ch'ao-ting Chi was a Communist. Dr. Ch'ao-ting Chi was a man shown to have been an associate of the witness, and the witness admitted the association. But Mr. Lattimore testified that no one had told him that Chi was a Communist, or shown him a report that Chi was a Communist, or given him any reason whatever to believe that Chi was a Communist.

On the other hand, Professor Karl Wittfogel of Columbia University, a witness before this committee, and E. Newton Steeley of the Review Board of the Civil Service Commission, have given testimony that flatly contradicts Mr. Lattimore's clear and unequivocal assertions in this regard.

Another instance concerns the question of whether Mr. Lattimore knew that a certain German Communist who wrote under the pseudonym of "Asiaticus" for the publication *Pacific Affairs* while Lattimore was editing it, was, in fact, a Communist. Mr. Lattimore has flatly asserted that he did not know or have reason to believe this writer to be a Communist. Contra, the record contains the testimony of Professor Karl Wittfogel that he did tell Mr. Lattimore about the Communist background and the Communist affiliation of "Asiaticus." Minutes of meetings in Moscow, taken from the files of the Institute of Pacific Relations, and a letter written by Mr. Lattimore, are among the items of evidence in the record which also purport to show that Mr. Lattimore knew or believed "Asiaticus" to be a Communist writer.

One of the most important, relevant, and substantial questions respecting which the committee has been seeking the truth is whether, when this witness was working with, and publishing articles for, certain Communists, he knew them to be Communists. The finding on this question is essential to a proper characterization of a whole series of actions by Mr. Lattimore, and will directly affect the committee's ultimate findings with respect to the Institute of Pacific Relations.

The shaping of United States Policy with respect to China was a factor in the success of Communism in that land, in the establishment of firm roots for Soviet influence in all Asia and in the subsequent ordeal through which United States boys now are being taken in Korea. If this policy in its initial stages, or at any time, was affected by acts or stratagems on the part of anyone having any slightest purpose except the welfare of this Nation, it would be a matter not to be lightly dealt with, nor one which the American people should easily overlook or forget. The intimate knowledge which this witness had of Asia and of Asiatic affairs, coupled with his deliberate and adroit attempts to mould American thinking with respect to those affairs, including his effort to establish certain concepts in the mind of the Chief Executive of the United States, necessarily bring this witness within the orbit of any realistic appraisal of this whole situation. When, in the face of the record, he undertook before this committee a deliberate attempt to deny or cover up pertinent facts, this witness placed himself in a most unenviable position.

THE *New York Times* REPORT, BY WILLIAM S. WHITE: [2]

WASHINGTON, March 21 [1952]: . . . Tonight Professor Lattimore issued a statement asserting that he had been "vigorous" but not "contemptuous," and had only "stood up to a savage and harassing examination, persisted in for so many days that it has, I am told, broken all Congressional records."

He added that Mr. McCarran had labeled as "an untruth every lapse or conflict of memory in my answers to questions ranging over many years and complicated events — many of them trivial and all of them related to events many years ago."

As to his manner on the stand, the professor said: "I cannot be temperate about an attack upon my loyalty, whatever its source or the forum. I refuse to defend myself by cringing and I do not believe my fellow citizens expect it of me."

. . . Professor Lattimore in his statement tonight asserted that Senator McCarran's summing up and the conduct of the hearings "justify the rueful prediction that I made in my opening statement that I could not expect a fair hearing."

He was not "defiant" of the Senate, he added, "but I do not believe that this means that a citizen must knuckle under or allow himself to be subjected to outrageous attack without striking back in self-defense."

[2] Such deletions as occur in this *Times* story deal solely with Senator McCarran's statement.

APPENDIX III

Dubinsky on Carter

On the stand before the McCarran Committee, Edward C. Carter discussed Harriet C. Moore as follows:

MR. MORRIS: Was [Miss Moore] a Communist?

MR. CARTER: No.

MR. MORRIS: You were associated with Russian War Relief?

MR. CARTER: I was.

MR. MORRIS: Do you remember if she was secretary of Russian War Relief?

MR. CARTER: Yes.

MR. MORRIS: Do you remember David Dubinsky, the head of the International Ladies' Garment Workers' Union, who refused to make any contributions to [Russian War Relief] as long as Harriet Moore remained as secretary?

MR. CARTER: . . . Oh yes, I had several hours with Mr. Dubinsky later after he made his protest. He conceded there must have been another Harriet Moore. That Harriet Moore was ten years older and six inches shorter than the other Harriet Moore.

Morris immediately wrote to David Dubinsky, asking him for his version of the disagreement over Miss Moore. Dubinsky's answer, inserted in the record twelve days later, raised some interesting questions about Carter's veracity as well as his politics.

Exhibit No. 69–A

INTERNATIONAL LADIES' GARMENT WORKERS' UNION
NEW YORK, N.Y., *August 3, 1951.*

Mr. Robert Morris,
Special Counsel, Internal Security Subcommittee,
Committee on the Judiciary, United States Senate,
Washington, D.C.

DEAR MR. MORRIS:

I have your letter of August 1, together with excerpts of testimony given by Edward C. Carter before the Senate Internal Security Subcommittee on July 26, in which my name and that of the International Ladies' Garment Workers' Union, of which I am president, are mentioned.

I note Mr. Carter's statement to the effect that our refusal to participate in Russian War Relief because of the important position held in that organization as secretary by Miss Harriet Moore was based on mistaken identity.

At the outset, I want to emphatically deny his statement that I have ever "conceded" that my objection to Miss Moore was based on an error of identity. Mr. Carter's correspondence in 1941 did not even bring up the subject of another Miss Moore to whom he now refers.

Our attitude concerning Miss Moore and her record has not changed in the slightest, although we later on contributed funds to Russian War Relief. This being the case, I deem it advisable to give a little of the history of the entire matter.

When Russian War Relief was organized in 1941 and an appeal was made to us to contribute to it, we had a study made of the officers because of our opposition to participating in any Communist-front organization. A member of our staff was assigned to this task and he submitted to us the enclosed memorandum. Based on this report, we definitely refused to be associated with Russian War Relief in any way and decided to make our contribution for Russian relief through the American Red Cross.

Several months later, Russian War Relief also made an appeal to the Rockefellers, who, having learned of our union's opposition to Russian War Relief, were interested in ascertaining the reason for our position in this matter. We thereupon submitted this same memorandum to them, and they too, based on the facts contained in the memorandum, refused to participate in the fund. Mr. Carter, fearful that this may affect the drive generally, formally inquired as to the reason for our opposition to Russian War Relief.

While this memorandum raised questions in our minds about Mr. Carter's own associations, it gave concrete evidence that Miss Moore was definitely tied up with communistic activities. We therefore contended that, so long as she remained in the key position of secretary, our union would refuse to cooperate with Russian War Relief. We were subsequently notified by Mr. Carter that Miss Moore had resigned her post. Thereupon we changed our position and transmitted to Russian War Relief approximately $500,-000 over a period of a number of years.

Quite sometime later, we learned that Mr. Carter, although complying technically with his promise to us as the head of the organization, in typical Communist fashion placed Miss Moore in another equally important position in Russian War Relief.

Now I learn that Mr. Carter is using my name and that of the International Ladies' Garment Workers' Union to alibi himself and Miss Harriet Moore in the proceedings before you.

Sincerely yours,

DAVID DUBINSKY,

PRESIDENT, INTERNATIONAL LADIES' GARMENT WORKERS' UNION

APPENDIX IV

Memo to Marshall

CONFIDENTIAL

June 10, 1947

From: Senate Appropriations Committee

To: Secretary of State, George C. Marshall

It becomes necessary due to the gravity of the situation to call your attention to a condition that developed and still flourishes in the State Department under the Administration of Dean Acheson.

It is evident that there is a deliberate, calculated program being carried out not only to protect Communist personnel in high places, but to reduce security and intelligence protection to a nullity.

Regarding the much-publicized MARZANI case, the evidence brought out at his trial was well known to State Department officers, who ignored it and refused to act for a full year.

MARZANI and several other department officials, with full knowledge of the State Department, and with government time and money, promoted a scheme called PRESENTATIONS, INC., which contracted with a Communist dominated organization to disseminate propaganda.

Security objections to these and other even more dangerous developments were rebuffed by high administrative officials; and there followed the substitution of unqualified men for these competent, highly respected personnel who theretofore held the intelligence and security assignments in the department. The new chief of controls is a man utterly devoid of background and experience for the job, who is and at the time of his appointment was known to those who appointed him to be, a cousin and close associate of a suspected Soviet espionage agent. The next development was the refusal of the FBI, G–2, ONI and other Federal investigative agencies to continue the wholehearted cooperation they had for years extended to the State Department.

On the file in the department is a copy of a preliminary report of the FBI on Soviet espionage activities in the United States, which involves a large number of State Department employes, some in high official positions. This report has been challenged and ignored by those charged with the responsibility of administering the department with the apparent tacit approval of Mr. Acheson. Should this case break before the State Department acts, it will be a national disgrace.

Voluminous files are on hand in the department proving the connection of the State Department employes and officials with this Soviet espionage ring. Despite this, only two persons, one of whom is MARZANI, were released under the McCarran rider because of their subversive activity.

1. * * * * *		6. * * * * *
2. * * * * *		7. * * * * *
3. * * * * *		8. * * * * *
4. * * * * *		9. * * * * *
5. * * * * *		

are only a few of the hundreds now employed in varying capacities who are protected and allowed to remain despite the fact that their presence is an obvious hazard to national security. There is also the extensive employment in highly classified positions of admitted homosexuals, who are historically known to be security risks.

The War and Navy Departments have been thwarted for a year in their efforts to carry out the German Scientist program. They are blocked by one man in the State Department, a protégé of Acheson named *****, who is also the chief instrument in the subverting of the over-all security program.

This deplorable condition runs all the way up and down the line. Assistant Secretary Braden also surrounded himself with men like ***** and with ***** who has a notorious international reputation. The network also extends into the office of Assistant Secretary Benton.

SUBCOMMITTEE OF SENATE APPROPRIATIONS COMMITTEE

APPENDIX V

Investigation of State Department

Excerpts re State Department, from transcript of meeting of Loyalty Review Board February 13, 14, 1951, Washington, D. C.:

February 13, 1951

Chairman Bingham: . . . As you all know, and especially those of you who live in this vicinity, we have been under fire now pretty seriously for some time, and particularly recently. That is due to two events — one the appointment by the President of a new Board to oversee us and examine our records and see what we have been doing and why, and also to examine what is going on in the general field of security in the country. Also, the Senate has finally adopted the resolution of Senator McCarran and given him money enough to start his investigation — a sub-committee of Judiciary Committee to investigate the Loyalty Program, particularly with reference to the State Department.

You perhaps saw in the paper yesterday that they have already started to function; and by a surprise move, using their powers of subpoena, they went up to Massachusetts and entered a barn or a place of refuge there from which they took a truckload of important documents belonging to the Institute of Pacific Relations and brought them down to Washington. I believe they are up on the Hill and about to be investigated. I am told that there may be some very interesting documents in that file. Also, as has not been publicized, the Appropriations Committee of the House is now starting its work on the new appropriation bills, and they are making a special point of asking members of the different departments how many persons in their office have been investigated, what the results of these investigations were, how many have been fired, if not, why not, etc.

So, your new Chairman, only five or six weeks on the job, is now faced with three investigations, and the Board is under fire. I am told there was an article in the morning paper — the *New York Times* — by Mr. Krock, answering, in a way, the attacks made on us by Senator Ferguson on the floor of the Senate the other day. Senator Ferguson said some things about the Board which were at least exaggerated, if not entirely unfair, and Mr. Krock, I believe, has pointed out the difference.

I have had conferences with four of the Senators who have attacked us on the floor of the Senate. I had very pleasant meetings with Senator Ferguson, Senator McCarran, Senator McCarthy, and Senator Hickenlooper. The general impression which I have gathered is that our troubles are due, in large part, to the words of the standard as set up by the Presidential Order — Executive Order 9835 — which set up this Board and gave us the standard. [pp. 5–6]

Consequently, it is not strange that the two Government departments which are most closely concerned with such matters [infiltration of Communists into the Government, etc.], namely, the State Department and the Department of Commerce, who have more to do with foreign nations and with export controls and with our plans and dealings than any other departments — should both be anxious to have this change to [standard of "reasonable doubt"] made by the President.

Clark: One of the most interesting cases we have had is not in the ordinary run, but it had to do with a man who had written a great deal. He had broadcast for the State Department, but years before, he had been separated from the service on a charge of disloyalty while working out West. There was a red flag in the records on him, yet the evidence was completely persuasive that his conduct had been loyal right along. In getting a position which he had been holding with — I think it was the International Labor Organization — he had failed to reveal the fact that his service in one of the agencies — I have forgotten which one it was — had been terminated on that ground. He simply omitted it from his statement.

. . . It was a very stupid thing to conceal the fact that that had happened to him, but there was no question in our minds that there was not reasonable ground to believe that he was disloyal; yet we felt that there was a question as to security risk where a man concealed a material fact with regard to his record, and we so reported, as a Committee of this Board, and I understand that that practically bars him from future service. It was a very hard thing for us to do. We debated about it. I think Mr. Shattuck and Mr. LaRoe and I sat on that for a long time, and yet we did feel that concealment of that fact while applying for a position, which was not in our Civil Service, was an act that indicated untrustworthiness on his part . . . so he is now forever barred.

I think that all of us have felt that with regard to incumbents, the present test, if we could only get the evidence, is a fair test. . . . In the case of applicants, I am strongly in favor of the suggested change. . . . [pp. 17–18]

Chairman: . . . The situation with regard to a few of the cases that I have had the opportunity of studying has led me to the belief that we should change. For instance, in the State Department there is a case of a man who might be said to be a rather "weak sister." There is no evidence that he is a Communist. His wife, on the other hand, who is not in the State Department, has a very close association with Communists. She, at one time, saw a good deal of them in the days before they went underground in Washington. I will try to make this as short as possible.

I came to this conclusion: That living with his wife, he was undoubtedly loyal to his wife; and from all the evidence he couldn't be loyal to his wife and at the same time be loyal to the U.S. Government in the sense in which I think loyalty deserves to be used. There is no way in which you can get him out of the Government service under the present rule, but you can certainly have reasonable doubt as to his loyalty. . . . [p. 21]

Hoag: . . . As far as the State Department is concerned, I don't understand their position at all, because although their board has not held their people ineligible under the loyalty test, who should have been held ineligible under that test, they have plenty of power to remove them as a security risk. *Why haven't they exercised it?* They haven't exercised it, in spite of all the searchlights that have been turned upon them. It seems to me that we should decide whether we are going to consider security risk (apropos of earlier statements by Chairman, etc.) and if we want to stick to loyalty, let's stick to loyalty as it is written down. In the minds of the public, there would be no difference. If there is reasonable doubt of a man's loyalty, it's going to be just as hard on him as if it is believed that he is disloyal, in spite of Webster's Dictionary.

Lee: I of course concur with Mr. Hoag with reference to the security risk business, because I think that it is the most important thing that we have, and it is my intention to discuss it later, but at this time you do not wish to discuss it. You wish to take up security later, is that correct?

Chairman: We did not put security on the agenda. It involves such a wide field that I'd hate to get away from the matter before us, because, notwithstanding what Mr. Hoag said, I am informed by a good many people here in the Government that if we change — if the President will change it to "reasonable doubt" — it will about double the number of cases that can be thrown out which cannot be thrown out now. In fact, I have had various members of the Board tell me that there were cases before them, under which, if they had been able to use the words "reasonable doubt" which were used in President Roosevelt's original War Service Regulations, they could have found the incumbent ineligible; whereas under the present rule, they couldn't so find him, so I hope that we will not get into a security discussion.

Lee: . . . If, as the Chairman has said, the Secretary of Commerce and the Secretary of State, as well as a number of other people in Government, urge the changing, and there may be a great deal of good, and I certainly urge that this Board recommend that the change be made. . . . [pp. 24–26]

Mr. Amen: Mr. Chairman, I have always gone on the theory, and I think other members of the Board have also, that if a person was shown to be a Communist or there was serious evidence to that effect at any time in the past, there was a presumption that that condition continued up to and including the present time, unless there was positive evidence of some rejection of the previous philosophy. Consequently, I don't see that there would be any practical difference at all that would result from the change of wording.

For instance, in the Remington case, if the panel here had found that in the past Remington was a Communist and nothing had happened to change it in between time, which certainly does not appear to have happened, then they would find under the present tense that at the time of the hearing he was disloyal, so I don't see how the tense — the changing of the wording — is actually going to change the consideration. . . . It may be that the State Department thinks so, or it may be that they are merely apologizing for something, but as a practical matter, I can't see any real difference in the test that would result from the alternative wording that we are talking about. Of course, it is true that we could say so — in a way, apologizing or explaining for a lot of decisions which have become unpopular, but, actually, I don't see any difference, as far as incumbents are concerned.

Alger: I think that the changing of the rule now will reflect on every case which we have previously decided. The assumption would be that if we had only had a different rule, a long line of these people would have been thrown out. I don't think it would have made any real difference, but if you change the rule now, after three years of efforts, and say, "If we had had this rule before, we could have thrown more people out," it simply reflects on every case that we have decided in three years.

Miss Glass: Does it have a bit of a look that we are currying favor with the Nimitz Committee before it gets under way? I don't like that, if that's what we are doing.

Chairman: May I say that I had talked with quite a number of people and faced the situation which I now face before anyone ever thought of the Nimitz Board. In fact, I had taken the position that it seemed to me very difficult to operate the Board in wartime under the present rule. . . . [pp. 27–28]

Mr. Lee (to Miss Perkins): On this loyalty business — now, take the Service case, where the record shows that the man was living over there with a Chinese woman who we know and the record shows was under the pay of the Russian Government, and he's in love with that woman, and you say that he can be loyal, perfectly loyal to this Government, and he's a safe employee for the State Department, when we know that he's living with a woman who's under the pay of the Russian Government, but we are prohibited from passing on that or finding him disloyal. [Perkins had stated, p. 33, on discussion of meaning of loyalty, etc., "I cannot say that I think from a knowledge of human nature that because we can see that a man is loyal to his wife necessarily means that he is a Communist and disloyal to his country. He is not required . . . in the sacrament of matrimony to promise he will support her in all of her political and economic views, and I cannot see that there would be the slightest difficulty to an individual faced with that. . . . I think we should be very slow to conclude that a marriage, or a relationship of father and daughter—there was one such in the Commerce Department—involves the individuals in a divided loyalty. . . .]

Perkins: I would say he was unsuitable for public service.

Lee: But under the present rule, this Board is bound to report him as a loyal employee [anent discussion about Board not permitted to pass on suitability].

Perkins: But you can report him to the Civil Service Commission.

Lee: No, we are prohibited from doing that. And the status of it is that we have been committing a fraud on the public. . . .

Clark: In this particular case he came over to this country with the intention of divorcing his wife who had borne him two children so that he could marry this Chinese girl.

Chairman: I am informed that when the Civil Service Commission finds a person suitable in the first place, and he becomes an employee, that the Civil Service Commission is not in any position to go back on its original action.

James Mitchell: That is correct.

Perkins: But we do frequently bring to the attention of the employing agency information which comes to us and which we think they should consider as to the retention of the employee. He could be placed under charges for that and dismissed for unsuitable conduct—conduct unbecoming an officer of the Government.

Lee: It would take three or four years to get rid of employees that way.

Meloy: The agencies had all these cases before them. They had gone through their loyalty boards and their security officers before they reached us.

You were talking about the Service case—that was passed on

three times by the State Department's Loyalty and Security Board, and now it's before us for post-audit; so all the information we have has been known to them for two years. All the cases that come to us come to us either on post-audit after going through the lower board or on appeal after going through the lower board. . . . [p. 39]

[Page 52 — motion to authorize Chairman to propose to Nimitz Board, and to President through Civil Service Commission, change of standard to "reasonable doubt" was passed 13 to 5.]

[Re Item III on Agenda, Composition of Agency Board Panels: (Reference to Veterans Administration case; two of three board members were friends of employee, etc.; also refers to board of three who are subordinates of employee, etc.)]

Meloy: In the third case, we found that the State Department had a hearing and only the Chairman, Mr. Snow, sat through the entire hearing. In fact, there was a series of hearings — probably three — but the other members of the Board changed and no member, other than Mr. Snow, sat throughout the case. We thought that we should admonish the boards that when they hear a case the hearing panel should consist of the same persons and go completely through the case, rather than keep changing the members as the case progressed through its hearing.

Collins: That ought to be a directive. [Motion to that effect.]

Chairman: . . . I am familiar with the case, having studied it myself. There was only one member of the Board who confronted all the witnesses. After the first hearing or two, one Board member in the State Department was sent abroad on a mission to Gibraltar, or some other place, and then after the next hearing, another member of the Board was given some other duty. Also, in that particular case, there were several occasions, as I read the testimony, where the Chairman of the State Department board permitted remarks to be made off the record, which is all you have in studying the case — what is said. In that case, also, he permitted the wife of the incumbent to be present during all the hearings and to coach her husband on what he had said in the affidavit.

Twohy: He probably got off.

Chairman: That was against the rule. . . .

Meloy: We've —

Chairman: I called attention to the Secretary of State myself to the fact that "You've got to tell the Loyalty Board members to behave themselves." [Motion i.p.s. carried.] [pp. 75–77]

Meloy: Item No. IX grows out of a practice which the State Department has pursued more vigorously than any other agency. In our regulations we provide that after the hearing the agency board, under mitigating circumstances and where national security is not involved, may permit the man to resign, rather than have a finding of ineligibility against him.

Now that, primarily, as I remember it, at the time we put it in the regulations was so that the service records of the Government would show a resignation, rather than a discharge for loyalty, but it has come to my attention that the State Department, throughout the program for two and one-half years, has not discharged a single person on the grounds of loyalty. What they do is to bring the employee in and say, "Now, we are going to file charges against you unless you resign," so the man resigns, or they'll hold a hearing and bring him in and tell him, "We are about to render a decision of ineligibility against you unless you resign." I have called their attention two or three times to the fact that that section was put in there for the protection of the employee, but they have taken the opposite position and say, "Now, you folks put it in. We're going to use it," and they've used it in that way, and have caused seven people to resign where they would normally have gone on through the hearing.

Now, I don't object to that so much up to that point, but they even go up on appeal to the person who hears it from the Secretary, and if he comes out adversely, they permit the appellant to resign.

They have gone a step further. In their regulations submitted to us just recently, they provide that they are going to permit people to resign. No other agency has done that in any of their regulations, and the State Department is taking the initiative in forcing people to resign under that section. It affects the Civil Service Commission in this way:

The Civil Service Commission rules and regulations say that if a person resigns from an agency, if there is anything in his record which affects his re-employment, on Form 50, which is a Personnel Action Sheet of which Civil Service gets a copy, the agency is supposed to put down under "Remarks" those factors that may affect his re-employment, such as an investigation pending under Executive Order 9835.

When they operate as they do — merely showing a resignation of the individual and he has this copy from the State Department — he immediately goes over to another agency and says, "I have worked for the State Department for five years. Here's my Personnel Action Sheet. I resigned a few weeks ago." There's nothing on the Personnel Action Sheet to tell the Personnel Officer that there is an investigation on that person. He gets a job, or the person may be interested in him for other employment, and has to go running around to the Government to find out that there is an investigation on the man.

I think, in view of the fact that the State Department is taking advantage of our own regulations in forcing people to resign, we should revoke the regulation. People are resigning every day in the Government, and it wasn't our intention to give departments and agencies a weapon with which to club the employee over the head to make him resign, but it is to be used in extraordinary circumstances where the Board felt that there were mitigating circumstances, even after finding him ineligible.

The State Department hasn't had a single rating of ineligibility, and it is due to this one thing. They are going to tell that to the Admiral's board and they are going to tell that to McCarran's board, and I think we are just sticking our necks out here and protecting the State Department when we didn't intend it to be used that way at all.

Shattuck: Mr. Chairman, might that not be taken care of by having such situations flagged in the record as a resignation while charges were pending, and have that appear in the record as a warning?

Meloy: Yes, we flag every case of resignation that comes to us, but there are probably 10,000 places where people could be employed in the Government today and they don't have the benefit of flag records. Furthermore, it takes quite a long while to put the flag records into all the positions where they could flag the man. It isn't a question of flagging. It is a question that we have given the State Department a weapon with which to beat the individual over the head.

Hoag: If you revoke this, why can't they follow the same procedure and say, "If you don't resign, we'll hold a hearing?"

Meloy: They can, but they won't be hiding behind our regulations. . . . [Provision re resignation revoked — pointed out employee can still resign if he wants to. As to noting circumstances of resignation, Meloy states that is merely a staff problem to see that agencies carry out their duty — Chairman says to take up with Civil Service Commission.] [pp. 90–96]

[Discussion of security risks; ten agencies have power to "summarily dismiss for security," Meloy notes, ". . . security not LRB field. . . ."]

Meloy: . . . Here's a problem that came to me recently: I had a call from the Army. They said, "We have a man over here, and we don't know what to do with him. Maybe you know him. You remember when the two flyers left Russia last summer and flew to Germany and they were brought to the U. S.? We have one of those persons on our payroll and here's our problem: Central Intelligence Agency, the State Department, and one other department brought this man to the U. S. and they vouched for him. We've got to feed him, I guess." They got him over here, so they put one of them on the Army payroll. The Army put through the Form 84 for his security search, but the FBI said, "We won't search him. You brought him over here, you know he is a Russian, and you are responsible for him." So the FBI won't get into this.

The State Department said, "We got him over here. We think he is a security risk. We don't say he's loyal. We have no use for him, but we are getting information from him. The FBI won't investigate him, and your regulations say that we have to put in a Form 84. Can you help us out?" I know the Government today is hiring disloyal people in some jobs in order to get information from them.

Now, the agency knows that man is a security risk, but they're getting something from him that they want. As soon as they get it, he is off, so I don't think the question of security is our job at all — to tell an agency that an employee is a security risk when they have their own security officer and their own security setup.

Alger: Why should he be an employee at all?

Meloy: He shouldn't be one at all.

Alger: What they ought to have is some money so they could get some people, but not make them Federal employees.

Meloy: You have 900 citizens from Germany here today. They have been over here for months and months. Fortunately, we have never run across them. They put them under public law contract and pay them so much a day, and they stay off our program. They could take these Russians and pay them $10 a day under Public Law 726 and then they wouldn't fall under our program. . . . But . . . if we get into security, we are going to get into something we can't handle . . . loyalty and security are all ramifying. [pp. 101–2]

Clark: What are you going to do when the attorney who is presenting the charges acts as though he were the attorney for the incumbent? I read 100 pages of a record where the three members of the board were acting as attorneys for the employee.

Meloy: You are talking about an agency case, I presume — the Elliott case?

Clark: No, I am talking about the —

Meloy: Oh, you're talking about the State Department. They're taking the attitude that they're there to clear the employee, and not to protect the Government. We've been arguing with them since the program started.

Hoag: That brings up a question that has been on my mind a little, and I have been accused a few times in connection with it. I have been disturbed about the State Department — their remarkable record of never having fired anybody for loyalty, and yet we do nothing about it as far as the Board is concerned.

I don't doubt that Larry [Meloy] does all he can in the echelons that he can reach, but I have been troubled about whether or not we owe the duty of having somebody call the attention of the President, for example, to the fact that the program simply does not work in that department, and let him worry about it. It seems to me we assume some responsibility when we sit back for three years and know that the country rests in a false sense of security that we are looking after their interests here when we know darn well that it is completely ineffective in one of the most important departments of the Government, and I wonder whether we ought to say anything to anybody about it.

Our functions under the Order are not only those of the appellate court, but to supervise. It is quite intended that we shall keep a weather eye on the whole problem and presumably do something about it when we find that there are fallacies and weaknesses, and I wonder if any of the other members of the Board have a like feeling.

Chairman: Your present Chairman thought about that for a couple of weeks and took counsel of two persons in whom he had confidence, and then asked for an appointment with the Secretary of State. The Secretary of State, who is a very busy man, very graciously gave me an appointment last Friday afternoon. As I say, he is a very busy man. He has all this business of the great debate and of the United Nations, etc., on his mind. I called his attention to the fact that his board was out of step with all other agency boards. In the Post Office Department, 10 percent of all persons examined were found to be worthy of separation from the Government. In the Commerce Department, 6½ percent. The average was about 6 percent. The State Department, zero.

The Secretary of State was very much impressed by what I said. He received my remarks very kindly. He asked me one or two questions about resignations, and so on. When I showed him my confidential statement, he was greatly impressed. He said, "I will take the matter up at once." That was Friday afternoon.

He obviously took it up Monday morning, because Monday afternoon at 2:30 one of his security officers called to know whether anybody at the State Department had been up here to oppose any change in the regulations. I talked over with the Secretary of State the change which you authorized me to suggest to the President yesterday, and he was very heartily in favor of it and very anxious about it. He said no one in the State Department could possibly have said a word against it. It has now been called to their attention. There are quite a number of cases pending before that board. I feel quite certain from the attitude of the Secretary of State that there was very great attention paid to what I told him.

I hadn't been instructed by the Board to do it, but I thought it was my duty to do it, so it is known now to the Secretary of State, and as he is very close to the President, I presume it will be known to him. I also called the attention of the Secretary of State to the fact that the Nimitz Board might ask us a question with regard to these different departments; that I was fairly sure that the new McCarran Committee of five would ask us about the record of dismissals, and so forth, and also that I knew that the present Appropriations Committee in the House was asking the departments that come before it how many they had fired. So the matter is known now to the Administration and I think will be taken care of.

I trust that the Board feels that I did not overstep my authority in going to the Secretary of State. I felt that it was my duty to call his attention to the fact, because, after all, we are working for the United States Government and for the security of the nation.

Clark: Mr. Chairman, I move we enthusiastically ratify the action of our Chairman.

Index

ACHESON, DEAN, 50, 125, 159, 161n.,
167, 168, 169, 170, 173, 196, 197,
198, 200, 201, 204, 205, 207n., 209,
235, 236
Achilles, Theodore, 150
Adler, Solomon, 132, 132n., 133, 133n.
"Alex" (pseudonym), 49, 68
All-China Labor Federation, 43
Allen, James S., 183
Alsop, Joseph, 177n., 218
Amerasia Magazine, 125, 133, 135, 140,
142–149, 151–153, 164, 165, 166, 167,
182, 192
Amerasia Case, xi, 125–169, 172–173,
175–176, 178, 182, 199, 209
American Council of Learned Societies,
145, 162, 183
American Council on Soviet Relations,
144
American Friends of the Chinese People,
144
American League for Peace and Democ-
racy, 144
American Peace Mobilization, 182, 187n.,
191
Amsterdam Handelsblatt, 70
Anderson, Donald, 164
Anti-Comintern Pact, 4, 69, 97, 99
Arcos Ltd., 37
Arent, Albert, 165
Army Pearl Harbor Board, 120, 121
Asahi Shimbun, 29, 33
"Asiaticus" (pseudonym), 186, 187n.,
230

BALLANTINE, JOSEPH, 160
Barmine, Alexander, 184, 185, 186

Barnes, Joseph F., 183
Barnett, Robert W., 179
Barsky, Edward, 144
Battle Hymn of China, 55, 56
Bentley, Elizabeth T., 90, 132n., 133n.,
162n., 184, 187n.
Benton, William, 236
Bergen Kurier, 70
Berkey, Russell S., 204
Berliner Tageblatt, 86
"Bernhardt" (pseudonym), *see* Wendt,
Bruno
Berzin, General, 41, 43, 46, 67, 68, 69,
185, 186
Beuren, Archbold van, 135, 140
Bielaski, Frank Brooks, 136–142, 148
Bingham, Hiram, 170, 171
"Bird, Alice" (pseudonym), *see* Smedley,
Agnes
Bisson, T. A., 124, 125, 136, 227, 228
Blaine, James G., 181
Bloch, Kurt, 179
Bluecher, Vassily C. (pseudonym), 30
32, 51
Blumenthal, Annette, 150, 152, 164
Borg, Dorothy, 179
Borodin, Michael, 30, 31, 32, 51
Bowles, Chester T., 191n.
Braden, Spruille A., 236
Breakfast Group, 87, 116
Brecht, Bertold, 12
Brewster, Owen, 207n.
Bridges, Styles, 199n., 204
Browder, Earl, 43, 57, 144, 174, 186,
190
Brunauer, Esther Caukin, 194
Budenz, Louis, 174, 184, 186

Bukharin, Nikolai, 18, 28, 36
Burma, viii
Bykov, Boris, 33*n.*
Byrnes, James, 167, 196, 199

CARLSON, EVANS, 124, 183
Carnegie Endowment for International Peace, 178, 183
Carter, Edward C., 103, 118, 119, 143, 179, 180–182, 184*n.*, 185, 186, 187–189, 190, 191, 192, 233, 234
Celler, Emanuel, 162
Central Intelligence Agency, 246
Chambers, Whittaker, 33*n.*, 76, 77, 141*n.*, 162*n.*, 172
Chavez, Dennis, 174
Chen Han-seng, 118*n.*, 186, 216
Chennault, Claire Lee, 218–219
Chiang Kai-shek, vii, ix, 30–32, 38, 51, 52, 53, 59, 65, 66, 97, 104, 106, 117–118, 119*n.*, 124, 125, 126, 127–132, 135, 139, 178, 180, 190, 199, 201–204, 205, 207–208, 208*n.*, 213–219
Chiang, Mme., 140
Chicago Sun, 148, 167
Chi Ch'ao-ting, 180, 185, 186, 220–223, 229
China Aid Council, 205
China Civil Rights League, 43
China Daily News, 220–222
China Forum, 63
China's Destiny, 216
China Story, 124*n.*, 204
China Today, 63*n.*, 136
Chinese Communists, viii, ix, x, 30–32, 33, 38, 40, 42, 43, 44, 50, 51, 52, 54, 55–56, 59, 66, 86, 119*n.*, 123, 124, 126–131, 135, 139, 149, 151, 157, 178, 182, 183, 185, 186, 187, 188, 190, 191*n.*, 199, 200, 201–209, 214, 218–219
Chinese Economic Theory, 216
Chinese Nationalists, vii, ix, 29–32, 38, 44, 51, 55–56, 66, 119, 127, 129–132, 187, 189, 198, 200–201, 208*n.*, 214–219
Chou En-lai, ix

Christian Science Monitor, 182
Ch'uang-Tsao-Sheh group, 33
Chuo Koron, 77
Churchill, Winston, 64, 128
Colegrove, Kenneth, 205
Collier's, 148
Comintern, 12, 20–22, 23, 28, 30–32, 35–44, 56, 66–67, 68, 72, 180*n.*, 222
Comintern Sixth World Conference, 36*n.*, 44
Communist International, Second, 12; First, 13; Third, *see* Comintern
Communist Party of Great Britain, 3, 6, 37; Germany, 18, 19–23, 28, 46; Austria, 21*n.*; Russia, 23, 40, 43, 44, 67; Japan, 27, 82, 114, 125; United States, 33, 36, 74, 136, 141, 166, 167, 182*n.*, 183, 186, 205; Brazil, 44, 141*n.*; France, 73
Connally, Tom, 201
Considine, William, 198
Cooke, Charles M., 201, 202, 203, 204
Currie, Lauchlin, 103, 106, 117–119, 182, 187*n.*, 228

Daily Worker, 155–156, 176, 182, 183, 184, 189, 209, 221
Daughter of Earth, A, 77
Davies, John P., Jr., 124, 125, 128, 151, 213
Davis, Elmer, 159
Davis, Forrest, 167
de Jong, Ellen van Zyll, 179
Dennett, Raymond, 103
Dennis, Eugene, 44, 57
Dilemma in Japan, 156
Dirksen, Herbert von, 83, 97
Dondero, George, 146, 153*n.*
Donovan, William, 140–142, 179
Dooman, Eugene, 107, 157, 159–161, 167–169, 178*n.*, 209*n.*
Doriot, Jacques, 38
Dreiser, Theodore, 63
Dubinsky, David, 232–234
Duggan, Laurence, 141, 182
Dulles, John Foster, 187

EASTLAND, WILLIAM O., 160, 161
Eastman Kodak Company, 69n.
Eastman, Max, 50, 189
Ebert, Friedrich, 19
Einstein, Albert, 63
Eisler, Gerhart, 21n., 36, 41, 43, 44
Emmerson, John, 125, 151
Epstein, Israel, 183, 187–189, 193
Ewert, Arthur, 44

FAIRBANK, JOHN K., ix, 125
Far Eastern Survey, 167, 178n., 187
Farley, Miriam S., 118n., 179
Federal Bureau of Investigation, 138, 142, 147–154, 156, 163, 164, 175, 246
Feldman, Lieutenant Colonel, 44
Ferguson, Homer T., 184, 185, 195, 196n., 201–203, 238
Feuchtwanger, Lion, 63
Field, Frederick Vanderbilt, 6, 136, 182, 185, 186, 189, 191, 193, 228
Field, Noel, 33, 122, 141n.
Financial News, British, 86
Fischer, Ruth, 21n., 23
Foreign Policy Association, 125, 183
Formosa, 25, 26, 66, 135, 204, 207–209
Forrestal Diaries, 156, 157n.
Forrestal, James V., 142, 151, 157, 158, 159
Fortier, Louis J., 207n.
Fortune, 179
Fourth Bureau (Red Army Intelligence), 8, 11, 40–44, 46, 49–50, 60, 63, 67–69, 71–73, 84, 85, 97, 100, 111, 113, 122, 185
Frankfurter Zeitung, 33, 55, 70, 79, 83
Freeman, 167
Friedman, Irving, 181
"Froelich" (pseudonym), see Theo
Fulbright, J. William, ix
Funakoshi Hisao, 61

GAUSS, CHRISTIAN, 140
Gayn, Mark, 147–149, 151–153, 161, 163, 167
Geiger, Theodore, 174, 194

"Genkichi Kusano" (pseudonym), see Ozaki Hozumi
Geopolitik, 79
German Seaman's Union, 46
Gestapo, 4, 12, 69, 70, 115
"Gloemberg-Ott" (pseudonym), 44, 46, 47
Gold, Mike, 63n.
Golos, Jacob, 184
GPU, see NKVD
Granich, Grace, 63, 183
Granich, Max, 63, 183
Graves, Mortimer, 145n., 162
Greater East Asia Co-prosperity Sphere, 26
Green, Theodore, 173
Greenberg, Michael, 187
Grew, Joseph C., 102, 107, 109, 155–162, 167, 169, 226
Groves, Leslie R., 198
Gurnea, Myron, 126, 142–149, 151

HARTFIELD, JOSEPH M., 162
Hickenlooper, Bourke B., 175, 220, 238
Hipper, Admiral von, 18
Hiss, Alger, 7, 24, 33, 75, 76, 122n., 141, 156, 172, 178, 183, 194
History of the Far East in Modern Times, 19–31
Hitchcock, Robert, 162, 164–166
Hitler-Stalin Pact, 81, 100, 191, 227
Hobbs Subcommittee Investigation, 136–139, 142–149, 172
Hoffman, Paul, 174
Holcombe, Arthur, 206
Holmes, Julius, 140, 141
Hong Chew-sih, 220–222
Hoover, J. Edgar, 142, 156
Hoover, Herbert, 65
Hornbeck, Stanley, 178n.
Hull, Cordell, 104–109, 117–120
Hull-Litvinov Agreement, 53
Hurley, Patrick J., 65, 126, 131, 151

ICKES, HAROLD, 197
Imperial Rule Assistance Association, 112

Independent Social Democratic Party, 17, 19
India, viii
Indonesia, viii
Infantry Journal, 131n.
"Ingrid" (pseudonym), 94
Inprecorr, 28
Institute of Pacific Relations, xii, 86, 87, 103, 109, 116, 118–119, 125, 136, 143–148, 150, 167, 177–193, 199, 200, 209, 237
IPR Popular Pamphlet Series, 180, 183
International Union of Revolutionary Writers, 63
Inverchapel, Lord (Sir Archibald Clark-Kerr), 123
Isaacs, Harold, 63
Ito Ritsu, 114
Ives, Irving S., 187
I Was There, 198

JAFFE, AGNES NEWMARK, 143
Jaffe, Lenore, 144
Jaffe, Philip, 126, 133, 136, 137, 142–144, 146, 147–153, 161, 162–169
Japan Advertiser, 74
Jefferson School of Social Science, 143
Jessup, Philip C., 191, 195, 206, 207
"Jim" group, 45, 47, 48
Joffe, Adolph, 30, 31
"Johnson" (pseudonym), *see* Sorge, Richard
Joint Anti-Fascist Refugee Committee, 144
Journey from the East, 147
Justice Department, 134, 153–155, 162–167, 175–176

KARAKHAN, LEO, 31
Kawai Teikichi, 60, 61, 115
Kazami Akira, 87
Kennan, George, 158n.
Kerensky Government, 17
Khrushchev, Nikita, x
King, Ernest, 198, 201n.
Kisch, Egon Erwin, 63
Kitabayashi Tomo, Mrs., 73, 114
Kito Ginichi, 33
Kizer, Benjamin, 136, 206

Klausen, Max, 45–48, 49, 82, 84, 85, 86, 89, 92–97, 113n., 114, 115
Klausen, Anna, 47, 84, 85, 92, 93, 115
Knitel, Renée Louise, 146
Knox, Frank, 109
Kohn, Nathan, 144
Konoye Fumimaru, 87, 98, 106, 107, 110, 112, 181
Korea, vii, viii, 26, 127, 157, 169, 178, 185, 192, 208n., 209, 230
Koshiro Yoshinobu, 75
Krivitsky, Walter, 23, 69, 73, 186
Krock, Arthur, 238
Kuomintang, *see* Chinese Nationalists
Kurusu Saburo, 103, 104
Kuusinen, Ottomar, 23, 39, 40, 68

LADD, MILTON D., 152–153
La Guardia, Fiorello, 141n.
Lamont, Corliss, 183, 190
Lamont, Thomas W., 190
Larsen, Emmanuel Sigurd, 144, 145, 147, 148, 151, 152, 163, 164–167, 173
Larsen, James Lewis, 144
Lassalle, Ferdinand, 27, 28
Lattimore, Owen, ix, 103, 117–119, 124, 125, 136, 157, 159, 160, 161, 165, 167, 168n., 176n., 180, 184n., 185–187, 189–192, 205, 206–207, 208n., 220–231
Leahy, William, 198
Left Opposition, 22, 37, 38, 39
Lenin, Nikolai, 12, 17, 18, 21, 27, 28, 31, 37, 84
Lesse, Karl, 44, 46
Liebknecht, Karl, 16, 17, 19
Li Li-san, 32
Lilliestrom, Tycho, 45, 47
Lin Yu-tang, 132
Li Ta-chao, 31
Little, Brown and Company, 187–188
Lockwood, William W., Jr., 179
Lodge, Henry Cabot, 175
London *Times,* 230
Lozovsky, George, 23, 38
Luce, Claire Booth, 132
Luce, Henry R., 181

Ludden, Raymond P., 125, 151
Luxemburg, Rosa, 4, 16, 90

MacArthur, Douglas, xii, 3, 50, 109, 116, 168, 179n., 197, 198
MacArthur Hearings, 197, 199–200, 207n., 209n.
MacLeish, Archibald, 159
McCarran Committee, xii, 103n., 109, 116, 118–119, 125n., 159–161, 168, 177–193, 195, 201–207, 209n., 218–219, 222–231, 237, 238, 245, 248
McCarthy, Joseph R., 169, 170, 172, 173–174, 175, 176, 177, 185, 191n., 194, 195, 196, 238
McInerney, James T., 151, 162–163, 164–165
McMahon, Brien, 154, 173
McNaughton, Ernest B., 206
Mainichi, 61
Malaya, viii
Manchuria Daily News, 145
Manchurian Incident, 53, 59, 64
Mandel, Benjamin, 177
Manuilsky, Dmitri, 23, 38, 68
Mao Tse-tung, ix, 32, 38, 42, 103, 125, 132, 149, 180n., 201, 209
Marshall, George Catlett, 106, 159, 177, 187, 188, 197, 199–200, 201–203, 205, 206, 207, 235
Marx, Karl, 11, 13, 17, 42, 69
Marzani, Carl Aldo, 141, 235
Massing, Hede, 41, 63n., 69, 70, 122, 141n., 182
Matsuoka Yosuke, 104, 181
Maxwell, General, 179
Mein Kampf, 69
Meisinger, Joseph, 83, 93, 115
Merisaki Genkichi, 29
M-Group, 21
Mikado, 78, 102, 107, 108, 157, 158–161, 192
"Minami Ryuichi" (pseudonym), see Miyagi Yotoku
Minster, Leon, 63
Mishin, Constantin, 46, 47
Mitchell, James M., 162

Mitchell, Kate, 137, 142, 143, 147, 151–153, 162, 163, 167
Miyagi Yotoku, 73–76, 78, 88, 95, 96, 114, 115
Mizuno Shige, 61
Modus vivendi, 108–109, 116–120, 199
Molotov, Vyacheslav M., 63
Monigan, Major, 140
Moore, Harriet C. (Lucy), 183, 232–234
Morgan, Edward S., 179n.
Morgenstern, George, 118n.
Morgenthau, Henry, 119, 182
Morris, Robert, 174, 177, 178n., 203, 232, 233
Morse, Wayne, 187
Motylev, V. E., 184n., 185n.
Muenzenberg, Willi, 11, 43, 63

Nagano Osami, 104
Nation, 155, 167, 183
National Council of American-Soviet Friendship, 143, 144
Nazi Party, 69, 70
New Masses, 143, 182, 189
New Republic, 155
Nevins, Allan, xii
New York Compass, 183, 208n.
New York Herald Tribune, 156, 183
New York Post, 155, 161, 176
New York Times, 147, 183, 189, 190, 197, 223, 231, 238
N-Group, 22
Nichols, Louis B., 153–154
Nimitz, Chester, 198
Nimitz Committee, 241, 243, 245, 248
Nixon, Richard M., 172
NKVD, 23, 40, 84
Nomonhan Incident, 98
Nomura Kichisaburo, 103, 105, 106, 107, 119
Noske, Gustav, 19
Noulens Defense Committee, 42–43, 63
Noulens, Hilaire, 44, 63

Office of Naval Intelligence, 137, 138, 140, 144, 145, 236
Office of Strategic Services, 135–142, 175

Office of War Information, 132, 137–138, 152, 157, 159, 220–222
Official Gazette (*Kampo*), 75
"Olga" (pseudonym), *see* Stahl, Lydia Tchekalov
On Active Service in Peace and War, 64
Open Door Policy, 25, 53, 65, 105
Ordeal by Slander, 185*n.*
Osaka Asahi, 29, 76
Osborne, Clay, 157
Ott, Eugen, 83, 98, 99, 100, 111, 112, 115
Ozaki Hozumi, xi, 3–9, 25–29, 32–34, 45, 57, 59–60, 63, 67, 72–78, 82, 86–88, 92, 95–98 103, 110–116, 178, 209

Pacific Affairs, 187, 230
Pan Pacific Trade Union Secretariat, 43
"Paul" (pseudonym), 60, 61
Pearl Harbor, ix, 4, 64, 101, 102–121, 178, 179, 188, 201*n.*
Pearl Harbor Inquiry, xii, 102, 106*n.*, 109
Pearl Harbor, the Story of the Secret War, 118*n.*
Pearson, Drew, 185*n.*
Peffer, Nathaniel, 206
"Petroikos, Mrs." (pseudonym), *see* Smedley, Agnes
Peurifoy, John, 194, 196
"Philips, J. W." (pseudonym), *see* Jaffe, Philip
Piatnitsky, 23, 38, 40, 68, 69
Pieck, Wilhelm, 19
Plain Talk, 173
PM, 148, 155, 167
Political Affairs, 161*n.*
Porter, Catherine, 179
Posniak, Edward, 194
Potsdam Agreement, 116
Powell, J. B., 50, 189
Presentations, Inc., 235
President's Loyalty Review Board, 169, 170
Proctor, James M., 165, 166
Proletarian Arts Society, 74

RADEK, KARL, 12, 28, 68
Rand, Christopher, 189
Rapp-Coudert Committee, 177
Reader's Digest, 189
Reischauer, Edwin O., 207
Reiss, Ignace, 41
Rhetts, C. E., 128*n.*
Rockefeller Foundation, 178, 182–183
Roosevelt, Franklin D., 53, 64, 102, 105–109, 113, 117, 119, 120, 130, 141, 180, 198, 213, 217, 218, 240
Root, Elihu, 193
Rosinger, Lawrence K., 125, 182, 183, 192, 205, 207
"Ross, Nat" (pseudonym), *see* Kohn, Nathan
Roth, Andrew, 136, 144, 146–152, 156, 161, 163, 167, 182
"Roy" (pseudonym), 74
Royall, Kenneth S., 197
"Ruegg, Paul" (pseudonym), *see* Noulens, Hilaire
Rusk, Dean, 203, 209
Russian War Relief, 232–234
Russo–Japanese War, 66, 98

SAIONJI KINKAZU, 87, 110, 115, 116, 178, 181
Salisbury, Lawrence, 178*n.*
Sansom, George, 89
SCAP report, *see* Willoughby report
Second International, *see* Comintern
Seeds of Treason, 72*n.*
Senate Appropriations Subcommittee, 235–236
Senate Foreign Relations Committee, ix
Senate Internal Security Subcommittee, *see* McCarran Committee
Service, John Stewart, ix, 125–133, 145*n.*, 149, 150*n.*–153, 155, 162, 163, 167, 169, 213*n.*–218, 241
Seven Decisions that Shaped History, 106
Shanghai Weekly, 60
Sheinberg, Arthur, 162
Sherwood, Robert, 102
"Shirakawa Jiro" (pseudonym), *see* Ozaki Hozumi

Sillen, Samuel, 189

Silvermaster, Nathan Gregory, 90, 103, 182

Smedley, Agnes, 5, 24, 33, 34, 43, 50, 52, 54–57, 58, 59, 60, 61, 63, 67, 70, 72, 77, 123, 124, 127, 178, 183, 197

Snow, Conrad, 170

Snow, Edgar, 124

Social Democratic Party of Germany, 11, 27–28

Society of Friends of the Soviet Union, 63

Solution in Asia, 168n., 192

Sorge, Adolph, 13

Sorge, Richard, xi, 3–25, 33–41, 43–45, 47–54, 56–63, 67–87, 89, 91–101, 103, 109, 110–116, 123, 126, 178, 181n., 182, 197, 199, 209, 210

South Manchuria Railway, 87, 114

Spartacus Bund, 19

Stachel, Jack, 186

Stahl, Lydia Tchekalov, 72, 73

Stahmer, Heinrich, 99, 115

Stalin and German Communism, 21n.

Stalin, Joseph, 4, 8, 10, 12, 23, 28, 36, 37, 38, 39, 53, 66, 84, 100, 103, 122n., 181, 201

Stark, Harold, 106

Stassen, Harold, 205, 206

State Department, 102, 104–109, 124–127, 132, 134–135, 137–138, 140–141, 146, 148, 155, 156, 158, 160–161, 165, 167–171, 173–175, 178, 179n., 182, 183, 185, 187, 191–197, 199, 200, 204–209, 224, 225, 233–234, 244–248

State Department Loyalty Security Board, xii, 126, 145n., 150, 152, 170, 242–244, 247

State of Asia, 183n.

Statistisches Jahrbuch für das Deutsche Reich, 113n.

Steele, Arch, 189

Steeley, E. Newton, 229

Stein, Guenther, 5, 82, 86, 89, 92, 93, 95, 124, 126, 127, 132, 178, 182

Steinhardt, Lawrence, 104

Stettinius, Edward, Jr., 140–142, 178n., 198

Stewart, Maxwell S., 125, 183

Stilwell, Joseph, 123, 124, 126, 129, 213, 218–219

Stimson, Henry L., 53, 64, 65, 109, 119, 120, 159, 165, 198

Stone, William T., 165, 192

Strength of the Great Powers in China, 77

Stripling, Robert S., 132n.

Strong, Anna Louise, 136

Stuart, Leighton, 125, 189, 204

Sun Fo, 157, 189

Sun Yat-sen, 29, 30, 31

Sun, Mme., 63, 182, 189

SWINK (State, War, and Navy Coordinating Committee), 160, 167, 168n.

Swope, Gerard, 193

TAIWAN NICHI NICHI SHIMBUN, 25

Technische Rundschau, 70

T-Group, 22

Theo, Major General, 44

Theses on the Revolutionary Movement in the Colonies and Semi-Colonies, 44

Third International, *see* Comintern

This Deception, 69

Times, London, 230

Tojo Hideki, 111

Trachtenberg, Alexander, 144, 184

Tripartite Pact, 105, 108

Trotsky, Leon, 18, 23, 36, 37, 66

Truman, Harry S., xii, 50, 116, 151, 159, 167, 169, 170, 172, 176, 177, 191n., 195, 196, 226

Tukhachevsky, Mikhail, 98, 100

Turner, Bruce, 181

Twenty-one Conditions, 21

Twenty-one Demands, 26

Tydings Committee Investigation, 139–140, 176n., 194

Tydings Hearings, 151, 152–154, 162–165, 166, 169, 173–175

Tydings Exhibits, 131n., 164–167, 214–217

Tydings, Millard E., 152–154, 173–175, 176, 205n.

Unfinished Revolution in China, 187
Uritsky, General, 84
Ushiba, 181
United Nations, 248
United States Civil Service Commission, 180, 220–222, 229, 242, 243–246
Utley, Freda, 124, 204

VANDENBERG, ARTHUR H., SR., 187
"Vandercruysen" (pseudonym), see Noulens, Hilaire
Versailles Treaty, 12, 26
Vietnam, vii, x, 169
Villard, Oswald Garrison, 63
Vinacke, Harold M., 31, 99
Vincent, John Carter, 63, 125, 160, 167, 168, 169, 187, 189, 200, 203
Virendranath Chattopadhyaya, 55
Voice of China, 63
Voroshilov, Klementi, 84
Voukelitch, Branko de, 72–74, 88, 89, 95, 96, 115
Voukelitch, Edith de, 73, 89
Vue, 73
Vutokevitch, Sergei, 94

WADLEIGH, HENRY JULIAN, 75
Wallace Brown, Inc., 144
Wallace, Henry A., 192, 218
Wallenius, Anna, see Klausen, Anna
Wallenius, Martti K., 47
Walsh, J. Raymond, 163
"Walsh, Paul" (pseudonym), see Dennis, Eugene

"Wang" (pseudonym), 58, 59
Washington Post, ix, 70
Watkins, Arthur, 195n.
Wednesday Group, 87
Weill, Kurt, 12
Weingart, Joseph, 48, 49
Welles, Benjamin, 189
Welles, Sumner, 102, 106, 132, 141n., 187, 189
Wells, Kenneth E., 135
Wendt, Bruno, 73, 83
White, Harry Dexter, 103, 118, 119, 122, 178, 182
White Paper on China, 5, 200, 202
White, William S., 229
Wiedemeyer, Irene, 33, 57, 62
Willkie, Wendell, 132, 181
Willoughby, Charles A., 116, 195
Willoughby report, xii, 28, 81–82, 197
Wilson, Woodrow, 26
Wittfogel, Karl A., 192, 229–230
Woidt, Dr., 94
Woltman, Frederick, 134
World War I, 11, 13–16, 17–18, 26
World War II, 19, 97, 100–101, 102–121, 124, 125, 201n.

YABE SHU, 88
Yalta Conference, 54, 159, 197–199, 204
Yamazaki Yoshiko, 89

ZACHARIAS, ELLIS, 145n.
Zaitzev, Victor S., 94
Zeitgeist Bookshop, 33, 57, 62
Z-Group, 22
Zinoviev, Gregory, 12, 36, 40